The Wars of
the Roses

The Wars of the Roses

J. R. Lander

SUTTON PUBLISHING

First published in 1965 by Secker & Warburg Ltd

First published by Sutton Publishing in 1990

This edition first published in 2000 by
Sutton Publishing Limited
Phoenix Mill · Thrupp · Stroud · Gloucestershire · GL5 2BU

A catalogue record for this book is available from the British Library

ISBN 0 7509 2464 0

*Cover: A manuscript illustration depicting a battle of the Wars of the Roses
(by courtesy of the Trustees of the British Library).*

Typesetting and origination by
Sutton Publishing Limited.
Printed in Great Britain by
Cox & Wyman, Reading, Berkshire.

Contents

Preface

The materials for English history in the mid-fifteenth century are notoriously intractable. Many a bewildered investigator must have echoed the despairing cry of a seventeenth-century historian, William Nicolson, who, after attempting to write an account of Edward IV's reign, admitted himself too perplexed 'to form a regular History out of such a vast Heap of Rubbish and Confusion.' Though government records oppress posterity by the hundredweight they are mainly concerned with administrative and judicial detail, composed in 'Indenture English', the prolix, inelegant language of the government department. Only occasionally are they suitable for quotation in a book of this type. I make no apology, therefore, for choosing (with few exceptions) extracts from chronicles and letters already printed – many of which (if any justification is needed) are in editions out of print, often rare and accessible only to scholars or in the better-equipped libraries.

At the time this book was first published, in 1965, general histories gave a deceptively clear account of the events of the mid-fifteenth century. In fact such narratives were a patchwork of legend and rumour mingled with and all too often, taken for fact. A convincing history of the period had yet to be written. During the last two decades a younger generation of scholars has produced a large variety of articles putting forward more detailed investigations of the economic and social structures of the times, which has led to new and more plausible political interpretations. Even so, in the absence of intimate personal correspondence and detailed state papers such as we are accustomed to for later ages, the motives of politicians, must in most cases, still be deduced from their actions and the results of those actions – a highly fallible hit and miss process.

Many of the letters and narratives quoted in this book purvey biased opinion, wild rumour, meretricious propaganda and the foulest of slander as well as historical truth. Baffling though they are, the smears of unscrupulous politicians and the credulous misconceptions of London merchants and country gentlemen are not to be despised. What people thought, their affections and their prejudices have often been as important in history as truth itself. I have tried to indicate some of the wilder vagaries of this kind: it would be impossible to note them all even with a vast (and quite out-of-place) critical apparatus.

Although there are grave objections to such a method, for easier reading I have, as far as possible, modernized spelling and punctuation while leaving tense and sentence structure in their original form to retain the savour of the originals – though it is impossible to be entirely consistent in such matters. Exact references are given for all extracts and scholars may therefore easily trace the originals for themselves. Where possible I have used existing translations from Latin and French sources. Other translations are my own. Mr F. Learoyd, Professors P. Chavy and Irene Coffin gave valuable advice and assistance in translating passages from French and Professor P.J. Atherton assisted with the extract from Abbot Whethemstede in Chapter 2.

Introduction

That great historical romancer, Sir Walter Scott, invented 'The Wars of the Roses'* to embellish a moral, almost tragical pattern of fifteenth-century English history, first set out by an Italian cleric, Polydore Vergil of Urbino. By the beginning of the sixteenth century the diplomatic and propaganda value of humanistic Latin had risen so high that the monarchs of northern Europe found it wise to justify both their ancestry and their ways to the world in the fashionable prose of Italian historians. Paolo Aemiliani was already writing such a history at the French court when Polydore arrived in England in 1502 as the deputy of Adriano Castelli, diplomat and collector of the obsolete papal tax, Peter's Pence. Encouraged by Henry VII, Polydore soon began to collect the materials for a history of England and by 1513 he had completed the first draft of his *Anglica Historia*. The theme of this soon notorious work became the exemplar for all the more accomplished historians writing in Tudor England. The Henrician chronicler, Edward Hall, extended, coloured and almost hallowed the conceptions of his Italian predecessor and passed them on to Shakespeare who, ignoring the historian's pedantic regard for 'old mouse-eaten records', as Sir Philip Sydney called them, with a poet's licence ignored or changed inconvenient facts to dramatize the moral theme.[1] Polydore Vergil drew the design of a world where institutions were more or less stable across the ages and where, within this stable framework, the personalities of individual kings determined the fate of their realms. Three powerful sentiments swayed the minds of the generations about whom he wrote – God's watchful presence over the affairs

*In *Anne of Geierstein* (Ch. vii). I owe the phrase and the information to Professor S.B. Chrimes. Pointing out that the red and the white roses were only two amongst many badges used by the Houses of Lancaster and York, Professor Chrimes condemns the term as misleading and would like historians to abandon it. See *History*, xlvii 24, 1963 and *Lancastrians, Yorkists and Henry VII,* pp. xi–xiv, 1964.

of princes, the inviolate nature of a family's inheritance and the sanctity of an anointed king.

Fifteenth- and sixteenth-century authors were lavish with evidence of God's intervention in the affairs of princes. Philippe de Commynes set down his conviction that the rulers of this world, too powerful to be controlled by other men, were subject in their doings to the peculiar interventions of the Almighty. Although the judicial duel was no longer respectable for the settlement of ordinary legal cases it survived in the affairs of princes through the idea of the judgment of God in battle. Edward IV, according to the hints of some contemporary writers, put off his coronation until God had blessed him with victory at the battle of Towton. There was hierarchy even in wickedness. As the Lord watched more closely over princes, so he visited their transgressions with a heavier rod even in this world, and they bought their soul's peace in the next with masses on a scale which their subjects could only envy.

'Only God can make an heir.' The landed classes of the time regarded the exclusion of an heir from his lawful rights – though it was a frequent enough occurrence – as one of the worst of all crimes. As Shakespeare, following Polydore Vergil and Hall, tells the tale, Richard II first banished Henry Bolingbroke, then on the death of his father, John of Gaunt, unlawfully deprived him of his patrimony, the Duchy of Lancaster. Henry returned from exile to recover it with the help of part of the nobility. Henry Hotspur claimed that he had seen Bolingbroke:

> A poor unminded outlaw sneaking home,
> My father gave him welcome to the shore;
> And, when he heard him swear, and vow to God,
> He came but to be Duke of Lancaster,
> To sue his livery, and beg his peace
> With tears of innocency and terms of zeal,
> My father, in kind heart and pity mov'd,
> Swore him assistance, and perform'd it too.[2]

Bolingbroke himself implied that he had returned to England with no intention of usurping the Crown. Events had dragged him to his high estate – and had punished him with everlasting calamities:

> Heaven knows, my son,
> By what by-paths and indirect crook'd ways
> I met this crown; and I myself know well,
> How troublesome it sat upon my head.[3]

To deprive a man of his inheritance was one great sin to provoke God's anger. To slay a king was sin mortal and incomparable – 'heinous, black, obscene' – words could scarce express the horror such a sin evoked. The Lord's Anointed partook of the Lord's mystery. He shared in God's sanctity and could not be slain without divine retribution. Even at the thought of his subjects daring to condemn Richard II the Bishop of Carlisle warned of the wrath to come:

> And shall the figure of God's Majesty,
> His captain, steward, deputy-elect,
> Anointed, crowned, planted many years,
> Be judged by subject and inferior breath,
> And he himself not present?

If such things happen:

> The blood of English shall manure the ground,
> And future ages groan for this foul act;
> Peace shall go sleep with Turks and infidels,
> And, in this seat of Peace, tumultuous wars,
> Shall kin with kin, and kind with kind confound;
> Disorder, Horror, Fear and Mutiny
> Shall here inhabit, and this land be call'd
> The field of Golgotha and dead men's sculls.[4]

The dread theme of guilt unfolds itself time and time again. Even on the night before Agincourt Henry V brooded on sin and expiation:

> Oh, not today! – Think not upon the fault
> My father made in compassing the crown!
> I Richard's body have interred new;
> And on it have bestow'd more contrite tears,

> Than from it issued forced drops of blood.
> Five hundred poor I have in yearly pay,
> Who twice a day their wither'd hands hold up
> Toward heaven, to pardon blood.[5]

Henry V escaped the curse. It descended to his son, Henry VI, whose weakness and inability to control a quarrelsome aristocracy gave Richard of York the opportunity to revive his own stronger, legitimate claim to the throne. Tragedy developed within tragedy. Each new crime brought its own fitting retribution. The murder of Edward IV's two sons, the Princes in the Tower, punished the perjury which he had committed on his return from exile in 1471 – to gain support he claimed, at first, that he had returned to recover only the Duchy of York, his family lands, not the Crown. Bosworth Field finally wiped out in blood a monstrous consummation of crime in Richard III and united the Houses of Lancaster and York in Henry VII and Elizabeth Plantagenet: 'Now civil wounds are stopp'd, peace lives again.' All was set for the peace and prosperity of Tudor England.

The needs of the stage forced Shakespeare to transmute all action into personal terms. He compressed the dreary annals of politics and war into an unhistorical but tragic unity so intense that it overwhelms us with horror: like Margaret of Anjou we know 'the realm a slaughter house'. From the Duchess of Gloucester's demand for revenge in Richard II, through Prince Henry's horrifying boast that he would extinguish his frivolity in 'a garment all of blood', through the scene at Towton where father slays son and son father, the reek of death and horror rises to Queen Margaret's last envenomed taunt to the Duchess of York:

> Forth from the kennel of thy womb hath crept
> A hell hound, that doth hunt us all to death.
> That dog, that had his teeth before his eyes,
> To worry lambs, and lap their gentle blood;
> That foul defacer of God's handy work;
> That excellent grand tyrant of the earth,
> That reigns in galled eyes of weeping souls,
> Thy womb let loose, to chase us to our graves.[6]

This bloodthirsty moral theme cannot, however, be entirely laid to the door of Polydore Vergil and the Tudor writers. Its genesis may be found in Yorkist propaganda. The claim of the House of York was not as clear as this symmetrically designed history mesmerises us into believing. In fifteenth-century England there was no definite public law governing the descent of the Crown and it was deduced, with some confusion, from the rules governing the descent of real property. In this there were conflicts of interest between the heirs male and heirs general of aristocratic families. The rules of primogeniture gave both title and estates to the heir male but if there were no son an affectionate father might well favour the claims of a daughter (the heir general) over those of a younger brother or a nephew. Such conflicts of interest were from time to time settled by awarding the title and part of the estates to the heir male and the rest of the property to the heir general. It was obviously impossible to apply such a compromise conclusion to the Crown and Kingdom of England. No division could be made in such a way.

The Lancastrians claimed as heirs the male line of Edward III, denying the right of Richard of York, as heir general descending through a female* – thus assuming in England a kind of Salic law which they themselves denied in France. When Richard of York forced the issue in 1460 his claim, in the way already noted, was argued through prolonged discussions with the law of real property. By this analogy the nobility, assembled in parliament, finally – and grudgingly – conceded the claim to be valid. The compromise then arranged, which recognized York as Henry VI's heir to the exclusion of Henry's son, Prince Edward, soon broke down. When Richard of York was killed a few weeks later at the battle of Wakefield and Margaret of Anjou had defeated another Yorkist army under the Earl of Warwick at the second battle of St Albans, to save a desperate situation a mere fragment of a faction made York's son, the Earl of March, king, as Edward IV. The new king's supporters were by no means numerous. Necessity drove him to use every possible means to support his weak position. During his enthronement at Westminster on 4 March 1461 a speech was made setting forth his title, a statement repeated almost verbatim when his first parliament met the following November. The king and his advisers took their stand upon a declaration which his father had made a few months before – 'though right for a time rest and be put to silence yet it rotteth not nor shall not perish.'

---

*Richard of York was also descended in the male line from Edward III's fifth son, Edmund of Langley, but he never put forward his claims on this ground.

They assumed that no one could possibly question the validity of Edward's title and in scathing words attributed the recent disorders of the kingdom to God's judgment upon it for tolerating so long the cancer of Lancastrian usurpation and the unjust denial of their rightful inheritance to the House of York. According to this interpretation Henry IV had taken:

> upon him usurpously the crown and name of king and lord of the same realm and lordship; and not therewith satisfied or content, but more grievous thing attempting, wickedly of unnatural, unmanly and cruel tyranny, the same King Richard, king anointed, crowned and consecrate, and his liege and most high lord in the earth, against God's law, man's liegance, and oath of fidelity, with uttermost punicion, a-tormenting, murdered and destroyed, with most vile, heinous and lamentable death; whereof the heavy exclamation in the doom of every Christian man soundeth into God's hearing in heaven, not forgotten in the earth, specially in this realm of England, which therefore hath suffered the charge of intolerable persecution, punicion and tribulation, whereof the like hath not been seen or heard in any other Christian realm . unrest, inward war and trouble, unrightwiseness, shedding and effusion of innocent blood, abusion of the laws, partiality, riot, extortion, murder, rape and vicious living have been the guiders and leaders of the noble realm of England.[7]

The government saw to it that such propaganda had the widest possible circulation and the reading of this particular statement in parliament would alone ensure that it was well known. Polydore Vergil could not have escaped from the background of such vehement opinions. For Edward IV's reign he relied on both a popular oral tradition and the reminiscences of men in high places who had lived through the events of those days – or who had at least heard of them from their fathers. He therefore reflected the judgment of Englishmen of his own day, a judgment strongly influenced by Yorkist propaganda, on the end of the House of Lancaster. The 'Yorkist myth' so strongly propagated in 1461 must surely have grown into the stem on which he grafted the more 'Tudor myth'.

Since this myth prevailed generations of authors have obviously enjoyed writing about the fifteenth century as a degraded, blood-drenched anti-climax to the great constructive period of the Middle Ages. It was, by modern standards, a turbulent and disorderly period; whether it was so much worse than the fourteenth or sixteenth centuries and whether its disorders were due to the civil wars are other, and contentious questions. The highly theatrical, richly-coloured conflation of picturesque fables, bloody battles, proscriptions and attainders, quick reversals of fortune, desperate flights and sudden victories, is a deceptive guide to the state of the country. Most probably England was no more war-ridden in the fifteenth century than in earlier centuries. Between 1066 and 1377 there were only two periods of more than thirty consecutive years when general peace prevailed in the land.[8] During the Wars of the Roses the total period of active campaigning between the first battle of St Albans (1455) and the battle of Stoke (1487) amounted to a little more than one year – one year out of thirty-two years.[9] Henry VII's progress from his landing in Milford Haven to his victory at Bosworth Field lasted only fourteen days.

These almost miniature campaigns bear no comparison with the scale of warfare in the rest of Europe. The first battle of St Albans has been described, with little exaggeration, as a 'short scuffle in a street'.[10] Only at Towton (1461), the greatest battle of the period, did the numbers engaged possibly approach 50,000. Training and tactics alike were elementary. The law required every free-born Englishman between the ages of sixteen and sixty to bear arms, but such regulations did not make an army. With the exception of the Calais garrison (not in any case a field force), and from 1468 the king's personal bodyguard of two hundred archers, there was no standing military force in the country receiving constant military training. The troops which fought the battles of the Wars of the Roses were hastily – and many of them unwillingly – collected as each particular climax mounted to its crisis and were as quickly disbanded once it was over. Neither side could afford the cost of anything better.[11] Strategy was equally elementary. At the second battle of St Albans Warwick was unaware of Queen Margaret's approach. Towton was fought in a snowstorm, Barnet in an April fog and even Edward's famous pursuit of the Lancastrian army to Tewkesbury in 1471 was marked more by dogged tenacity than strategic ability.

Though several English towns were sacked from 1459 to 1461, none suffered a prolonged siege. None burned their suburbs to make it easier to defend them from besieging forces as several French towns had been forced to do in the course of the Hundred Years War. This urban immunity is the more significant if we call to mind that English towns were more open to attack than any in Europe. Owing to the early unification of England and the power of the central government, defences had become less necessary than they were elsewhere. Little fortified market towns, so common in France, were almost unknown in England. Even major towns like Reading and Oxford lacked fortifications.[12] The dilapidated condition of the walls of London may well, in part, account for the readiness of the city fathers to negotiate with both Yorkists and Lancastrians in the 1450s and 1460s. If so, they continued to feel secure enough to take risks. A few years later they remained almost contemptuously negligent of a vigorous mayor's efforts to rebuild the fortifications.

The architecture of the day shows few concessions to warfare. After the end of Richard II's reign the science of military fortification was almost unknown in England until Henry VIII, between 1538 and 1540, built a chain of coastal artillery forts in a revolutionary foreign style. The Wars of the Roses produced nothing comparable to the fortifications and earthworks built up during the great civil war in the seventeenth century.[13] 'Castles' like Tattershall, Caister, Ashby-de-la-Zouch and Hurstmonceux (the first two built in the then fashionable French or Rhenish style) were, despite their delusive military air, more magnificent dwellings than fortresses.

The private castles erected during the fifteenth century might never have existed as far as their significance in the Wars of the Roses was concerned. Lesser houses were very unmartial indeed. When John Norreys built Ockwells during one of the most acute phases of the civil war – it was not quite finished when he died in 1465 – he saw fit to build a house notable for the number and size of its windows, to a design based on simple but harmonious mathematical ratios worked out for their aesthetic effect, quite unrelated to thoughts of defence.[14] Of the older royal castles only Harlech, for reasons now obscure, withstood a long blockade. The rest of the Welsh castles and the famous strongholds of northern England which figure so prominently in the struggles of the early 1460s never held out against a besieging force for more than a few weeks – often it was only a matter of days.

Looting was not unknown – it never can be in any war. Yet complaints of it were singularly rare. The war was highly localized. Any damage inflicted was small in comparison with the destruction wrought by the devastating raids of the Scots and the English 'scavengers' leagued with them in the early fourteenth century when, in the years between the battle of Bannockburn and the death of King Robert I of Scotland, the tithes of the churches appropriated to the monastery of Durham fell in value from £412 to £10 a year.[15] In the fifteenth century disorders certainly occurred less in England than in its poorer neighbour Scotland. Seen against events in the northern kingdom – two kings assassinated within twenty years and the interminable bloody feuds of the Black and the Red Douglases, the Crichtons and the Livingstones – the Wars of the Roses seem less ferocious. Again, England seems a haven of quiet if compared with the faction fights of contemporary Bohemia.

Louis XI's councillor, Philippe de Commynes, once remarked: 'England enjoyed this peculiar mercy above all other kingdoms, that neither the country nor the people, nor the houses were wasted, destroyed or demolished; but the calamities and misfortunes of the war fell only upon the soldiers, and especially on the nobility.'[16] Although Commynes himself admitted that he was somewhat hazy on the details of English politics, his comparisons of conditions in different countries are exceedingly shrewd.

The English hardly suffered at all compared with the damage which they had inflicted on many of the provinces of France during the Hundred Years War. The fortified church, almost unknown in England, once again as in earlier times became a familiar landmark in France. The chronicler, Molinet, devoted a long poem entirely to the destruction of the French abbeys. They fell into poverty of a kind they had not known since the Dark Ages: monasticism in France never recovered from the effects of this English destruction.[17] When the English were finally driven out of Gascony in 1453 they left thirty per cent of the villages ravaged or seriously damaged.[18] Nothing in English experience could compare with Limoges where it was said that in 1435 only five people were left alive in the town. Recovery took twenty years and more. As late as the 1480s some districts still suffered from the wartime destruction of draught animals: men, women and children were still being harnessed to the ploughs.[19] Around Amiens the damage had been so great that all the city's parish churches and most of the religious houses in the district had to be rebuilt – and they were rebuilt between about 1470 and 1490.[20] It took about the same time to clear up another of the war's more serious legacies – a tangle of conflicting property rights – for during the fighting both sides had made grants of the same estates, often several times over – causing legal confusion and social conflict far more extreme than anything that resulted in England from the confiscations and acts of attainder inflicted on the various combatants during the civil wars.[21]

England escaped the horrors of invasion by a foreign power: an immunity which has led historians to treat the Wars of the Roses too exclusively as an incident in English history. Although the civil conflicts began in a domestic crisis they were by no means an insular affair. Neither Lancastrians nor Yorkists scrupled to call in foreign help when they could get it and the rapid changes of English politics upset the calculations of statesmen in courts as far distant as Milan, Naples and Aragon. John of Calabria, Margaret of Anjou's brother, still pressed his family's claim to the throne of Naples and his Italian ambitions reacted upon his sister's fortunes in England. In the early 1450s the French still feared a renewed English invasion: in the second half of the decade they were obsessed by a dread of Burgundy. From about 1456 to the death of Charles the Bold in 1477 the politics of north-western Europe turned upon the mutual suspicions of these two powers. In this bitter conflict no holds were barred. The insincerity, chicanery and ruthlessness of its diplomacy could have taught Machiavelli as much as he ever learned from the quarrels of Italian states. As diplomacy failed war took its place. Both sides competed for an English alliance and for many years their ambitions made worse the squalid confusions of English politics.

From 1459 onwards Francesco Sforza, Duke of Milan, wished to unite England and Burgundy in an invasion of France in order to frustrate French support for John of Calabria's ambitions in Genoa and Naples. He employed as his agent the papal legate, Francesco Coppini, who unscrupulously used his position to support Warwick and his friends when they mounted their invasion from Calais in 1460. In 1462 Louis XI France, dreading once more an Anglo-Burgundian alliance, countered by supporting Margaret of Anjou, only to leave her in the lurch at the end of the year when the danger to his kingdom had passed away. France and Burgundy continued to compete for the English alliance. Charles the Bold unsuccessfully tried to persuade Edward to join with the League of the Public Weal against Louis. Later it was a temporary success on the part of France which drove Charles to marry Margaret of York, and according to one chronicler, he bitterly remarked that to avenge himself on the King of France he had been constrained to marry a whore. Reacting strongly Louis (probably as early as 1468) toyed with the idea of bringing together Queen Margaret and Warwick: the almost fantastic plan which led to their successful invasion of England in 1470 – and ultimately failed because Louis, going too far, pushed his puppet Lancastrian government into an invasion of Burgundy. Duke Charles, who until that point had shown scant sympathy for the woes of his exiled brother-in-law, then quickly supported Edward's plans for a counterinvasion. Margaret and Warwick on the one side, Edward on the other, owed their triumphs, in part at least, to foreign interests which supported them for their own purposes. Even after Edward's restoration in 1471 his invasion of France, delayed until 1475, took place only after a bewildering progression of truces, counter-truces and contradictory negotiations between the three rivals. Henry VII invaded the country with Breton help and for many years nearly every court in northern Europe found it expedient at some time or another to support the claims of the Yorkist pretender, Perkin Warbeck.

Though by continental standards England escaped the horrors of war it was a turbulent enough land. Long before and long after the civil wars its inhabitants complained bitterly and endlessly of 'lack of governance' and the prevalence of violent crime. In the minds of medieval men a period of good order had always ; existed in some erstwhile golden age and the conditions of their own day were found wanting by this legendary standard.[22] As evidence accumulates of the extensive crime of earlier centuries it beggars credulity to think of any massive deterioration of public order in the mid-fifteenth century. The execution of criminal law had always been weak[23] and the criminal records of any period in medieval or sixteenth-century England present a grim and lurid picture.* The respectable classes of society were as much given to violent crime as the rabble. Fifteenth-century letters often show in their writers a disturbing irascibility of temperament. Respectable members of the Mercers' Company drew their knives on each other at the company's meetings. Landed families who accused each other of whole catalogues of crime from forcible entry to arson and mayhem were soon on good terms again and even arranging marriages between their members. Even under Henry V outrageous assaults and the like were frequent. In 1415 servants of the members of parliament for Shropshire waylaid and attacked the tax collectors for the county.[24] A fine example of the gentleman thug

---

*In the early thirteenth century over three hundred crimes of violence were committed in one year in the county of Lincoln alone, and as late as 1600–1 the Council in the Marches of Wales during the same short period of time levied two hundred and seventy fines for riot.

was John Newport, a veteran of the French wars, whom the Duke of York had appointed as his steward of the Isle of Wight. In 1450 the inhabitants of the island complained:

> . . . the said John Newport, hath at this day no livelode to maintain his great countenance, but by the oppressing of the people in the country that he sit in, through the which he hath greatly enpovred and hurt the poor island ready; for what time he was Steward of the isle, he had but ten marks of fee, and kept an household and a countenance like a lord, with as rich wines as could be imagined, naming himself Newport the Galant, otherwise called Newport the rich, whom the country cursen daily that ever he come there . . . [25]

One of the widest streams of violence flowed unceasingly from a combination of land hunger and the fantastic involutions of the law of real property. Under-developed agrarian societies are always fiercely litigious. During the later Middle Ages and the sixteenth century men seized every chance of adding acre to acre. Few landed families went for more than a few years unentangled in a lawsuit of some kind. The law of real property was in no state to meet the demands of so acquisitive a society. Quite apart from the appalling protractions and delays of common law procedure, no statutes of limitation had been passed since Edward I's day. In real actions the term of legal memory still went back to 1189. It was not until 1540, and again in 1623, that legislation applied some limited remedies for these evils.[26] Bad titles everywhere had become one of the curses of social and economic life. Many of the notorious attacks upon the Paston properties were supported at least by the pretext of a suddenly discovered, antiquated legal claim. Many men, in angry frustration at the delays and inadequacies of the common law, took to violence to impose their 'rights'. It is hardly straining the evidence to suggest that the obsolete deformities of the common law caused more disorder than the sporadic incidents of the civil wars. Disputes over land could be expensively exacerbated by the corrupt support of powerful men,[27] the crime of maintenance, as it was known at the time. On the other hand conditions were ameliorated by a considerable revival of arbitration – sometimes by neighbours, sometimes under the aegis of influential baronial councils.

The dramatic crises of history distort our vision of the past. Despite the periodic, spectacular clashes between them, cooperation in the government of the realm was the normal relationship between the king and the nobility. While writers from the fifteenth century to the present day have rightly condemned the intransigent ambitions of the overmighty subject – the menace to the king of the nobleman 'equipollent to himself' as Sir John Fortescue (1394?–1477?) put it – they have too often passed over the less interesting, because merely mighty, subjects.

Edward IV and Henry VII would have regarded as little more than simple-minded the once popular interpretation of history which saw them putting down the nobility and basing their rule on the middle classes. Politics are not played out *in vacuo*: those who rule must work in the conditions they find. Even if the monarchs of the day had been capable of thinking in terms of ignoring the nobility, harsh realities would never have permitted them such anachronistic illusions. In the countryside royal servants of less than noble rank were unreliable. The sheriffs' offices had long been notorious centres of corruption. From their very inception experienced judges like Geoffrey le Scrope had looked upon the justices of the peace with grave – and justified – doubts about their probable efficiency.[28] The society of the day was incapable of organizing an effective bureaucracy and in its absence no government could possible ignore the nobility. Sir John Fortescue, himself one of the official class, had no illusions about the power of officials. He ranked it as less than that of the aristocracy – 'For the might of the land, after the might of the great lords thereof, standeth most in the king's officers.'[29] Again Bishop Russell described them in a draft sermon of 1483 as the firm islands and rocks in an unstable sea and added that it was obvious 'the politic rule of every region well ordained standeth in the nobility.'[30]

At the same time the English nobility were hardly typical of their generation in Europe. Provincial feeling in England was weak for it was a small country early united under strong kings. It had nothing to compare with what Shakespeare aptly called France's 'almost kingly dukedoms', with their separatist tendencies and, at times, near-independence of the central power. As the intelligent Venetian envoy pointed out in 1497, by continental standards the English nobility, lacking compact territories and extensive judicial powers, were nothing more than rich landlords. They expected to be, and were, treated with greater consideration than other men, from such small matters as having bread baked for them on Sundays (otherwise forbidden by law) when they arrived unexpectedly in strange towns, to declaring their income on oath instead of being assessed for taxation, and having the king and council settle their major quarrels instead of suing in the law courts like other men.

Yet limited as their powers were compared with those of their peers in France, Italy and Germany, they were far too powerful for the insecure Houses of York and Tudor to ignore them. Their ultimate success makes us forget that both Edward IV and Henry VII were so precariously seated on their thrones that they were compelled to make use of whatever support they could command, enforce or bribe. Their shifts and turns and essential opportunism may lend their actions a somewhat haphazard and contradictory air, but far from suppressing the nobility they welcomed the adherence of old opponents. Eighty-four per cent of the attainders passed against nobles in the Wars of the Roses were reversed. The wars had no significant effect on the numbers or wealth of the English landed classes. Edward IV and the early Tudors, far from suppressing the nobility were prepared, as and when particular circumstances made it necessary, to increase the wealth and influence of those who were loyal and to discipline, by whatever means they could, those who were as politically unreliable as they were highly placed, or whose low intelligence, positive eccentricities or erratic conduct were likely to make them a danger to the state. The influence of the Percys, if not indispensable, was at least highly desirable in governing the north. Just as Edward IV restored Henry Percy IV to his earldom of Northumberland in 1469–70 to offset the power of the Nevilles, so Henry VII soon released him from imprisonment after the battle of Bosworth to make him warden of the East and Middle Marches.

There is little to commend the traditional idea that kings at this time created a new and more subservient nobility as a counterpoise to the older aristocracy. The idea of 'old nobility' has been very much overworked. Baronial families in general seem to have died out in the male line about every third generation or so and the Wars of the Roses made little difference to this aristocratic mortality. The honours of a large section of the lay peerage did not go very far back. Between 1439 and 1504 sixty-eight new peerages were created (excluding promotions from one rank to another). Of these twenty-one went to the husbands or sons of heiresses to old titles: forty-seven creations were completely new. The ranks of the nobility were constantly recruited from below, by promotion from a group of rich, untitled families whose way of life and political instincts differed little, if at all, from those of the lesser nobility. Some such peers were created, and splendidly endowed, by the king with a consciously political purpose in mind. In 1461 Edward ennobled William Hastings and by granting him the forfeited Leicestershire estates of the Earl of Wiltshire, Viscount Beaumont and Lord Roos transformed him from a middling landowner into a magnate capable keeping loyal what before 1461 had been a strongly Lancastrian district in the central Midlands.[31]

Such men through their connections with the local gentry, a mixture of patronage and dominance summed up by the contemporary term 'good lordship', in no small measure kept the countryside in peace and quiet. The new Lord Hastings in the course of twenty-two years sealed legal indentures with no less than eighty-eight retainers, ranging from two other noblemen to knights and squires, spread over at least five counties. The noble retinue, the affinity, in other words the 'bastard feudalism' which has been so often condemned as an unmitigated evil, was an essential part of Yorkist and Tudor government. The lack of a police force and a standing army left the personal bond between lord and man, exercised as Lord Hastings' indentures state 'as far as law and conscience requireth', essential for the peace of the countryside.[32] Law and conscience, it is true, were often conspicuously absent from these relationships. The magnate had to be given a fairly free hand in his own district; in return for his loyalty the government did not probe over-carefully into his activities.

The potential success or failure of the system lay in the personality of the king: on whether he could hold the balance between turbulent men too powerful to be ignored, prevent them from gaining undue control of his resources in land, men and money, and see that by and large they used their own in his and the general interest. This Henry VI conspicuously failed to do. All through the Middle Ages and until well into the reign of Elizabeth I the monarch and the royal council spent an inordinate amount of their time on settling the personal and territorial problems of the great.[33] Bastard feudalism, by putting coercive power into the magnates' hands, undoubtedly gave them the means to take advantage of Henry's irresolute character and to fight out their quarrels *vi et armis* free from the normal restraints of royal discipline. Consequently in the 1440s and the 1450s more and more families took to violence to settle their disputes. This progressive deterioration of public life and the discredit which its final, swift defeat in the Hundred Years War had brought upon the government gave Richard of York the opportunity to pit his legitimist claim to the throne against the prescriptive right of the House of Lancaster. Even so, whenever York tried to impose his will by force upon the king during the 1450s it is remarkable how little support he commanded amongst the nobles. Though turbulent and excessively prone to take to arms to settle their own quarrels, they were not prepared to cross the line which separated violence from treason. York's great rival, Somerset, may have been unpopular, but there is no evidence that York was greatly loved. York's programme, if such it can be called, was the programme of an ambitious magnate, not a party. In the 1450s the nobility was certainly not divided into Yorkist and Lancastrian. More men than we know may well have sympathized with York's complaints, and their sympathy may well have increased as support for the Lancastrian dynasty waned in the later 1450s before the court's increasing weakness. In spite of this only after York's attainder at the Parliament of Devils in 1459 did any significant part of the nobility begin to support him. Even then at first they – and even his closest friends amongst them – were unaware that he planned to revive his dormant claim to the throne. The parliamentary discussions of 1460 show above all things reluctance to accept and the impossibility of peacefully rejecting the duke's challenge. York himself was never able to topple Henry VI from his throne: he was forced to accept a compromise – recognition as Henry's heir. A few months later a mere fragment of the Yorkist faction which had grown up since 1459 made his son king as Edward IV – impelled by the desperate circumstances which had developed from York's lone policies rather than by conviction and wide support.[34]

Treason, once committed, tends to breed treason. Four political revolutions in a quarter of a century tarnished ideas of loyalty and the vision of kingship and bred an atmosphere tainted with sedition, at least amongst certain types of people. The 'union of the two noble and illustre families' of York and Lancaster in the marriage of Elizabeth of York and Henry of Richmond failed to stifle treason. There were more and wider conspiracies against Henry VII than there had ever been against Henry VI though the conspirators came mainly from lower social groups. Although, if a spy's report can be believed, even after 1500 some of the highest in the land could discuss the question of the succession without even mentioning the king's son; the nobility and the greater gentry remained aloof from both the monarchy and from treason. The political misfortunes of two generations had made them cautious and wary. They, after all, had most to lose by active involvement when high politics led to violence. Events had shown how very small were the forces which could topple a king with disastrous results for those on the losing side. Nor did the stability of the settlement of 1485 inspire much confidence. Only a small family group of nobles had then actively supported Henry VII and, as far as we know, only two peers actively fought for him at Bosworth. Lord Stanley remained aloof although his troops fought and the Earl of Northumberland stood by and watched the fight. During Henry's reign, as Sir Francis Bacon perceptively remarked, 'for his nobles, though they were loyal and obedient, yet did not cooperate with him, but let every man go his own way'. Henry returned the suspicion in even greater measure. During the Yorkist period two-thirds of the peerage had been under attainder, more or less suspended sentences of attainder or enormous financial bonds and recognizances to be of good behaviour. Under Henry the proportion increased to four-fifths.

Finally in recent years historians have debated the economic condition of fifteenth-century England. Such debates still vigorously resound. After some years in which it was generally regarded as a stagnant if not a declining economy it is now recognized that conditions were much more complicated. The country could hardly be called a unified economy. Regional variations were enormous. Some great landlords undoubtedly suffered from declining rent rolls until the last quarter of the century when there was a modest, if slow and uneven, revival. The fortune of the towns likewise varied and some undoubtedly suffered serious decline, while others vigorously prospered on the growing cloth trade. On the other hand there is a general consensus that the century was a golden age for the peasant, the labourer and the artisan. Economic change was due not to technological innovation but to demographic movements. Before the Black Death of 1349 and the further outbreaks of bubonic plague which followed it the country had been disastrously over-populated. Population had outrun agrarian resources so that the greater part of the population was seriously impoverished and its living standards depressed. The subsequent decline of population by at least one-third resulted in greater productivity per head of the population and, therefore, greater prosperity – a situation which was again reversed in the sixteenth century with a long term recovery of the population level which depressed large sections of the population into ever-increasing poverty. A detailed discussion of these highly technical problems is impossible here except to note that the civil wars had little or no effect upon agrarian and commercial life and to note a certain connection between financial power and the revival of the monarchy.[35]

The period of the 'New Monarchy' as J.R. Green in his *History of the English People* called the decades after 1461, or the 'Tudor Despotism' as others until about a couple of decades ago used to call its later phases, has often been analysed in a way which gave it a deceptive appearance of strength; a kind of incipient autocracy based on strong royal finances, the decline of parliament and an aristocracy weakened and demoralized by the Wars of the Roses – or alternatively as the medieval monarchy restored to new heights of secure power. In reality it was neither. Its stability must be sought in other causes.

There was no greater fundamental opposition between the king and parliament in the later Middle Ages than between the king and the aristocracy. Parliament occupied no static place in the constitution: it varied with circumstances. Normally its role was to cooperate with the king in the government of the realm. The great periods of parliamentary drama, apart from the peaks of revolution, were periods of financial mismanagement and financial strain, when the Commons, suspicious and resentful of heavy royal expenditure which the king expected them to defray by taxation, demanded financial reforms and concessions. The so-called 'New Monarchy' coincided with one of the longest periods in English history free of prolonged and expensive foreign warfare. Between 1453 and 1544 campaigns abroad were short and took place at long intervals. The end of the Hundred Years War was itself enough to end the principal drain on the royal coffers.[36] Edward IV, more by luck than judgment, avoided prolonged war with France and his single expedition abroad ended in his return home the richer by a valuable pension from Louis XI. Henry VII enjoyed the like good fortune. With no wars to fight, men expected the king to 'live of his own' and thus remove the most nagging dissonance between the king and his subjects in parliament. With the great shift in English trade from the export of wool to the export of cloth, revenue from the customs duties had become much smaller than it had been in the fourteenth century. Rather than risk political discontent by radically reforming the customs dues and, even more, by reforming the antiquated and unproductive system of taxation on personal property to take account of changes in the distribution of wealth, Edward IV quickly adopted as his official policy demands which the Commons had forced on Henry VI between 1449 and 1453 – demands for less taxation and for the conservation and more businesslike management of the crown lands, by cancelling grants from these estates, adding to them by a rigid enforcement of feudal rights, and placing them under a strict administration copied from the most up-to-date methods of seigneurial estate management. The whole transferred from the Exchequer and entrusted to the Chamber (a department of the royal household) the organization of which was more flexible and more adaptable for this particular purpose, though its actual achievement was somewhat patchy. Meanwhile the Exchequer of Receipt was also improving its procedures for the handling of cash and debt. Edward IV also added a more meticulous control of the customs service to avoid evasions of payment, his French pension and the considerable profits of his private trading ventures; he redeemed the monarchy from chronic debt and died rich – the only English king to do so since the time of Henry I. Parliament sank into the background, content enough to accept an administration which made no demands on its purses. Henry VII continued these practices, profiting from Edward's experiments which time and his own attentive care made even more profitable.[37]

Edward IV and Henry VII, in spite of the dramatic incidents of their careers, were by no means adventurous men. Conventionally minded to a large degree, they worked within the social and political facts of the world in which they lived, not against them. Cunning to the extent of perjury if it served their turn, their moral outlook was no worse – and no better – than that of the men through whom they had to work. Though both could be hard and cruel, they were, on the whole, merciful towards their opponents, partly because the political conventions of the day demanded it, partly because they could not afford to be anything else. Financially, by modern standards, or even by the standards of some of the more magnificent and warlike medieval kings, their ancestors, their state was hardly a state at all. With inflexible incomes derived from contracted sources, capable of only limited expansion, they were compelled to shift more after the ways of a college bursar than of a modern minister of finance. To call such a monarchy strong is to mistake shadow for substance. The English monarchy emerged from the Wars of the Roses under firm, strong guidance, but inherently it was a ramshackle structure: its survival depended on the protection of the sea, serving 'as a moat defensive to a house, against the envy of less happy lands' as John of Gaunt, 'time-honoured Lancaster', proclaimed. A generation later even the reforming schemes of Henry VIII's minister, Thomas Cromwell, failed to obliterate its inherited weaknesses. By continental standards it was one of the shallow little backwaters of monarchy.[38]

NOTES

1. E.M.W. Tillyard, *Shakespeare's History Plays* (1944); D. Hay, *Polydore Vergil, Renaissance Historian and Man of Letters* (1952).
2. *Henry IV, Pt. I*, Act IV, Sc. III.
3. *Henry IV, Pt. II*, Act IV, Sc. IV.
4. *Richard II*, Act IV, Sc. I.
5. *Henry V*, Act IV, Sc. I.
6. *Richard III*, Act IV, Sc. IV.
7. See below, pp. 96–7.
8. F.M. Stenton, 'The Changing Feudalism of the Middle Ages', *History*, xix (1935), 289–301.
9. J. Gillingham, *The Wars of the Roses: Peace and Conflict in Fifteenth Century England* (1981), p. 14.
10. C. Oman, *The Political History of England, 1377–1485* (1920), p. 367.
11. For the sheer financial and administrative difficulties of keeping an army together see J.R. Hooker, 'Notes on the Organisation and Support of the Tudor Military under Henry VII', *Huntingdon Library Quarterly*, xxiii (1959), 19–31.
12. *Medieval England*, ed. A.L. Poole (1958), i, 65–67.
13. B.H.StJ. O'Neil, *Castles and Cannon* (1960), pp. 1–64.
14. J. Evans, *English Art, 1307–1461* (1949), p. 134.
15. J. Scammell, 'Robert I and the North of England', *E.H.R.*, lxxiii (1958), 385–403.
16. *Commynes*, ii, 231, Bohn's trans., i, 394.
17. J. Evans, *Art in Medieval France, 987–1498* (1948), pp. 264–7.
18. R.S. Lopez, 'Hard Times and Investment in Culture', in *The Renaissance: A Symposium* (New York, 1953), pp. 19–32.
19. See below, pp. 227–8.
20. J. Evans, *Art in Medieval France*, op. cit., p. 282.
21. A. Bossuat, 'Le rétablissement de la paix sociale sous le règne de Charles VII' *Le Moyen Age*, 4 Ser., ix (1954), 137–62.
22. See E.G.L. Stones, *E.H.R.*, lxxii (1957), 111–2.
23. T.F.T. Plucknett, *Edward I and Criminal Law* (1960), chs. III and IV.
24. E.F. Jacob, *The Fifteenth Century, 1399–1485* (1961), p. 134.
25. R.P., v, 204–5.
26. W. Holdsworth, *The History of English Law*, iv (3rd ed., 1945) 415–61, 484ff;

C. Ogilvie, *The King's Government and the Common Law, 1470–1641* (1958), pp. 1–33; K.B. McFarlane, 'The Investment of Sir John Fastolf's Profits of War' in *T.R. Hist. S.*, Ser., vii (1957), 111–14.

27. A. Smith, 'Litigation and Politics: Sir John Fasfolt's Defence of his English Property', in *Property and Politics: Essays in later Medieval English History* (ed.) T. Pollard (Gloucester, 1984), pp. 59–75.

28. M. McKisack, *The Fourteenth Century, 1307–1399* (1959), pp. 202–3.

29. J. Fortescue, *The Governance of England*, (ed.) C. Plummer (1885), pp. 150–1.

30. '*Grants Etc. from the Crown During the Reign of Edward V*', (ed.) J. G. Nichols (Camden soc., 1854), p.ixl.

31. For the nobility see T.L. Kingston Oliphant, 'Was the old English Aristocracy destroyed by the Wars of the Roses?' in *T.R. Hist. S.*, i (1875), 437–43; J.R. Lander, 'Council, Administration and Councillors, 1461–1485', *B.I.H.R.*, xxxii (1959), 151–5; 'Attainder: and Forfeiture, 1453–1509', *The Historical Journal*, iv (1961), 119–51; 'Marriage and Politics in the Fifteenth Century: The Nevilles and the Wydevilles', *B.I.H.R.*, xxxvi (1963), 148–9; reprinted in J.R. Lander, *Crown and Nobility 1450–1509* (1976).

32. W.H. Dunham IV, 'Lord Hastings; Indentured Retainers, 1461–1483', *Transactions of the Connecticut Academy of Arts and Sciences*, 39 (1955), Appendices A and B.

33. W. T. MacCaffery, 'Talbot and Stanhope: an Episode in Elizabethan Politics', *B.I.H.R.*, xxx (1960).

34. J.R. Lander, *Marriage and Politics*. etc. op. cit, pp. 123–9.

35. A.R. Bridbury, *Economic Growth: England in the Later Middle Ages* (1962), criticized by E. Miller, 'The English Economy in the Thirteenth Century'; *Past and Present*, 28 (1964), W.G. Hoskins, *The Making of the English Landscape* (London, 1955), J.L. Bolton, *The Medieval English Economy, 1150–1500* (London, Totawa, N.J., 1980) chs. 7, 8 and 9 which also supplies an excellent bibliography on the topic.

36. G. Holmes, *The Later Middle Ages, 1272–1485* (1962), ch. 12.

37. B.P. Wolffe, *The Crown Lands, 1461–1536* (London, 1970) and *The Royal Demesne in English History: The Crown Estates in the Governance of the Realm from the Conquest to 1509* (1971); J.D. Alsop, 'The Exchequer in Late Medieval Government, c. 1485–1530', in *Aspects of Late Medieval Government and Society: Essays Presented to J.R Lander* (Toronto, 1986), 179–212.

38. G.L. Harriss, 'Medieval Government and Statecraft', *Past and Present* (25), 1963.

ONE

The House of Lancaster

When in 1399 Henry of Derby, the heir of John of Gaunt, Duke of Lancaster, fourth son of the great Edward III, usurped the throne from his cousin, Richard II, he concealed the flaws in his title in a vague and evasive declaration in parliament:

> In the name of Father, Son and Holy Ghost, I Henry of Lancaster challenge this realm of England, and the crown with all the members and the appurtenances, als I that am descended by right line of the blood coming from the good lord King Henry third, and through that right that God of his grace hath sent me, with help of my kin and of my friends to recover it: the which realm was in point to be undone for default of governance and undoing of the good laws.(1)

In so doing he ignored the claims of the Mortimer family, descending through a woman, Philippa, the daughter of Lionel of Clarence, the third son of Edward III. These claims after 1425 passed to her great-grandson, Richard, Duke of York. There was no certain rule of succession to the English crown at this time. Should the inheritance descend to the heir male or to the heir general? For the time the claims of the heir general lay dormant – but potentially dangerous. Only success could justify the House of Lancaster in continued possession of the throne. Henry V's renewal of the Hundred Years War in France soon lost its appeal for any except the soldiers who directly profited from his campaigns and the merchants who victualled his armies. Henry bought his triumphs against the Valois at the cost of mounting resentment at the high taxation which he levied on the rest of the community to pay for them. By 1421 many men echoed the indignant wail on which Adam of Usk ended his Chronicle:

> And, seeking to avenge it* yet more, our Lord the King, rending every man throughout the realm who had money, be he rich or poor,

---

*i.e. the English defeat at Bauge, 22 March 1421.

designs to return again into France in full strength. But, woe is me! mighty men and treasure of the realm will be most miserably fordone about this business. And in truth the grievous taxation of the people to this end being unbearable, accompanied with murmurs and with smothered curses among them from hatred of the burden, I pray that my liege lord become not in the end a partaker, together with Julius, with Asshur, with Alexander, with Hector, with Cyrus, with Darius, with Maccabaeus, of the sword of the wrath of the Lord!(2)

After Henry's premature death the following year, the English in France, led by his brother John, Duke of Bedford, for a time extended their conquests. From about 1429, however, the French began to gain ground against the English. By 1435, with the death of John of Bedford and the failure of peace negotiations – the result of almost insanely presumptuous demands which the English made at the conference of Arras – the French war had reached a crisis. Sir John Fastolf, one of the most experienced of the war captains, advised that Henrys V's policy of conquest and consolidation by the maintenance of garrisons had become too expensive. Terror and a 'scorched-earth' policy were his recommendations for the future:

. . . First, it seemeth . . . that the king should do lay no sieges nor make no conquest out of Normandy, or to conquest by way of siege as yet; for the sieges hath greatly hindered his conquest in time passed, and destroyed his people, as well lords, captains, and chieftains, as his other people, and wasted and consumed innumerable good of his finances, both in England and in France, and in Normandy. For there may no king conquer a great realm by continual sieges, and specially seeing the habiliments and ordnances that be-eth this day used for the war, and the knowledge and experience that the enemies have therein, both in keeping of their places and otherwise; and also the favour that they find in many that should be the king's true subjects.

Wherefore . . . it is thought right expedient, for the speed and the advancement of the king's conquest and destroying of his enemies, to ordain two notable chieftains, descreet and of one accord, having either of them seven hundred and fifty spears of well chosen men, and they to

*i.e. to lead an army, wage war.

hold the field continually and oostay,* and go six, eight or ten leagues asunder in breadth, or more or less after their discretion; and each of them may answer to other and join together in case of necessity. And that they begin to oostay from the first day of June continually unto the first day of November, landing for the first time at Calais or Crotoy, or the one at Calais and the other at Crotoy, as shall be thought expedient; and so holding forth their way through Artois and Picardy, and so through Vermandois, Lannoy, Champagne and Burgundy, brenning and destroying all the land as they pass, both house, corn, vines, and all trees that bearen fruit for man's sustenance, and all bestaile* that may not be driven, to be destroyed; and that that may be well driven and spared over the sustenance and advictualling of the hosts, to be driven into Normandy, to Paris, and to other places of the king's obeisance, and if goodly them think it to be done. For it is thought that the traitors and rebels must needs have another manner of war, and more sharp and more cruel war than a natural and anoien† enemy . . . to th'intent to drive th'enemies thereby to an extreme famine.(3)

In these unhappy circumstances Henry VI and his later foe, Richard, Duke of York, came to the forefront of politics for the first time. Henry, at the age of fifteen, signed his first royal warrant in December 1436. Richard of York had taken part in a Great Council at Westminster in April and May 1434 and in January 1435 (he was then twenty-four) the royal council appointed him Lieutenant and Governor of France and Normandy. Many years later John Blacman, a Carthusian monk who had been one of Henry's chaplains, wrote a memoir of his master. He depicted an extreme form of a contemporary type of intense lay piety – an English variation of the *devotio moderna*: bliss to a monk of a strict contemplative order, disastrous for a people in days when a king must rule as well as reign:

He was, like a second Job, a man simple and upright, altogether fearing the Lord God, and departing from evil. He was a simple man, without any crook of craft or untruth, as is plain to all. With none did he deal craftily, nor ever would say an untrue word to any, but framed his speech always to speak truth.

---

*i.e. livestock.
† i.e. honourable(?).

He was both upright and just, always keeping to the straight line of justice in his acts. Upon none would he wittingly inflict any injustice. To God and the Almighty he rendered most faithfully that which was His, for he took pains to pay in full the tithes and offerings due to God and the church: and this he accompanied with most sedulous devotion, so that even when decked with the kingly ornaments and crowned with the royal diadem he made it a duty to bow before the Lord as deep in prayer as any young monk might have done ...

... And that this prince cherished a son's fear towards the Lord is plain from many an act and devotion of his. In the first place, a certain reverend prelate of England used to relate that for ten years he held the office of confessor to King Henry; but he declared that never throughout that long time had any blemish of mortal sin touched his soul ...

.... A diligent and sincere worshipper of God was this king, more given to God and to devout prayer than to handling worldly and temporal things, or practising vain sports and pursuits: these he despised as trifling, and was continually occupied either in prayer or the reading of the scriptures or of chronicles, whence he drew not a few wise utterances to the spiritual comfort of himself and others ...

... This King Henry was chaste and pure from the beginning of his days. He eschewed all licentiousness in word or deed while he was young; until he was of marriageable age, when he espoused the most noble lady, Lady Margaret, daughter of the King of Sicily, by whom he begat one only son, the most noble and virtuous Prince Edward; and with her and toward her he kept his marriage vow wholly and sincerely, even in the absences of the lady, which were sometimes very long: never dealing unchastely with any other woman. Neither when they lived together did he use his wife unseemly, but with all honesty and gravity.

... It happened once, that at Christmas time a certain great lord brought before him a dance or show of young ladies with bared bosoms who were to dance in that guise before the king, perhaps to prove him, or to entice his youthful mind. But the king was not blind to it, nor unaware of the devilish wile, and spurned the delusion, and very angrily averted his eyes, turned his back upon them, and went out to his chamber, saying:

'Fy, fy, for shame, forsothe ye be to blame.'

At another time, riding by Bath, where are warm baths in which they say the men of that country customably refresh and wash themselves, the king, looking into the baths, saw in them men wholly naked with every garment cast off. At which he was displeased, and went away quickly, abhorring such nudity as a great offence, and not unmindful of that sentence of Francis Petrarch 'the nakedness of a beast is in men unpleasing, but the decency of raiment makes for modesty ...*

... I would have you know that he was most eminent for that virtue of humility. This pious prince was not ashamed to be a diligent server to a priest celebrating in his presence, and to make the responses at the mass, as *Amen, Sed libera nos*, and the rest. He did so commonly even to me, a poor priest. At table even when he took a slight refection, he would (like a professed religious) rise quickly, observe silence, and devoutly give thanks to God standing on every occasion. Also on the testimony of Master Doctor Towne, he made a rule that a certain dish which represented the five wounds of Christ as it were red with blood, should be set on his table by his almoner before any other course, when he was to take refreshment; and contemplating these images with great fervour he thanked God marvellous devoutly ...

Also at the principal feasts of the year, but especially at those when of custom he wore his crown, he would always have put on his bare body a rough hair shirt, that by its roughness his body might be restrained from excess, or more truly that all pride and vain glory, such as is apt to be engendered by pomp, might be repressed.(4)

York,† with little or no experience of warfare, took up his first command in the most depressing circumstances. The French had penetrated to the very gates of Rouen and in Easter Week they captured Paris. The following year, despite a modest success, rejecting urgent protests from the royal council, he

---

*For the extremely louche customs of the people of Bath which drew upon them the rebuke of their bishop see *The Register of Thomas Bekynton, Bishop of Bath and Wells, 1443–1465*, ed. Sir H.C. Maxwell-Lyte and M.C.B. Dawes, *Som. Rec. Soc.*, i, 1934–5, 116–17.

†Unfortunately, no corresponding description of York's character exists.

insisted on giving up his charge. Re-appointed in July 1440, he lingered in England, ignoring urgent appeals that he should cross the Channel, until in June 1441 the council at Rouen predicted total defeat unless he immediately went to their rescue. As the following warrant shows the government spared no efforts to provide the money his forces required:

Henry by the grace of God King of England and of France and Lord of Ireland. To the Treasurer and Chamberlains of our Exchequer greeting. For as much as for the setting over the sea of our cousin the Duke of York into our realm of France and Duchy of Normandy for the conservation and keeping of them and also the th'entretenue of our subjects in our obeisance in the same us needeth in haste great and notable sums of money. Whereof we be not as now purveyed neither cannot be without chevisance of our subjects or sale or departing from us of parcel of our jewels. And in so much as the chevisance* that we can make at this time for the said cause will not suffice for the contenting of the said army over ready money by us perforce paid and that we would not for th'ease of us and of all Our true subjects but that the same army shall by the grace of our Lord take good effect and exploit it to the good relief and succours of our said realm, duchy and of all our subjects. We will therefore and charge you straitly that anon after the sight of these ye do break, cune,† sell and lay to wedde‡ such and as many of our jewels as over the payments by you made for the said army and over ready apprestes§ to us made for the same will reasonably suffice for the setting over of the said army, and as far as the said jewels will stretch if ye can and may do it. And these our letters shall be unto you here your sufficient warrant and discharge. Given under our privy seal at our castle of Windsor the second day of February the year of our reign XIX.(5)

During the next few months York, advised by Talbot, the greatest of the war veterans, made no less than five valiant onslaughts to relieve the besieged

*i.e. borrowing.
†i.e. coin.
‡i.e. pledge.
§i.e. advances.

fortress of Pontoise. At last their troops, unable to live on the ravaged countryside, fell back on Rouen and Pontoise surrendered to the French. York accomplished very little after the summer of 1442, despite factions and plots at the French court which weakened his opponents in the field. When the English and French concluded a truce in April 1444 he had seen less than three years' active campaigning during the five years of his second command, and the English position was hardly better than it had been in 1440. York himself, may well have brooded in bitterness of spirit over obstructive political intrigues at home* and, as a royal warrant of 1446 clearly shows, by the recent failure of the government to meet his expenses:

Henry by the grace of God, King of England and of France and Lord of Ireland. To the Treasurer and Chamberlains of our Exchequer greeting. We let you weet that we have understand by a supplication of our cousin the Duke of York that where as now late we commanded you by our letters of warrant to content him of all this that should be found due unto him of his appointment of £20,000 yearly for five years ended at Michaelmas last past for the keeping and entretening of our realm of France and Duchy of Normandy as in his indentures thereupon made it appeareth more at large, it is so as he saith that and he should be counted with and paid after the tenor of the said indentures there should be found due unto him of the fourth year of the same five year £18,666 13s. 4d., and of the fifth year the whole sum of £20,000 which amount to the sum of £38,066 13s.4d.† And how

*In 1443 John Beaufort, Duke of Somerset, was appointed Captain-General of France and Guienne. His commission was limited to parts outside York's control. The force which he led overseas, and which diverted money from York, was a failure, and York naturally resented the appointment. See J. Ramsay, Lancaster and York, ii, 48–55, 1892.
†The correct amount is, of course, £38,666 13s. 4d. It is generally said that Henry VI's ministers treated York most unscrupulously in money matters and that financial grievances roused his bitter discontent. This particular warrant, at first sight, seems to indicate that York was exceptionally badly treated. Yet other and poorer men were treated in a similar way, e.g., the Earl of Warwick and the Earl of Devonshire. Shortly before this a mere squire, John Nanfan, had surrendered 8,938 out of 22,938 *livres tournois* in order to obtain payment of the balance (PRO, E. 404/57/157). A few years later Sir John Fastolf's secretary, William Worcester, alleged that such bargains were common practice. (*The Boke of Noblesse*, pp. 80–81.)

be it that he hath promitted the lords, captains and soldiers of our garrisons within our said realm and duchy to content them of their wages which he cannot without he may have payment of the said sums, yet natheless he hath agreed him considering the great charges that we have in hand to rebate £12,666 13s. 4d. of the said £38,006 13s. 4d. so that he might be payed of have sufficient assignment of the residue which amounteth to the sum of £26,000. Wherefore we will and charge you that unto our said cousin ye make payment or sufficient assignment of the said £26,000. Given under our privy seal at our Tower of London the 2nd day of June the year of our reign XXIV.(6)

Whether or not the English had wantonly followed Sir John Fastolf's scorched-earth policy, his secretary, William Worcester, a few years later admitted that their administration had become oppressive and savage in the extreme. As the following account, written by the Norman ecclesiastic, Thomas Basin, shows, in their demoralized ferocity they reduced to utter misery wide areas of the borderlands of northern France where their control was constantly disputed:

Thus after the death of his father . . . Charles VII succeeded to the throne of France, at the age of twenty-two or thereabouts. In his day, as well through the effect of continual wars, civil and foreign, as through the negligence and idleness of those who conducted business or commanded under his orders as through lack of military order and discipline and the greed and slackness of the men-at-arms the said kingdom was reduced to such a state of devastation that from the Loire to the Seine the peasants had been slain or put to flight. Most of the fields for long remained, over the years, not only uncultivated but without men enough to till them, except for a few odd pieces of land where it was impossible to extend the little that could be cultivated away from the cities, towns and castles owing to the frequent forays of the robbers.

Nevertheless, the Bassin and the Cotentin and Lower Normandy which, under the sway of the English, were far enough away from the enemy's defence line, less easily and less often exposed to the robber raids, remained a little better cultivated and populated, though often borne down by great poverty, as will more clearly appear in what follows:

> We ourselves have seen the vast plains of Champagne, of Beauce, of Brie, of the Gâtinais, Chartres, Dreux, Maine and Perche, of the Vexin, French as well as Norman, the Beauvaisis, the Pays de Caux, from the Seine as far as Amiens and Abbeville, the countryside round Senlis, Soissons and Valois right to Laon and beyond towards Hainault absolutely deserted, uncultivated, abandoned, empty of inhabitants, covered with scrub and brambles; indeed in most of the more thickly wooded districts dense forests were growing up. And, in a great many places it was feared that the marks of this devastation would long endure and remain visible unless divine providence kept better watch over the things of this world.
>
> All that could be cultivated at this time in these parts, lay only about and within the cities, towns or castles, close enough that from the tower or look-out the watchman's eye could see the brigands approaching. Then by the sound of the alarm-bell or horn or any other instrument, he gave everybody working in the fields or amongst the vines the signal to withdraw to the fortifications.
>
> Such things were common and frequent almost everywhere, so much so that the oxen and draught horses once released from the plough, when they heard the watchman's signal, trained by long habit, without being told would, panic-stricken, gallop to the refuge where they knew that they were safe. Sheep and pigs had developed the same habit. But as in the said provinces over the whole extent of the land, cities and fortified places were rare, as besides, either many had been burned, destroyed, sacked by the enemy or were empty of inhabitants the little land cultivated as if surreptitiously round the fortified places seemed very little indeed, almost nothing in comparison with the vast expanse of completely deserted fields with no one to cultivate them.(7)

With a France rejuvenated by success opposed to an England leaderless under a *fainéant* king, success in war was a forlorn delusion. Early in 1444 William de la Pole, the leader of those who wished to rid the country of Henry V's now disastrously ambitious legacy, fully aware of the risks he ran from embittered diehards at home led an embassy to France, which resulted in the betrothal of Henry VI to Margaret of Anjou and the conclusion of a two-year truce. Margaret, a dowerless bride of sixteen, landed at Portsmouth in April 1445.

The king's uncle, Humphrey, Duke of Gloucester, the Lancastrian heir apparent and the most intransigent of the warmongers, violently opposed the truce, maintaining that the French would take advantage of an interval of peace to build up their forces for a more determined attack on Normandy. Although Suffolk and his friends had almost completely destroyed Gloucester's influence with the king his opposition to an agreement to surrender Maine to the French* grew so outspoken that they determined, at all costs, to silence him. Early in 1447 they summoned a parliament to Bury St Edmunds to condemn him for treason. Richard Fox, a monk of St Albans, wrote the following account of the Bury Parliament:

... the parliament began the 10th day of February.

And on the 16th day of the same month mustered the men of the same country on the north side of Bury on Henow Heath to the number of 40,000.

And on the morrow they showed themself on the south-east party of the town of Bury. And there they brake up their watch, and every man went to his own dwelling-place, some thirty mile, some twenty mile, ten mile, four mile, g some more, some less, and no doubt of it was a fervent cold weather and a biting. And on the morrow, that is to say the 18th day of February and Shrove-Sunday's Even, come the Duke of Gloucester from Lyneham; and ere he come by half a mile or more met with him Sir John Stourton, treasurer of the king's house, and Sir Thomas Stanley, controller of the king's house in message from the king, was [sic] as it was reported by some of the foresaid duke's

---

*Charles VII of France and René of Anjou, Queen Margaret's father, had instructed her to persuade Henry VI to make this concession. This was later held against her though most probably, inexperienced as she was at this time, she acted as an unwitting tool. Since 1441, when he had been discredited by the condemnation of his wife, Eleanor Cobham, for attempting to cause the king's death by witchcraft, Gloucester had taken very little part in politics.

meinie:* 'that forasmuch as the foresaid Duke of Gloucester had laboured in that fervent cold weather, it was the king's will that he should take the next way to his lodging, and go to his meat.' And indeed he entered in at the Southgate about eleven on the clock afore noon. And by estimation there come with him to the number of four score horse. These foresaid messengers, when they had do the king's commandment, took leave of the duke, and returned again to the king.

And the foresaid duke rode into the horse-market, and took the way on his left hand to the Northgate ward, and he entered into a lewd lane. And then the duke asked a poor man that dwelled in the same lane, 'What call me this lane?' The poor man answered and said, 'Forsooth, my lord, it is called the Dead Lane.' And then the good duke remembered him of an old prophecy that he had read many a day before, and said, 'As our lord will, be it all;' and rode forth to the North Spital to his meat. And anon as he had eaten, come to him by the king's commandment the Duke of Buckingham, the Marquess of Dorset, the Earl of Salisbury, the Viscount Beaumont, the Lord Sudeley. And the Viscount Beaumont arrested the said Duke of Gloucester; and by the commandment of the king there waited upon the said duke two yeomen of the Crown and a sergeant of arms: Bartholomew Halley and Pulford, yeomen of the Crown, and Thomas Calbrose, sergeant of arms.

And that same afternoon, between eight and nine, were arrested by the king's officers Sir Roger Chamberlain and Sir Henry Wogan knights, Thomas Herbert, Thomas Weryot, John Wogan, Howell ap David Thomas, and mo other, etc.

And on the Sunday was John Hobergere commanded to ward against even.

And on the Shrove-Tuesday, in the latter end of their meat, in the hall were arrest Sir Robert Vere, Sir John Cheyne, knights, John Buckland, controller with the said duke, Arteys, Thomas Wild, Richard Middleton, Wallerown, Bassingbourn, squires; Richard Needham, John Swafylde, yeomen; and mo other, to the number of twenty-eight. And these were sent to divers places to prison, some to the Tower of London, some to Winchester, some to Nottingham, and some to Northampton, and to other divers places, as pleased the king and his council.

---

*i.e. retinue, band of servants or retainers.

And on the Thursday next following after the arresting of the said Duke of Gloucester, he died soon upon three of the bell at afternoon, at his own lodging called St Salvator's, without the Northgate: on whose soul God have mercy. Amen.(8)

Although as a politician Gloucester had been senseless and worse, he deserves to be remembered as one of the first English patrons of humanism. An anonymous chronicler wrote:

And in the 26th year [of his reign] died the Duke of Gloucester, Humphrey, the son of Henry IV, brother of Henry V and uncle of Henry VI, at the Parliament of Bury on the eve of the feast of St Matthew the Apostle,* about midnight. This duke was a man of letters, and a true enthusiast for learning, the faith, the church, the clergy and the realm. He endowed and enriched the University of Oxford with precious, beautiful and sumptuous books of every science and branch of learning; and his name and the remembrance of him are and shall be for ever engraved there in memory both human and divine.(9)

Gloucester's death left York heir to the throne – and he was the next to be dealt with. His lieutenancy in France had expired in 1445. For many months he hoped for its renewal. Finally, in the autumn of 1447, it was given to Suffolk's ally, Edmund Beaufort† (created Duke of Somerset in March 1448). Beaufort from this time forth became the target of all York's suspicions. He was descended from John of Gaunt and therefore had a claim of sorts to the throne and from at least 1450 York dreaded him as a possible competitor for the succession. In September 1447 the court banished York to a kind of honourable exile by appointing him Lieutenant of Ireland for ten years.‡At the same time to soften the blow he received a number of valuable grants from the king.

---

*26 February.
†Abbot Whethamstede of St Albans saw the origins of the Wars of the Roses in this incident (*Registrum Abbatiae Johannis Whethamstede*, ed. H.T. Riley, R. S., 1872–3, i, 1 59ff), but this part of his work is altogether too literary and imaginative.
‡He remained in England until July 1449.

Suffolk's triumph was short. François de Surienne, an Aragonese knight in English pay, wantonly broke the Anglo-French truce, by attacking the Breton town of Fougères on 23 or 24 March 1449. Suffolk and Edmund Beaufort may well have been privy to this reckless enterprise. If so, they were the architects of their own ruin. Charles VII of France came to the help of his cousin, the Duke of Brittany, and counter-attacked in Normandy. A fatal combination of stratagem and treachery, defection of Englishmen eager to make their own terms with the enemy and so retain their Norman estates, and inadequate forces weakened by the indiscipline of their petty captains swept the English out of Normandy.

This catastrophe produced a wave of violent resentment against the king's ministers. Early in January 1450 one of Suffolk's principal supporters was murdered at Portsmouth:

> And this year, the Friday the 9th day of January, Master Adam Moleyns, Bishop of Chichester and Keeper of the King's Privy Seal, whom the king sent to Portsmouth, for to make payment of money to certain soldiers and shipmen for their wages; and so it happened that with boisterous language, and also for abridging of their wages, he fell in variance with them, and they fell on him, and cruelly there killed him.(10)

Suffolk, seriously disturbed by the turn events had taken, determined to stifle opposition by tactics which had served him well in 1445: to get parliament to place on record its approval of his conduct. The very day parliament met (22 January) he made a long speech dwelling on the loyal service which, over a generation and more, his family had given to the Lancastrian kings:

> Our aller most high and dread Sovereign Lord, I suppose well that it be commen to your ears, to my great heaviness and sorrow, God knoweth, the odious and horrible language that runneth through your land, almost in every common's mouth sowning to my highest charge and most heaviest dis-slander, again your most noble and royal person and your land, by a certain confession of the keeper of your privy seal, whom God assoil, should have made at his death, as it is said; which noise and language is to me the heaviest charge and burthen, that I could in any wise receive or bear as reason is, of the which our Lord

above that all thing seeth and knoweth, wot that I am full unguilty of: Beseeching your Highness, ye like of your good grace, to consider the true service that my Lord my father did to the king of noble memory your grandsire, in all the voyages in his days both by sea and land, that were made out of this land, in the which he was at all. And after in the days of the most victorious prince the king your father, in whose service he died at Harfleur; mine eldest brother after with him at the battle of Agincourt; mine other two brethren also dieden in your service at Jargeau, the day that I was taken but as a knight ought to be I trust to God, and paid £20,000 to my finance;* my fourth brother lying there for me in hostage, died also in your enemies' hands; myself hath be armed in the king's days your father, and yours thirty-four winters, and of the fellowship of the garter thirty, and continually within the time beforesaid abiden in the war there seventeen year withouten coming home or seeing of this land;† and sithen my coming home, have continually served about your most noble person fifteen year, in the which I have founden as great grace and goodness, as ever liegeman found in his Sovereign Lord, God reward your Highness therefore in heaven and in earth. And in this your realm, Sovereign Lord, I have my birth, and mine inheritance and estate to me, and to them that be, and shall come of me, to serve you, Sovereign Lord, and this your noble realm. And all these things well considered, if for a Frenchman's promise, where all thoo that I am comen of myself also, and all thoo that should come of me been enherited here in this your land that I am born of, there were none earthly punicion but that it were to little for me ... (11)

Suffolk badly misjudged the temper of his audience. This high-pitched invocation of past services availed him nothing, for the Commons detested him as much for his prolonged misgovernment at home as for the loss of Normandy. Suffolk's 'insaciable covetise' stank even in the nostrils of a generation far from nice in matters financial. Since 1437, following his

---

*i.e. ransom.
†Suffolk certainly exaggerated at this point. He may possibly have been in France for fourteen years (1417–31) without returning to England.

example, his friends amongst the nobles and courtiers had plundered the king's estates and other sources of income on an unheard-of scale.[1] The Commons bitterly resented demands for taxation to make good such losses.* Now they seized their opportunity. Four days after Suffolk's declaration they demanded his imprisonment. A little later they denounced him for treason and for corrupt and violent practices.† The following extracts are taken from their indictment:

> First, the said Duke, the 20th day of July, the 25th year of your blessed reign,‡ in your City of London, in the parish of St Sepulchre in the ward of Farringdon Infra, imagining and purposing, falsely and traitorously, to destroy your most royal person, and this your said realm; then and there traitorously excited, counselled, provoked and comforted the Earl of Donas, Bastard of Orleans, Bertrand, Lord Pressigny, Master William Cunyset, enemies to you Sovereign Lord, and other your enemies, subjects and ambassadors to Charles, calling himself King of France, your greatest adversary and enemy, to move, counsel, stir and provoke the same Charles, to come into this your realm, to levy, raise and make open war against you Sovereign Lord, with a great puissance and army, to destroy your most royal person, and your true subjects of the same realm; to th'intent to make John son of the same duke, king of this your said realm, and to depose you of your high regalie thereof; the same Duke of Suffolk having then of your grant, the ward and marriage of Margaret,§ daughter and heir to John, late Duke of Somerset, purposing to marry her to his said son, presuming and pretending her to be next inheritable to the crown of this your realm,

---

*From 1449 onwards the Commons were demanding Acts of Resumption, i.e. the revocation of all grants made by the king out of the royal lands and revenues.
†The treason charges were fantastic but modern research has shown the truth of other accusations made against Suffolk.
‡i.e. 1446–7.
§Lady Margaret Beaufort, later the mother of Henry VII, descended from John of Gaunt and Catherine Sywnford. Their children, born out of wedlock, were legitimized by Richard II. In 1407 Henry IV declared that this did not cover the succession to the crown. Henry's restriction was legally dubious.

for lack of issue of you Sovereign Lord, in accomplishment of his said traitorous purpose and intent, hath do the said Margaret to be married to his said son . . . *

. . . The said duke, the 16th year of your reign,† then being next and priviest of your council, and steward of your honourable household, then and many years sith, for covetise of great lucre of good singularly to himself, stirred and moved your Highness, the said 16th year, ye then being in prosperity and having great possessions, to give and grant much partie of your said possessions, to divers persons in your said realm of England, by the which ye be greatly impoverished, the expenses of your honourable Household, and the wages and fees of your menial servants not paid, your Wardrobe, the reparations of your castles and manors, and your other ordinary charges were not had, satisfied nor do; and so by his subtle counsel, importunate and unprofitable labour to your most high and royal estate, the revenues of the demesnes and possessions of your crown, your Duchy of Lancaster, and other your inheritances, have been so amenused and anientised,** that your commons of this your realm have be so importably charged, that it is nigh to their final destruction . . .

. . . Item, that where the Lord Sudeley, late your Treasurer of this your realm,‡ the time of his departure out of his said office, of his great truth and providence for the defence of your said realm, and support of the charges necessary of the same, left in your Treasury in ready money and sure payment, the sum of £60,000, of quinzimes, dismes,§ and other revenues of this your realm; which money, if it had be well dispended,

*On 18 August 1450 Pope Nicholas V issued a licence permitting the two children (Lady Margaret was born in 1441 and John de la Pole in 1442) to *remain* in marriage. They must have been hastily and secretly married earlier in the year.
†i.e. 1437–8
**i.e. diminished and destroyed.
‡Ralph Butler, 1st Lord Sudeley, Treasurer, July 1443–December 1446.
§Fifteenths and tenths were the standard form of taxation levied on personal property. Between 1429 and 1449 a fifteenth and tenth had been granted on average every second year, i.e., rather more than £15,000 p.a., much less than under Henry V but much more than in the 1420s.

and to such intent as it was left for in your Treasury, would greatly have holpen to the defence of the same; the great part of which £60,000, by labour and means of the said Duke of Suffolk, hath been mischievously given and distribute to himself, his friends and well-willers; for lack of which treasure, none army nor competent ordnance might be sufficiently in due time purveyed for these premises . . .(12)

The indictment, which is very long, also alleged (falsely) that Suffolk betrayed vital military information to the French and at home (basically correctly though with considerable exaggeration) accused him of corrupt administration, maintenance, oppression and the perversion of justice in his own interest and in the interests of his adherents.

To save him from condemnation Henry banished him. On his way to Calais he was murdered by persons unknown. On 5 May William Lomner wrote to John Paston:

Right worshipful sir, I recommend me to you, and am right sorry of that I shall say, and have so wash this little bill with sorrowful tears, that on ethes* ye shall read it.

As on Monday next after May day there come tidings to London, that on Thursday before the Duke of Suffolk come unto the coasts of Kent full near Dover with his two ships and a little spynner; the which spynner he sent with certain letters to certain of his trusted men unto Calais ward, to know how he should be received; and with him met a ship called Nicholas of the Tower, with other ships waiting on him, and by them that were in the spynner, the master of the Nicholas had knowledge of the duke's coming. And when he espied the duke's ships, he sent forth his boat to weet what they were, and the duke himself spake to them, and said, he was by the king's commandment sent to Calais ward, etc.

And they said he must speak with their master. And so he, with two or three of his men, went forth with them in their boat to the Nicholas; and when he come, the master bade him, 'Welcome, Traitor,' as men say; and further the master desired to weet if the shipmen

*i.e. scarcely.

would hold with the duke, and they sent word they would not in no wise; and so he was in the Nicholas till Saturday next following.

Some say he wrote much thing to be delivered to the king, but that is not verily known. He had his confessor with him, etc.

And some say he was arraigned in the ship on here manner* upon the appeachments and found guilty, etc.

Also he asked the name of the ship, and when he knew it, he remembered Stacy that said, if he might escape the danger of the Tower, he should be safe; and then he heart failed him, for he thought he was deceived, and in the sight of all his men he was drawn out of the great ship into the boat; and there was an axe, and a stroke, and one of the lewdest of the ship bade him lay down his head, and he should be fair ferd with,† and die on a sword; and took a rusty sword, and smote off his head within half a dozen strokes, and took away his gown of russet, and his doublet of velvet mayled,‡ and laid his body on the sands of Dover; and some say his head was set on a pole by it, and his men set on the land by great circumstance and praye.** And the sheriff of Kent doth watch the body, and sent his under-sheriff to the judges to weet what to do and also to the king what shall be do.(13)

By the end of May the men of Kent were under arms. Cade's rebellion had broken out. *Gregory's Chronicle* recounts the events of the next few weeks:

And after that the commons of Kent arose with certain other shires, and they chose them a captain, the which captain compelled all the gentles to arise with them. And at the end of the parliament they came with a great might and a strong host unto the Blackheath, beside Greenwich, the number of 46,000; and there they made a field, dyked and staked well about, as it been in the land of war, save only they kept order among them, for alls good was Jack Robin as John at the Noke,

*i.e. directly (?).
†i e. fairly treated.
‡i.e. covered with metal rings or plates.
**i.e. troop of men (?).

for all were as high as pigs' feet, unto the time that they should commune and speak with such states* and messengers as were sent unto them; then they put all their power unto the man that named him captain of all their host. And there they abode certain days to the coming of the king from the parliament at Leicester. And then the king sent unto the captain divers lords both spiritual and temporal, to wit and to have knowledge of that great assembling and gathering of that great and misadvised fellowship. The captain of them sending word again unto the king, that it was for the weal of him our sovereign lord, and of all the realm, and for to destroy the traitors being about him, with other divers points that they would see that it were in short time amended. Upon which answer that the king,** thither sent by his lords, did make a cry in the king's name of England that all the king's liege men of England should avoid the field. And upon the night after they were all voided and a-go.

The morning after, the king rode armed at all pecys† from St John's beside Clerkenwell through London; and with him the most party of temporal lords of this land of England in their a-best [ar]-ray. After that they were every lord with his retinue, to the number of 10,000 persons, ready as they all should have gone to battle into any land of Christendom, with bends above their harness that every lord should be known from other. And in the forward, as they would have followed the captain, was slain Sir Humphrey Stafford and William Stafford, squire, one of the manliest men of all this realm of England, with many moo other of mean persons at Sevenoaks, in Kent, in their out raging from their host of our sovereign lord's the king' Harry the VI. And the king lodged that night at Greenwich, and soon after every lord with his retinue rode home into their country.

And after that, upon the first day of July, the same captain came again, as the Kentishmen said, but it was another that named himself the captain, and he came to the Blackheath. And upon the morrow he came with a great host into Southwark, and at the White Hart he took

*i.e. Lords, people of high rank.
**i.e. as in MS.
†i.e. points.

his lodging. And upon the morrow, that was the Friday, again even, they smote asunder the ropes of the draw-bridge and fought sore a-manly, and many a man was murdered and killed in that conflict, I wot not what [to] name it for the multitude of riffraff. And then they entered into the city of London as men that had been half beside their wit; and in that furnace (furynys) they went, as they said, for the common weal of the realm of England, even straight unto a merchant his place y— named Philip Malpas of London. If it were true as they surmised after their doing, I remit me to ink and paper – *Deus scit et ego non*. But well I wot that every ill beginning most commonly hath an ill ending, and every good beginning hath the very good ending. *Proverbium:– Felix principium finem facit esse beatum*. And that Philip Malpas was alderman, and they spoiled him and bare away much good of his, and in specially much money, both of silver and gold, the value of a notable sum, and in specially of merchandises, as of tin, woad, madder, and alum, with great quantity of woollen cloth and many rich jewels, with other notable stuff of feather-beds, bedding, nappery and many a rich cloth of arras, to the value of a notable sum – *nescio, set Deus omnia scit*.

And in the evening they went with their simple captain to his lodging; but a certain of his simple and rude meinie abode there all the night, weening to them that they had wit and wisdom for to have guiding or put in guiding all England, also-soon at they had got the city of London by a mishap of cutting of two sorry cords that now be altered, and made two strong chains of iron unto the drawbridge of London. But they had other men with them, as well of London as of their own party. And by them of one party and of that other party they left nothing unsoffethe,* and they searched all that night.

And in the morn he came in again, that sorry and simple and rebellious captain with his meinie; that was Saturday, and it was also a St Martin his day, the dedication of St Martin's in the Vintry, the 4th day of July. And then divers quests† were i-summoned at the Guild Hall; and there Robert Horne being alderman was arrested and brought in to Newgate. And that same day William Crowmer, squire, and sheriff of

*i.e. unsought (?).
†i.e. inquests, inquiries.

Kent, was beheaded in the field without Aldgate at the Mile's End beside Clopton his place. And another man that was named John Bayle was beheaded at the White Chapel. And the same day afternoon was beheaded in Cheap afore the Standard, Sir James Fiennes, being that time the Lord Say and Great Treasurer of England, the which was brought out of the Tower of London unto the Guild Hall, and there of divers treasons he was examined, of which he knowledged of the death of that notable and famous prince the Duke of Gloucester.* And then they brought him unto the Standard in Cheap, and there he received his dues (jewys) and his death. And so forth all the three heads that day smitten off were set upon the Bridge of London, and the two other heads taken down that stood upon the London Bridge before. And at the coming of the captain into Southwark, he let smite off the head of a strong thief that was named Haywardyn. And upon the morrow the Sunday at high mass time a–let to be beheaded a man of Hampton, a squire, the which was named Thomas Mayne. And that same even London did arise and came out upon them at ten of the bell, being that time their captains the good old Lord Scales and Matthew Gough. And from that time unto the morrow eight of bell they were ever fighting upon London Bridge, and many a man was slain and cast in Thames, harness, body and all; and among the press was slain Matthew Gough and John Sutton alderman. And the same night, anon after midnight, the captain of Kent did fire the drawbridge of London; and before that time he broke both King's Bench and the Marshalsea, and let out all the prisoners that were in them. And upon the morrow betimes came my Lord the Cardinal of York, and my Lord of Canterbury, and the Bishop of Winchester,** and they treated between the Lord Scales and that captain, that the sore conflict and skirmish was ceased, and gave the captain and his meinie a general charter† for him and all his company in his name, calling himself John Mortimer, and through that mean

---

*Rumours were spreading that Gloucester had been murdered at Bury St Edmunds. It seems almost probable, suspicious though the circumstances were, that he died from natural causes.

**John Kemp, John Stafford, William Waynflete.

†i.e. a general pardon.

they were i-voided the most party. And the 6th day after that, the Saturday at even, the three heads were taken down off London Bridge, that is to say, the Lord Say his head, Crowmer's and the Bayle's, and the other two heads set up again that stood upon London Bridge before, and the body with head were i-buried at the Grey Friars at London. And upon the 12th day of July, the year aforesaid, the said captain was cried and proclaimed traitor, by the name of John Cade, in divers places of London, and also in Southwark, with many moo, that what man might or would bring the said John Cade to the king, quick or dead, should have of the king a thousand marks. Also who so ever might bring or would bring any of his chief counsellors, or of affinity, that kept any state or rule or governance under the said false captain John Cade, he should have to his reward of the king five hundred marks. And that day was that false traitor the captain of Kent i-take and slain in the Weald in the county of Sussex, and upon the morrow he was brought in a car (carre) all naked, and at the Hart in Southwark there the car was made stand still, the wife of the house might see him if it were the same man or no that was named the captain of Kent for he was lodged within her house in his pevys time of his misrule and rising. And then he was had into the King's Bench, and there he lay from Monday at even unto the Thursday next following at even; and within the King's Bench the said captain was beheaded and quartered; and the same day i-draw upon a hurdle in pieces with the head between his breast from the King's Bench throughout Southwark, and then over London Bridge, and then through London unto Newgate, and then his head was taken and set upon London Bridge.(14)

There were violent disturbances in other parts of the country. At the end of June the parishoners of Edington murdered the Bishop of Salisbury after he had said mass 'and spoiled him unto the naked skin, and rent his bloody shirt into pieces and bare them away with them, and made boast of their wickedness.' The refugee soldiers from Normandy still roistered about London, such a menace to the royal household that Lord Scales was given £50 to distribute for their relief. During Cade's rebellion York had watched events from Ireland. Now, taking advantage of a clause in his indentures allowing him to come to England in case of emergency he crossed the Irish Sea at the end of August. He complained bitterly that certain royal officers tried to intercept him, with the intention of incarcerating him in Conway Castle, 'striking off the head' of his chamberlain, Sir William Oldhall and imprisoning his advisers, Sir William Devereux and Sir Edward Mulsho.

On the other hand when York was accused of treason in 1459 the indictment stated that at this time:

> . . . he come out of Ireland with great bobaunce* and inordinate people, to your Palace of Westminster unto your presence, with great multitude of people harnessed and arrayed in manner of war, and there beat down the speres† and walls in your chamber, having no consideration to your high presence . . . (15)

His enemies later accused York of complicity in Cade's rebellion. There is no proof of it and we can only guess why he chose to leave Ireland. A letter which he wrote in May 1450 to his brother-in-law, the Earl of Salisbury, shows that he dreaded that failure there would destroy his reputation as failure in Normandy had already destroyed that of Suffolk and Somerset. He may well have thought it wise to come home and deny the sinister rumours now being murmured against him. An Ipswich jury, in fact, in February 1453 accused Sir William Oldhall of treasonable conspiracies at this time.

The jury reported:

> That William Assheton, late of Soham Comitis, Suffolk, knight, William Oldhall, late of Hunsdon, Herts, knight, Edmund FitzWilliam, late of Framlingham Castle, Suffolk, esquire, Charles and Otwell Nowell of the same, esquire . . (and others) . . . proposing to depose the king and put the Duke of York on the throne, realising that they could not do this while he remained powerful with his lords around him, on 6th March 28 Henry VI (1450) at Bury St Edmunds plotted the death and destruction of the king and the laws and discord among the people. They agreed to take divers bills and writings made and fabricated in sets of verses and ballads at Bury St Edmunds and elsewhere, and placed them on men's doors and windows, reciting in the same that the king

---

*i.e. pomp, ostentation.

†i. e. fixed screens or temporary wooden partitions.

through the counsel of the late Duke of Suffolk, the Bishops of Salisbury and Chichester, Lord Say and others round his person had sold the Kingdoms of England and France and that the king's uncle of France would reign in England. All this with the intention of withdrawing the love of the king's subjects from him and moving the said Duke of York to have the realm and crown of England.

And they sent letters to divers counties of England, especially Kent and Sussex, urging rebellion against the king, on account of which the Duke of Suffolk was murdered ... (16)

The next few years witnessed a ruthless duel for supremacy between York and Somerset: a bitter personal struggle to control the king. With Suffolk dead upon the Dover sands and financial reform already begun, no question of principle was involved. It was certainly not, as some historians once asserted, a contest between the forces of good and bad government. A letter written by William Wayte* to John Paston on the 6 October shows York, Oldhall and their friends supreme, for the time, at court and whipping-up support for themselves in East Anglia.

Sir, and it please, I was in my Lord of York's house, and I heard much thing more than my master writeth unto you of; I heard much thing in Fleet Street. But, Sir, my Lord was with the king, and he visaged so the matter that all the King's household was and is a-feared right sore; and my said Lord hath put a bill to the king, and desired much thing, which is much after the Commons' desire, and all is upon justice, and to put all those that been indicted under arrest without surety or mainprise,† and to be tried by law as law will; in so much that on Monday Sir William Oldhall was with the king at Westminster more than two hours and had of the king good cheer. And the king desired of Sir William Oldhall that he should speak to his cousin York, that he would be good lord to John Penycock,‡ and that my Lord of York should write unto his tenants that they would suffer Penycock's officers go and gather up

---

*Clerk to William Yelverton, one of the judges of the King's Bench.
†i.e. surety.
‡One of Henry VI's Squires of the Body.

his rents farms within the said duke's lordships. And Sir William Oldhall answered again to the king, and prayed him to hold my Lord excused, for though my Lord wrote under his seal of his arms his tenants will not obey it; in so much that when Sir Thomas Hoo met with my Lord of York beyond St Albans, the western men fell upon him, and would have slain him, had [not] Sir William Oldhall abe,* and therefore would the western men a-fall upon the said Sir William, and a-killed him and so he told the king.

Sir Borle Jonge and Josse labour sore for Heydon and Tuddenham† to Sir William Oldhall, and proffer more than two thousand pound for to have his good lordship . . . Sir, my master bade me write unto you that ye should stir the Mayor and all the Aldermen‡ to cry on my Lord that they mown have justice of these men that be indicted, and that my Lord will speak unto the king thereof. And, Sir, in divers parts of the town where my Lord cometh, there would be ordained many portions of commoners to cry on my Lord for justice of these men that are indicted, and tell their names, in special Tuddenham, Heydon, Wyndham, Prentys. Sir, I send you a copy of the bill that my Lord of York put unto the King; and, Sir, let copies go about the city now, for the love of God, which have you in his keeping.(17)

York, now supreme at court, was popular with the Commons at this time, for he had supported their demand for reforms, particularly financial reforms. When parliament met in November, the Commons, over a week before the duke arrived at Westminster, elected Sir William Oldhall as Speaker, although this is was the first time he had ever sat in parliament. Henry may now have tried to hold a balance between Somerset and York. If so he failed miserably. Various jejune chronicles, too meagre for quotation,

*i.e. have been (there).

†John Heydon, a Norfolk gentleman, Thomas Tuddenham, also of Norfolk, Clerk of the Great Wardrobe (1446–50), Treasurer of the Household, 1458–60, were notorious (according to their opponents) for their oppressions in East Anglia, encouraged by the Duke of Suffolk, and now feared that they would suffer at the hands of York and his friends.

‡Of Norwich.

and later indictments in the court of King's Bench, reveal that Somerset's house was attacked and looted, Oldhall himself taking part in the attack, besides inciting other acts of violence.* Somerset was imprisoned in the Tower but soon released. Then an anonymous chronicle relates:

> In the aforesaid parliament the commons asked the lord king to remove certain persons from about him (de familiaritate domini regis) etc. But nothing came of it. In the same parliament the Duchess of Suffolk was acquitted by her peers, and John Say and Thomas Daniell and other foresworn people of treason of which they were accused at the time of the insurrection. In the same parliament Thomas Yonge of Bristol, apprentice in law, moved that because the king had no offspring, it would be for the security of the kingdom that it should be openly known who should be heir apparent. And he named the Duke of York. For which cause the same Thomas was afterwards committed to the Tower of London.(18)

York himself must have inspired this last proposal, for Yonge was a lawyer whom the duke had employed in various ways for several years past. The product of York's fears about the succession, it was probably intended more as a warning to the Duke of Somerset than as an attack upon the king. Like many of York's political gestures it was badly timed. It might have succeeded had York arrived in England during Cade's rebellion, or even during the previous November. It had no chance of success now that the demoralized Beaufort affinity was regaining confidence. Parliament was immediately dissolved. York, as far from power as ever, retired to his estates in the Welsh Marches. Oldhall was again plotting treason by June 1451. York himself waited until the early months of 1452. He then issued two manifestos accusing Somerset of plotting his destruction and led a rebellion against the king.

As the following account taken from a London chronicle shows, York's attempt to impose his will by armed force failed completely:

---

*That is unless the indictments were perjured and malicious. For these and similar incidents in which Oldhall was involved in these years see J.S. Roskell, 'Sir William Oldhall, Speaker in the Parliament of 1450–1', *Nottingham Medieval Studies*, v, 1961.

The 30th year of King Henry the Sixth. This year on Wednesday the 16th day of February the king with the lords rode toward the Duke of York for to take him, because he raised people to come down and take the Duke of Somerset; but when the Duke of York heard here of, he took another way and so came toward London. And also soon as the king heard thereof he sent letters to the mayor, aldermen and commons of London, on St Mathies' day, that they should keep the city and suffer not the Duke of York to come therein; wherefore was made great watch in the city, the which was told the Duke of York, wherefore he left London way and went over Kingston Bridge. And on Sunday next after, that was the first Sunday of Lent, the king's vaward came to London early in the morning and lodged in Southwark. And on the Monday after, in the morning they were removed from thence into Kent. And at afternoon the same day the king came to London with his host, and so went into Southwark and lodged at St Mary Overeys. And the Duke of York pitched his field about Dartford with great ordnance. And whilst the king lay still at St Mary Overeys bishop* rode between the king and the Duke of York to set them at rest and peace. But the Duke of York said he would have the Duke of Somerset, or else he would die therefore. And on Wednesday next following† the king with his host rode to Blackheath, and forth over Shooters' Hill to Welling, and there lodged that day and the morrow. And on Thursday at afternoon there was made a pointment between the king and the Duke of York by the mean of lords.‡ And on the morrow, that was Friday, the king ensembled his host on the Blackheath afore noon; and there abode the coming of the Duke of York after the pointment made over even. And in the king's host was numbered 20,000 fighting men, and men said the Duke of York had as many with much great stuff and ordnance. And at the last the Duke of York came with forty horse to the king about noon, and obeyed him to his liegance; and with [him] the Earl of Devonshire and the Lord Cobham, the which held with the Duke of York and were in host with him. And the king took them to grace and all.(19)

*Possibly 'bishops'.
†1 March.
‡By the Bishops of Winchester and Ely, the Earls of Salisbury and Warwick and Lords Beauchamp and Sudeley.

One contemporary writer states that York surrendered on a promise that Somerset would be arrested and compelled to answer York's charges against him. If so, York was cheated and before an assembly of magnates at St Paul's he, the Earl of Devonshire and Lord Cobham were forced to swear an oath which was, in effect, a suspended sentence of attainder, involving the penalties of treason, including the forfeiture of all their property, in case of future misconduct.

The Commons' fury at Suffolk's notorious pillage of the royal resources and the dissipation of the Crown lands amongst rapacious courtiers and household officers had been one of the prime forces which swept him to destruction. In 1449 the Commons had demanded an Act of Resumption, that is an act of parliament revoking all grants made by the Crown. The courtiers and officials put up a prolonged, clever and subtle resistance, but in the end the Commons won. Having gained the day they showed a new generosity towards the king with a consequent diminution of York's influence. In the parliament which met at Reading in March 1453 they made an exceptionally large grant of taxation and provision for a force of 13,000 archers to maintain order at home. Months before parliament met the court had begun to prosecute some of York's supporters in the King's Bench. As early as November 1451 Sir William Oldhall had fled into sanctuary at St Martin-le-Grand. Parliament now attainted him and passed an act confiscating the property of those who had taken the field with York at Dartmouth and according to one very pro-Yorkist chronicler the Duke of Somerset rode to certain of York's 'townships' and hanged some of his adherents although the king had already pardoned them.

However on 21 November 1452 in the Star Chamber the two sides agreed upon a formula of reconciliation. York agreed to attend the king's 'great council'* on condition that his own advisers and servants should be allowed free access to him. Tragic events (for a time concealed by the court) quickly shattered this new concord and the recent modest revival of royal power.[2] By 10 August, at the latest, Henry VI had become insane. On 15 October his only child, Prince Edward, was born, thus destroying York's hopes of the succession.[3] When parliament re-assembled in November it was prorogued to February 1454. Even then most people were desperately

---

*The word can be transcribed either 'council' or 'counsel'.

anxious to avoid committing themselves on the vital question of the regency which York was determined to secure for himself in the teeth of opposition from the queen and Somerset. Attendance in the Lords, generally poor in the later Middle Ages, was exceptionally thin in February 1454. York who, as the king's nearest adult relation, the Great Council had commissioned to open parliament, wished for at least the appearance of widespread approval for his own plans. He was so disturbed by this marked abstention that he attempted to compel cooperation. For the first and only known occasion in English history peers were fined for non-attendance.[4] The king's illness and the debates of the Lords are described in the *Paston Letters* and the *Rolls of Parliament*:

. . . at the Prince's coming to Windsor, the Duke of Buckingham took him in his arms and presented him to the King in goodly wise, beseeching the King to bless him; and the King gave no manner answer. Natheless the Duke abode still with the Prince by the King; and when he could no manner answer have, the Queen come in, and took the Prince in her arms and presented him in like form as the Duke had done, desiring that he should bless it; but all their labour was in vain, for they departed thence without any answer or countenance saving only that once he looked on the Prince and cast down his eyen again . . .

. . . Item, the Queen hath made a bill of five articles, desiring those articles to be granted; whereof the first is that she desireth to have the whole rule of this land; the second is that she may make the Chancellor, the Treasurer, the Privy Seal, and all other officers of this land, with sheriffs and all other officers that the King should make; the third is, that she may give all the bishoprics of this land, and all other benefices longing to the King's gift; the fourth is that she may have sufficient live-lode assigned her for the King, and the Prince and herself. But as for the fifth article, I cannot yet know what it is . . .

. . . And for the more readiness of such fellowship to be had ready, that my Lord* send sad and wise messages to his servants and tenants in Sussex and elsewhere, that they be ready at London against his coming,

*i.e. York.

to await on my Lord; but let my Lord beware of writing of letters for them, lest the letters be delivered to the Cardinal* and the Lords, as one of my Lord's letters was now late, for peril that might fall, for that letter hath done much harm and no good.

And as for such tidings as been contained in the letter sent home by John Sumpterman, I cannot hitherto hear the contrary of any of them, but that every man that is of th'opinion of the Duke of Somerset maketh him ready to be as strong as he can make him. Wherefore it is necessary that my Lord look well to himself and keep him among his meinie, and depart not from them, for it is to dread lest bushments should be laid for him. And if that happed, and my Lord came hitherward, as he hath been used for to come, he might lightly be deceived and betrapped, that God defend. And therefore let my Lord make good watch and be sure.

The Duke of Somerset hath espies going in every Lord's house of this land; some gone as friars, some as ship-men taken on the sea, and some in other wise; which report unto him all that they can see or hear touching the said Duke. And therefore make good watch, and beware of such espies.(20)

The Lords commissioned twelve of their number to ride to Windsor and attempt to discuss matters with the king. On 25 March:

. . . the said lords spiritual and temporal, were at the King's high presence, and in the place where he dined; and anon after his dinner was done, the said matters were opened and declared by the mouth of the Bishop of Chester,† right cunningly, sadly and worshipfully, nothing in substance changed from the said instruction,‡ added ne diminished, as the said Bishop of Chester can I more clearly declare to their lordships. And thereupon the said Bishop of Chester shewed and declared, how that the opening and declaring of the said matters, by th'avis of the lords that were sent to Windsor, was put upon him, how

---

*Most probably Cardinal Kemp, the Chancellor.
†i.e. Chichester.
‡i.e. the instruction given by the Lords to the twelve who went to Windsor.

be it he thought himself right unable thereto; and that he first opened and shewed to the King's Highness the three first articles, as it was advised by the lords ere they went; that is to say, the humble recommendation of the lords to the King's Highness, the great desire of his hele,* and the great diligence of the lords in this parliament. And then for asmuch as it liked not the King's Highness to give any answer to the articles, the said Bishop of Chester, by th'avis of all the other lords, declared and opened to the King's Highness, the other matters contained in the said instruction; to the which matters ne to any of them they could get no answer ne sign, for no prayer ne desire, lamentable cheer ne exhortation, ne any thing that they or any of them could do or say, to their great sorrow and discomfort. And then the Bishop of Winchester said to the King's Highness, that the lords had not dined, but they should go dine them, and wait upon his Highness again after dinner. And so after dinner they come to the King's Highness in the same place where they were before; and there they moved and stirred him, by all the ways and means that they could think, to have answer of the matters aforesaid, but they could have none; and from that place they willed the King's Highness to go into another chamber, and so he was led between two men into the chamber where he lieth; and there the lords moved and stirred the King's Highness the third time, by all the means and ways that they could think, to have answer of the said matters, and also desired to have knowledge of him, if it should like his Highness that they should wait upon him any longer, and to have answer at his leisure, but they could have no answer, word ne sign . . .(21)

On 27 March, unable to avoid an embarrassing decision any longer, the Lords appointed Richard of York Protector. They did the very least they could in the circumstances, and hedged in his authority with drastic restrictions.†

---

*i.e. health.
†The Duke of Gloucester's authority had been restricted in very much the same way when he had been appointed protector during Henry VI's minority.

. . . the said duke shall be chief of the king's council, and devised therefore to the said duke a name different from other councillors, nought the name of tutor, lieutenant, governor, nor of regent, nor no name that shall import authority of governance of the land; but the said name of protector and defenser, the which importeth a personal duty of intendance to the actual defence of this land, as well against th'enemies outward, if case require, as against rebels inward, if any hap to be, that God forbid, during the king's pleasure, and so that it be not prejudice to my Lord Prince . . .(22)

By the end of the year the king had recovered. On 9 January 1455 Edmund Clere wrote to John Paston:

. . . Blessed be God, the King is well amended, and hath been since Christmas day, and on St John's day commanded his almoner to ride to 33 Canterbury with his offering, and commanded the secretary to offer at St Edward's.

And on the Monday after noon the Queen came to him, and brought my Lord Prince with her. And then he asked what the Prince's name was, and the Queen told him Edward; and then he held up his hands and thanked God thereof. And he said he never knew till that time, nor wist not what was said to him, nor wist not where he had be whilst he hath be sick till now . . .

And she told him that the Cardinal* was dead, and he said he knew never thereof till that time; and he said one of the wisest lords in this land was dead.

And my Lord of Winchester† and my Lord of St John's‡ were with him on the morrow after Twelfth Day, and he speke to them as well as ever he did; and when they come out they wept for joy.

And he saith he is in charity with all the world, and so he would all the lords were . . .(23)

---

*John Kemp, Cardinal Archbishop of Canterbury, died 22 March 1454.
†William Waynflete, Bishop of Winchester.
‡Robert Botyll, the Prior of the Order of St John of Jerusalem in England.

Somerset was released from the Tower.* York's short protectorate came to an end and he left the court. Defeated in the council chamber he took to arms, most probably instigated by the Nevilles, his brother-in-law the Earl of Salisbury, and Salisbury's son, the Earl of Warwick, anxious to make use of him for their own ends in their armed quarrel with the Percys. The king and Somerset, hoping to deal with York by peaceful means in a Great Council at Leicester,† remained unaware of his military preparations until they heard, when they were already on their way to Leicester, that he was marching south. Hasty, last-minute attempts to recruit and concentrate forces round St Albans were too late. When the royal army reached Watford on the night of the 21 May it consisted of little more than the household retinues of the peers who happened to be with the king – no more than 2,000 men. The forces of York and his friends, by this time at Ware, numbered possibly 3,000. The Yorkists later inscribed on the Parliament Roll their own equivocal apologia for the disaster which followed. Under their influence the king stated:

Our said cousins understanding and considering as they say, the labours made against them . . .‡ addressed them toward our presence, to declare them our true liegemen, the better accompanied for their surety, and to resist such malice as they verily deemed was purposed to have been executed against : them, at their coming upon us . . . and for other cause; and to th'intent that we should not wonder nor marvel of the coming of our said cousins afore- rehearsed toward us, nor of the manner thereof, nor have any suspicion or mistrust thereof toward our person, they wrote their letters at Royston the 20th day of May last passed, and them sent afore their coming unto us, for their declaration and desire, to the Most Reverend Father in God, th'Archbishop of Canterbury, our Chancellor of England, to be by him opened unto us, whereof th'endorsement and tenor followeth here after.(24)

---

*He had been imprisoned, for his own safety, during the protectorate.
†It had been summoned in the hope of reconciling the factions.
‡By Somerset, Thomas Thorpe and William Joseph upon whom the Yorkists tried to throw all the blame for the events.

The letter began with a strong affirmation of their loyalty, protested against their not being called to the recent council at Westminster and asked the prelate publically to pronounce the censures of the church at St Paul's Cross (more or less the equivalent of the broadcasting house of the day) against anybody intending harm to the king. The following day (21 May), so the apologia continued, York and his friends wrote to the king enclosing a copy of this letter which they had sent to the chancellor. They claimed that Somerset and his hangers-on, Thomas Thorpe and William Joseph, intercepted and suppressed these crucial documents. Finally the Yorkist army arrived, probably at about seven o'clock on the morning of the 22 May, and took up its position in the Key Field, somewhat to the east of St Albans. Henry and his supporters entered the town at about nine. There was no sudden clash of arms, for long-established tradition – broken only in 1461 at the second battle of St Albans and the battle of Towton – held that in a struggle of Englishmen against Englishmen there should be some attempt at mediation. Negotiations were, in fact, prolonged. They broke down on Henry's final, adamant refusal to surrender Somerset to his adversary. Several conflicting accounts of the battle which followed survive. The following, found in the *Archives de la Côte d'Or* at Dijon, was written within five days of the conflict, most probably by a foreigner resident in England.*

When the Duke of Somerset and those who were of his party then being in the City of London, heard that the Duke of York and may other lords in his company were advancing against them with a force of five thousand men and when he considered what he had done against the said duke of York and that he was also in very bad odour with the people of London, he came to the conclusion that he should not remain in the City of London for fear that the people would fall upon him the moment he† arrived. For which cause he persuaded the king to sally forth against the said Duke of York and his other enemies, their opponents, and hastily gathered the said third day after the feast of the

---

*I have preferred to retain the tone of this extract by giving a more or less literal translation, in spite of its many ambiguities, rather than destroy its peculiar flavour by introducing emendations.
†i.e the Duke of York.

Ascension[5] up to 3,500 persons and on the 21st day of May in the morning [they] issued out of London and went to lodge twenty miles away from there at a little village where there is an abbey called St Albans, near the which village at less than half a day's march their enemies were lodged. These, when they knew of the king's coming, immediately approached him and also the 22nd day of the said month very early the king sent a herald to the Duke of York to know the cause for which he had come there with so many men and that it seemed to the king something quite new that he, the duke, should be rising against him, the king. The reply made was that he was not coming against him thus, [he] was always ready to do him obedience but he well intended in one way or another to have the traitors who were about him so that they should be punished, and that in case he could not have them with good will and fair consent, he intended in any case to have them by force. The reply that was made from the king's side to the said Duke of York was that he* was unaware that there were any traitors about him were it not for the Duke of York himself who had risen against his crown. And even before this reply came to the Duke of York there begun the skirmish before the village by one side and the other. And thus when the Duke of York had the aforesaid reply the battle became more violent and both sides with banners displayed began to fight. And first the Duke of York's men incontinently approached the village and set a good guard at all the ways about and entered in with such great force that incontinent they took and blockaded the marketplace of the said village and part of his people found themselves in the middle of it and in this manner began to fight the one party against the other. The battle began on the stroke of ten hours in the morning but because the place was small few of the combatants could set to work there and matters reached such great extremity that four of those who were of the king's bodyguard were killed by arrows in his presence and the king himself was struck by an arrow in the shoulder, but it penetrated only a little of the flesh. At last when they had fought for the space of three hours the king's party seeing themselves to have the worst of it broke on one wing and began

*i.e. the king.

to flee and the Duke of Somerset retreated within an inn to save himself and hid. Which things seen by those of the said Duke of York [they] incontinent beset the said house all about. And there the Duke of York gave order that the king should be taken and drawn out of the throng and put in the abbey in safety and thus it was done. And in this abbey took refuge also with him the Duke of Buckingham who was very badly wounded by three arrows. And incontinent this done [they] began to fight Somerset and his men who were in this place within the inn and defended themselves valiantly. And in the end after the doors were broken down the Duke of Somerset seeing that he had no other remedy took counsel with his men about coming out and did so, as a result of which incontinent he and all his people were surrounded by the Duke of York's men. And after some were stricken down and the Duke of Somerset had killed four of them with his own hand, so it is said, he was felled to the ground with an axe and incontinent being so wounded in several places that there he ended his life. And while the said Somerset made this defence in the inn others of his party who remained outside all the time fought against those of the Duke of York so that three lords died there on Somerset's side, that is to say the Earl of Northumberland, Lord Clifford, which was a great pity for he was a brave man, and Sir Richard Harrington also a noble knight and a brave man and many other gentlemen and esquires as many of one party as the other so that in all there died 200 persons or thereabouts.* The battle lasted until two and a half hours after noon and this done the Duke of York's men took themselves to the abbey to kill the Duke of Buckingham and the treasurer, who is called the Earl of Wiltshire, who had retreated there with the king but the said Duke of York would not suffer it but sent his herald to the king to inform him that he must choose which he preferred, either to hand over the two lords as prisoners into his hands, or that they should be killed in front of him and to put himself in danger once more. Wherefore the king agreed freely to allow him to arrest the said two lords and so he did, in particular the Duke of Buckingham. The treasurer could not be found for disguising himself he fled in a monk's habit and even now the 17th

*The best modern estimate puts the deaths at no more than sixty.

May no one knows where he has gone. And when all these things were done the Duke of York entered within the abbey and went before the king's person and there went on his knees to him crying mercy for whatever way he might have offended and for the peril in which he had put his person and many other good and humble words, showing him that he had not gone against him but against the traitors to his crown, and in the end before the Duke of York went away from there the king pardoned him everything and took him in his good grace, and this day the king, the Duke of York and all the other lords came to London where they have been received with great joy and solemn procession. And the said Duke of York will now be without contradiction the first after the king and will have the government of all. God give him grace to carry out his tasks well and have pity on the souls of sinners. Amen.(25)

From a military point of view the first battle of St Albans was insignificant and settled nothing. Although York and the Nevilles were now 'first after the king' their victory was hollow and they stood in considerable danger. Parliament met on 9 July. Two days later Henry Windsor, one of Sir John Fastolf's circle, wrote to two friends in Norfolk:

. . . First, the King our sovereign Lord, and all his true Lords stand in hele* of their bodies, but not all at heart's ease as we. Amongst other marvel, two days afore the writing of this letter, there was language between my Lords of Warwick and Cromwell afore the King, in so much as the Lord Cromwell would have excused himself of all the stirring or moving of the male journey† of St Albans; of the which excuse making, my Lord Warwick had knowledge, and in haste was with the King, and sware by his oath that the Lord Cromwell said not truth, but that he was beginner of all that journey at St Albans; and so between my said two Lords of Warwick and Cromwell there is at this day great grudging, in so much as the Earl of Shrewsbury hath lodged him at the hospital of St James, beside the Mewes, by the Lord Cromwell's desire, for his safe guard.

*i.e. health.
†i.e. evil battle.

And also all my Lord of Warwick men, my Lord of York men, and also my Lord of Salisbury men go with harness, and in harness with strong weapons, and have stuffed their Lords' barges full of weapon daily unto Westminster.

And the day of making of this letter, there was a proclamation made in the Chancery, on the King's behalf, that no man should neither bear weapon, nor wear harness defensible, etc.

Also, the day afore the making of this letter, there passed a bill both by the King, Lords, and Commons, putting Thorpe, Joseph, and my Lord of Somerset in all the default; by the which bill all manner of actions that should grow to any person or persons for any offences at that journey done, in any manner of wise should be extinct and void, affirming all thing done there well done, and nothing done there never after this time to be spoken of; to the which bill many a man grudged full sore now it is passed.*(26)

Although York and the Nevilles with great difficulty suppressed public censure of their recent conduct, their tenure of power was, to say the least, precarious. They planned to consolidate it by making York protector a second time, on the pretext that the country, particularly the south-west, was so torn by riot and disorder that extraordinary methods were necessary to deal with it. Their plot was ready by the time parliament met for its second session on 12 November. The drama began on the second day of the session when William Burley, Knight of the Shire for Shropshire, not the Commons' Speaker† the obvious choice for such a task, but one of the Duke of York's clients and a member of his council, led a deputation from the Commons to put pressure on the Lords.

*This 'Parliamentary Pardon' laid the entire blame for St Albans on three men only, Somerset, Thomas Thorpe and William Joseph, secured all others from molestation for their part there and ingeniously barred any claim for losses by private people against the victorious Yorkists. It was greatly resented by many people. See C.A.J. Armstrong, 'Politics and the Battle of St Albans, 1455', *B.I.H.R.*, xxiii (1960) 58–61, (35)

†The Speaker was Sir John Wenlock.

... the 13th day of the said month of November, it was shewed to the Duke of York, the King's Lieutenant in this present parliament, and to the Lords Spiritual and Temporal, by the mouth of Burley, accompanied with notable numbers of the Commons, in name of all the Commons. That how it had liked the King's Highness for certain causes him moving, to assign the said Duke of York to be his Lieutenant in this present Parliament, and to proceed in matters of Parliament . . . Wherefore it was thought by them that were comen for the Commons of this land, that if for such causes the King hereafter might not entend to the protection and defence of this land,* that it should like the King by th'advice of his said Lieutenant and the Lords, to ordain and purvey such an able person, as should mowe entend to the defence and protection of the said land, and this to be done as soon as it might be, and they to have knowledge thereof, to that entent that they might send to them for whom they were comen to this present Parliament knowledge, who should be Protector and Defensor of this land, and to whom they should mowe have recourse to sue for remedy of injuries and wrongs done to them. And also where there been great and grievous riots done in the West Country, between th'Earl of Devonshire, and the Lord Bonvile, by the which some men have be murdered, some robbed, and children and women taken. It is thought that if such Protector and Defensor were had, that such riots and injuries should be sooner punished, justice largely ministered, and the law more duly to proceed . . . (27)

It was true that the Devonshire family had been terrorizing part of the south-west, at intervals, for over a year. In October 1455, as the following petition shows, their conduct reached a new peak of violence:

... The Thursday the 23rd day of October the year of your noble reign 38th, [Sir Nicholas Radford] was in God's peace and yours in his own

---

*The speech insinuates that the king might again become incapable of ruling. Though he may have been sick for a time he did not, in fact, become insane again at this time as many writers have alleged. See p. 76, n.3.

place called Uppecote in the town* of Cadley in the same shire.†There came the same day and year, Thomas Courtenay late of Tiverton in the said shire knight, son to Thomas Earl of Devonshire, Nicholas Philippe otherwise called Nicholas Gye late of the same town and shire, yeoman, Thomas Philippe late of the same town and shire yeoman, John Amore otherwise called John Penyale late of Exe Island in the same shire tailor – (and various others named, to the number of 94) – with other riotous persons whose names been yet unknown arrayed in manner of war, that is to say with jacks, salets, bows, arrows, swords, bucklers, langedebiff,‡ long daggers, and other weapons defensible, greatly against the peace of you sovereign lord at midnight of the same Thursday, the said place assaulted and beset it all about. The said Nicholas, his wife, and all his meinie, at that time being there in their beds. The which misdoers as soon as they had beset the said place they made there a great shout and the gates of the said place set a-fire. And the said Nicholas Radford woke, and hearing a great noise and stirring about his said place, arose and opened his window of his chamber. And he seeing the said gates on fire, asked what they were that were there and whether there were any gentlemen among them. And the said Nicholas Philippe answered and said, 'Here is Sir Thomas Courtenay.'

And then the said Sir Thomas Courtenay hearing the said Nicholas Radford speak, called to him, saying in this wise, 'Come down Radford and speak with me.' And then the said Nicholas Radford knowing the voice of the said Sir Thomas Courtenay knight answered saying to him these words: 'Sir, and ye will promise me on your faith and truth, and as ye are true knight and gentleman, that I shall have no bodily harm, ne hurt of my goods, I will come down to you.' And then the said Sir Thomas Courtenay knight answered the said Nicholas Radford again, and said to him in this wise: 'Radford come ye to me, and I promise you as I am true knight and gentleman ye shall be safe both of your body and of your goods.' Whereupon the said Nicholas Radford trusting faithfully upon that promise, came out of his chamber with

*i.e. 'tithing'.
†i.e. Devonshire.
‡i.e. 'langues de bœuf', halberds with tongue-shaped heads.

torch light, and did set open the gates and let him in – and then pressed in with him the said misgoverned people. And the said Nicholas Radford seeing so much people within his said place, was sore a-feared, and said to Sir Thomas Courtenay knight,'Sir, what do all this people here?' and he answered again and said 'Radford, ye shall have none harm,' and thereupon the said Sir Thomas Courtenay had the said Nicholas Radford bring him to this chamber where as he lay in, and he did so, and there the said Sir Thomas C both ate and raknk, and from thence came out into the hall, and the said Nicholas R with him, and there stood together at a cupbaord, and drank of his wine. And there the said Sir Thomas Courtenay subtly held the said Nicholas R with tales, while the said Sir T. Courtenay's men brake up the chamber doors and coffers of the said Nicholas R, and then and there the said misdoers above named and others, the said Nicholas Radford of £300 and more in money numbered being in his trussing coffers, and other goods and jewels, bedding, gowns, furs, books, and ornaments of his chapel, to the value of 1,000 marks and more, feloniously robbed, and the goods they trussed together and with the said Nicholas Radford's own horse, carried them away.

And among other rifling then and there, they found the said Nicholas Radford's wife in her bed, sore sick as she hath been this two year and more, and rolled her out of her bed, and took away the sheets that she lay in, and trussed them with the remnant of the said goods.

And after that the said Sir Thomas Courtenay left his talking with the said Nicholas R at the cupboard, and said to the said N. R.: 'Have do Radford, for thou must go with me to my lord my father', and he said he would go with him all ready, and made him ready to ride, and bade his servant make him ready an horse, and his servant answered him, 'Sir, your horse has been taken all away and charged with your goods' and the said Nicholas R hearing that said to the said Sir Thomas C: 'Sir, I am aged, and may not well go upon my feet, and therefore I pray you that I may ride' and the said Sir Thomas Courtenay answered again in this wise, 'Nor force Radford thou shalt ride enough anon, and therefore come on with me.' And he went forth with him a stone's cast and more from his said place within Cadley aforesaid, and there the said Sir Thomas Courtenay knight communed privily with the said Nicholas Philippe, Thomas P, and John Amore and forthwith spurred his horse and rode his way and said 'Farewell Radford. And the said Nicholas P, Thomas P and John Amore and other forthwith turned upon the said Nicholas Radford, and then and there the said Nicholas P with a glaive smote the said Nicholas Radford a hideous deadly stroke overthwart the face, and felled him to the ground, and then the said Nicholas Philippe gave him another stroke upon his head behind that the brain fell out of the head. And the said Thomas Philippe that time and then with a knife feloniously cut the throat of the said Nicholas Radford, and the said John Amore that time and there with a long dagger smote the said Nicholas Radford behind on his back to the heart. And so the said Nicholas P, T.P. and John Amore thus gave the said Nicholas Radford several deadly wounds, and him then and there feloniously and horribly slew and murdered . . . And forthwith after the said horrible murder and felony thus done, the said Sir Thomas Courtenay with all the said misdoers rode to Tiverton in the said shire of Devonshire where the said earl the Friday next after the said Thursday feloniously recetted, comforted, and the said Sir Thomas Courtenay, N.P., T.P., and J.M. [sic] and other misdoers above named, with the said remnant of misdoers with the said goods, knowing them to have done the said murder, robbery and felony in the form aforesaid.

And the Monday next after the said Thursday, Henry Courtenay late of Tiverton in the shire of Devon squire, brother to the said Sir Thomas C knight, and godson to the said Nicholas Radford, with divers of the said misdoers and other moo, came to the said place where as the body of the said Nicholas Radford lay, in his chapel of his said place in Cadley, and there and then the said Henry C and those misdoers took upon them the office of coroner without authority, and made one of them sit down, and called afore him an inquest of the persons that murdered the said Nicholas Radford, by such estrange names as no man might know them by, ne never men heard tell such dwelling in that country. The which misdoers by such names as they were called scornfully appearing, and made such a presentment as peased them, and such as is reported that they should indict the said Nicholas Radford of his own death, in great despite and derision of your laws. And anon after that, the said Henry and divers of the said misdoers with other misdoers to a great number, constrained certain persons there that were servants to said Nicholas Radford to bear his body to the church . . .

And there the said misdoers took the body of the said Nicholas Radford out of his chest that he was laid in, and rolled him out of his sheet in the which he was wound; and there and then cast the body all naked into the pit, and with such stuff of stones as the said Nicholas Radford had late purveyed for his tomb to be made there, cast upon his body and head, and it horribly brake and quashed, having no more compassion no pity than though it had be a Jew or a Saracen . . . (28)

A week after the murder, the earl and his sons assembled a gang of men at Tiverton, marched to Exeter, seized the city gates and held possession of the town until the Monday before Christmas. Meanwhile they went to Powderham Castle, menaced its owner Sir Philip Courtenay and maltreated two of the cathedral clergy in Exeter.

At Westminster Burley and his delegation outrageously pressed the Lords – they demanded three interviews in five days – for an answer to their demands about the protectorate. During the third interview with the Lords on 17 November Burley clinched his case with the latest wild rumours which had just arrived from Devonshire – rumours which had grown in horror as they passed to the capital.

. . . it was shewed to the said Lieutenant and all the Lords, by the mouth of Burley, accompanied in notable number of the Commons, in the name of all their fellows, that how the said Commons had divers times made requests to their good Lordships, that they should be good means to the King's Highness, that there might be chosen and made a Protector and Defensor of this land, of the which requests as yet they have none answer. And where as it is yet thought by them that be come to this high Court of Parliament for the Commons of this land; forasmuch as this day they have knowledge and understanding by such person which the said Lords send to them, that there be great and grievous riots done in the West Country at the City of Exeter, by th'Earl of Devonshire, accompanied with many riotous persons, as it is said with 800 horsemen, and 4,000 footmen, and there have robbed the Church of Exeter, and take the canons of the same church and put them to finance,* and also take the gentlemen in that country, and done

*i.e. ransom.

and committed many other great and heinous inconveniences; that in abridging of such riots and inconveniences, such a Protector and Defensor must be had, and that they might have knowledge of him, his power and authority; and that he in abridging of such riots and offences, should ride and labour into that country, for but if the said riots and inconveniences were resisted, it should be the cause of the loss of that land, and if that land were lost, it might be cause of the subversion of all this land . . . (29)

The Lords gave way. York made a formal denial of his fitness for the post, but nevertheless he had ready a long and detailed list of the conditions under which he was prepared to take office – a list which could not have been produced on the spur of the moment. But his triumph was short-lived. The Devonshire faction in the south-west by the end of the year had submitted when faced by a threat of force from the government. This rapid collapse must have left many people, never well disposed to York in the first place, feeling that two months before the duke had most unscrupulously forced the issue of the protectorate. Further – and tactless – armed demonstrations availed him nothing. In the third session of the parliament which opened on 14 January 1456 the way was clear for the king to remove him from power.

Towards the end of February Henry came in person to parliament and relieved York of his office. Although York did perform very good work in various parts of the kingdom in suppressing disorders, some sixty years later the Italian, Polydore Vergil, permitted himself to speculate on York's motives and alleged that he, the Nevilles and 'divers other noble men' had plotted to usurp the government and turn Henry VI into a *roi fainéant*. Though very biased against the duke Vergil's surmises are credible enough to ring true.

York was in no way vindictively treated,* yet all his violence and intrigues had left him in a worse position than before. Bitter jibes were being published against him. Bale's *Chronicle* tells that 'the 19th day of September in the night time were set upon the Standard in Fleet Street afore the Duke of York being there lodged in the Bishop of Salisbury place certain dogs' heads

---

*He was granted over £1,800, arrears of salary from his first protectorate and sums promised for expenses during the second. Also, as late as May 1456 he received the valuable grant of all the gold- and silver-bearing mines in Devon and Cornwall.

with scriptures in their mouths ballad wise which dogs were slain vengeably the same night.' Here are the 'scriptures'.

THE FIVE DOGS OF LONDON

Colle, primus canis londonie . . .
Whan lordschype fayleth, gode felowschipe awayleth.
My mayster ys cruell and can no curtesye,
ffor whos offence here am y pyghtye.
hyt ys no reson pat y schulde dye
ffor hys trespace, & he go quyte.

Grubbe, 2us canis:
Offte beryth pe sone the faderis gylte.
None so gylteles as y compleyne:
ffor ones pat y barkyd a-geynys pe mone,*
With myghty force here was y sleyne.
My tyme was come; my dcfcnys ys done.

Lugtrype, 3us canis:
The tonge breketh bone, zit in hym is none.
ffor fawte of curasse my throte was cutte.
y cryed for helpe – y was not herde.
y wolde my mayster hadde provide my butte;†
Thys hadde y for hym to my rewarde.

Slugge, 4us canis:
Off folowynge aventurous, pe Iugement is leperdous.
Wat planet compellyd me, or what signe,
To serue pat man that all men hate?
y wolde his hede were here for myne,
ffor he hathe caused all pe debate.

*i.e. to no effect.
†i e. Deliverance.

Turne-bole, 5us canis:
ffelix quem faciunt aliena pericula cautum.
The blasynge starne with his late constellacion,
ys pleynly determyned weyis batayle;
To soche a remedye y holde hyt geson,*
And yn rancur with-owte remedye ys none avayle.

Maysterys, taketh for no grewe† thewgh pat we be dede;
ffor they wylle walke be your fleke, In dyspyte of your hede.(30)

In spite of their political failure this last crisis left York and his friends with two valuable assets – the financial backing of the Merchants of the Staple, the most powerful organized financial group in the country, and possession of Calais. While he was in power the Staplers had, tardily and reluctantly, supported him for their own ends, to obtain payment of debts due from the Crown, and now found themselves too tangled in his affairs to withdraw from his schemes. Calais gave him a magnificent base from which to launch an attack on England.

After the battle of St Albans and the end of York's second protectorate it was impossible to re-establish normal political life. Confusion and hostility grew ever worse as the months went by. In October 1456 the court made its first hostile – and unwise – move by dismissing the chancellor, Thomas Bourchier, Archbishop of Canterbury and half-brother of the Duke of Buckingham, who at this time was apparently trying to hold a mediating position between the two hostile factions. In August 1457 Pierre de Brezé, the Grand Seneschal of Normandy, sacked the town of Sandwich, encouraged, according to rumours, by the queen herself. Early the following year some of the king's servants attacked the Earl of Warwick in the midst of a brawl in the royal household. The earl retired to Calais where, lacking victuals and money, he attempted, unsuccessfully, to support his garrison by piracy. In March 1458, after prolonged negotiations in a Great Council, an impressive but hollow reconciliation between the factions was staged at St Paul's. It solved nothing and from this time onwards a new mean, vicious note crept into Yorkist propaganda.

*i.e. agreed.
†i.e. victory.

An anonymous chronicle, compiled between 1461 and 1471, known from the name of its nineteenth century editor as *Davies' Chronicle*, insinuated that the Earl of Devonshire had been poisoned with the connivance of Queen Margaret,* that the king had been inveigled into giving away most of his patrimony and continues:

The queen with such as were of her affinity ruled the realm as her liked, gathering riches innumerable. The offices [sic] of the realm, and specially the Earl of Wiltshire treasurer of England for to enrich himself, peled the poor people, and disherited rightful heirs, and did many wrongs. The queen was defamed and dislandered, that he that was called Prince, was not her son, but a bastard gotten in avoutry; wherefore she dreading that he should not succeed his father in the Crown of England, allied unto her all the knights and squires of Cheshire for to have their benevolence, and held open household among them; and made her son called the Prince give a livery of swans to all the gentlemen of the country, and to many other throughout the land; trusting through their strength to make her son king; making privy means to some of the lords of England for to stir the king that he should resign the crown to her son: but she could not bring her purpose about.

The 38th year of King Harry, in the month of September, the year of our Lord 1459 on the Sunday in the feast of St Matthew, Richard Earl of Salisbury, having with him seven thousand of well arrayed men, dreading the malices of his enemies and specially of the queen and her company the which hated him deadly and the Duke of York and the Earl of Warwick also, took his way toward Ludlow where the said Duke of York lay at that time, to th'intent that they both together would have ride to the king to Coleshill in Staffordshire, for to have excused them of certain articles and false accusations touching their liegance laid against them maliciously by their enemies.

When the king heard of their coming, they that were about him counselled him to gather a power for to withstand them, and informed him that they came for to destroy him. Then lay the queen at

---

*The statement is completely false.

Eccleshall, and anon by her stirring the king assembled a great power whereof the Lord Audley was chief and had the leading of them, and went forth into the field called Blore Heath; by the which the said Duke of York and the earl must needs pass. And there both hosts met and countered together, and fought mortally. And there was the Lord Audley slain, and many of the notable knights and squires of Cheshire that had received the livery of the swans; and there were taken prisoners, the earl's two sons of Salisbury, Thomas and John, and Sir Thomas Harrington, and imprisoned in the castle of Chester; but soon after they were delivered. After this discomforture, the earl passed forth to Duke Richard at Ludlow, and thither came to them fro Calais the Earl of Warwick, and they wrote a letter unto King Harry.

The tenor of the letter was a long apologia once again protesting their loyalty, claiming that they had been maliciously slandered and that certain people around the king were determined upon their destruction with a view to grabbing their lands, goods and offices. Then:

After their excusation contained in this letter sent to the king, they withdrew them, and went into divers parties of beyond the sea, for the more surety of their persons: the Duke of York went into Ireland, where he was worshipfully received. The Earls of March, of Salisbury, and Warwick, not without great jeopardy and peril, as well in the land as in the sea, went unto Calais and abode there.(31)

These last few sentences of the chronicler's account were less than frank. The indictment against York and his friends made in parliament a few weeks later gives a very different account of these last hours at Ludlow:

Ye* having compassion of your people thus blinded by the foresaid Duke of York, and Earls of Warwick and Salisbury, made your proclamation of grace in your host, to all them being with the same duke and earls that would depart from them; and sent unto the same Duke of York and Earl of Warwick, that ye would give them pardon

*i.e. Henry VI.

and grace of their lives, lifelode and goods, and not only to them, but to all the people there with them assembled, if they would take your grace and humbly desire it, within six days next after the said proclamation made; except a few persons proclaimed after the death of the Lord Audley; which was notified to them by your high commandment, by heralds of arms, by writing signed with your hand, to the more authorising of your said proclamation; to the which the same duke and earls took no consideration, but abode still in their false and traitorous purpose. And the Friday, in the Vigil of the Feast of the Translation of Saint Edward King and Confessor, the 38th year of your most noble reign, at Ludford in the shire of Hereford, in the fields of the same, the said Richard Duke of York, Edward Earl of March, Richard Earl of Warwick, Richard Earl of Salisbury [and others named], with other knights and people, such as they had blinded and assembled by wages, promises, and other exquisite means, brought in certain persons before the people, to swear that Ye were deceased, doing Mass to be said, and offering all to make the people the less to dread to take the field. Nevertheless after exhortation to all the lords, knights and nobley in your host, made by your own mouth, in so witty, so knightly, so manly, in so comfortable wise, with so princely apport and assured manner, of which the lords and the people took such joy and comfort, that all their desire was only to haste to fulfil your courageous knightly desire, albe the impediment of the ways and straitness, and by let of waters, it was nigh even ere ye might come to take ground covenable for your field, displayed your banners, ranged your battles,* pighted your tents; they being in the same fields the same day and place, traitorously ranged in battle, fortified their chosen ground, their carts with guns set before their battles, made their eskirmishes, laid their enbushments there, suddenly to have taken the advantage of your host. And they intending the destruction of your most noble person, the same Friday and town, in the field there falsely and traitorously reared war against You, and then and there shot their said guns, and shot as well at your most royal person, as at your lords and people with You then and there being. But God in whose hands the hearts of kings been, made to be known, that

*i.e. a body of troops arrayed for battle.

they whose hearts and desires were only set to untruth, falseness and cruelty, subtly coloured, and feigned zealing justice, meant the greatest falseness and treason, most immoderate covetise that ever was wrought in any realm: in so much that by Robert Radclif, one of the fellowship of the said Duke of York, and Earls of Warwick and Salisbury, it was confessed at his dying, that both the Crown of England and Duchy of Lancaster they would have translated at their will and pleasure. But Almighty God, that seeth the hearts of people, to whom nothing is hid, smote the hearts of the said Duke of York and earls suddenly from that most presumptuous pride, to the most shameful fall of cowardice that could be thought, so that about midnight then next suing they stale away out of the field, under colour they would have refreshed them awhile in the town of Ludlow, leaving their standards and banners in their battle directly against your field, fled out of the town unarmed, with few persons into Wales; understanding that your people hearts assembled, was blinded by them afore, were the more party converted by God's inspiration to repent them, and humbly submit them to You, and ask your grace, which so did the great part ... (32)

The Burgundian chronicler, Jehan de Waurin, adds a vivid account of the cause of York's sudden flight:

... the Duke of York, like a valiant prince, ordered that, the following day in the morning, each should take himself to the field, which they did, and took themselves towards Ludlow hoping to find the king's company in disorder, but they did not do so, for the king's people still held together, so much so that they came to battle the one against the other, and my Lord of Warwick drew his forces putting Andrew Trollope* to lead the vanguard because he trusted him more than he trusted anybody else. The which Andrew had received news by a secret and extremely well written message from the Duke of Somerset which rebuked him because he was coming to wage war against the king his

*The Master Porter of Calais and one of the most famous soldiers of the day. It is possible that Warwick had assured him before leaving Calais that he would not be required to fight against the king.

sovereign lord, saying as well that the king had had published among his host that all those who were adherents to the opposing party but wished to return to serve the king he would pardon everything and would give them great rewards and would do much for them. Then the said Andrew Trollope secretly went away to all those of the Calais garrison and so exhorted them that they joined his party so that they all came together to the Earl of Warwick and told him that they did not wish to fight against their sovereign lord and incontinent turned from the other party without anybody being able to stop them.(33)

The parliament which met at Coventry on 20 November attainted* the rebels for treason. Opinion was very much divided about the attainders. The Yorkist lords in a manifesto which they sent from Calais again blamed their condemnation on the greed of their enemies:

The Earls of Wiltshire and Shrewsbury, and the Lord Beaumont, not satisfied nor content with the king's possessions and his good, stirred and excited his said highness to hold his parliament at Coventry, where an act is made by their provocation and labour against us the said Duke of York, my sons March and Rutland, and the Earls of Warwick and Salisbury, and the sons of the said Earl of Salisbury, and many other knights and esquires, of divers matters falsely and untruly imagined, as they will answer afore Almighty God in the day of Doom; the which the said Earls of Shrewsbury and Wiltshire and the Lord Beaumont provoked to be made to th'intent of our destruction and of our issue, and that they might have our lifelode and goods, as they have openly robbed and despoiled all our places and our tenements and many other true men ... (34)

Friar Brackley, one of the Pastons' acquaintances, and an ardent Yorkist, took the same line:

*An act of attainder was a condemnation by parliament without judicial trial, involving the penalties of treason, viz. death, forfeiture of property and corruption of the blood of descendants so that they could neither inherit nor transmit property.

Worshipful and most entirely betrusted master and special friend, after
duty of all lowly recommendation, ye shall conceive that I certify you
for truth. I communed late with a worshipful and a well named, a good
thrifty* man of this country, which told me in secret wise that he heard
Dr Aleyn say after the Parliament of Coventry that if the Lords that
time reigning and now disseised† might have standing in governance,
that Fortescue the justice, Doctor Morton, John Heydon, Thorp and
he, should be made for ever; and if it turned to contrary wise, it should
grow to their final confusion and utter destruction; for why, the
perilous writing and mischievous indicting was imagined, contrived,
and utterly concluded by their most vengeable labour, etc., and their
most malicious conspiracy against the innocent lords, knights, gendes,
and commons, and all their issue perpetual, etc.(35)

Other men were equally vehement against the rebels. An anonymous
pamphlet,‡ the *Somnium Vigilantis*, written some time during the early
months of 1460, between the Parliament of Devils (1459) and the invasion
of the earls from Calais, asserted that their prolonged recalcitrance had
brought a well-deserved punishment upon them, that their attainder was
necessary for the peace of the realm:

Is it any matter of mercy to be executed to the persons that ye speak
for?§ If it were their first offence the which had happened by
ignorance, or else yet by negligence, then mercy might challenge
(calenge) an interest therein. And perhaps such might be the cause that
justice should have nought a do therewith. But of a pure malice and
longtime precogitate wickedness, the which after the first indulgence
had relapse and recay in a greater and more pernicious offence than the
first was, and in the same so rebuked, not pondering the sweetness of
the recurat¶ mercy and pardon, without any erubescence hath the third

---

*i.e. thriving, prosperous.

† i.e. ousted.

‡Sometimes, though very dubiously, attributed to Sir John Fortescue.

§The pamphlet is in dialogue form.

¶i.e. recurrent (?).

time attempted and put him in his utmost devoir to accomplish his pernicious intent, doing such deeds with such circumstance that no very true man can it ascribe to any other purpose but to the final destruction of this gracious king and to the irreparable subversion of all his true lovers, is it herein any cause of mercy? . . . Then thus I conclude. It were none other but cruelness to have mercy upon them, the which so many times have offended . . .

As for the second point and article, wherein ye make a collation betwix their offence and the part that should fall in this realm by extermination of them,* if in this were any ground of reason I would in more ample wise answer to it. But it is so frivolous and full of derision that with a blast your reason may be annulled. Here is a similitude for it. I have a rotten tooth in my mouth that vexeth me night and day. Is it better to pull him out and so make a gap in my mouth, the which I wot well is not good, or else to plaster him to the confusion and undoing of all the other, and at the last he will fall according to his nature and do me a shrewd turn? For sooth if the king had no moo lords in this land than they, yet were it better without comparison to give them to the hands of Sathanas in perpetual subversion than to reconcile them, for the restoring of them were none other but a wilful submission and exposing of the king to their will, the which was never good nor never shall be, for as Saint Augustine saith *Veternose consuetudinis vis nimis alto radices habet.* They been inextirpable, they been incurable. And for that the king should be destituted, in the case presupposed, of lords and helpers for the tuition of his realm it were no maystre† to restore their places among so many and so true knights as the king hath beside them. And for the case we be versant in it, if the memory and remembrance of them were utterly extinct and quenched and of all other that been false, there been other enough that been true to succeed them. In conclusion that of this point I say that it is more needful to the realm that they be eternally depulsed‡ and utterly destroyed than to reconcile them in any wise . . . (36)

---

*Answering an argument that the defence of the realm would suffer by the loss of their power.

†i.e. matter or meaning 'of no importance'.

‡i.e. driven away.

NOTES

1. For these financial matters see B.P. Wolffe, 'Acts of Resumption in the Lancastrian Parliaments, 1399–1456', *E.H.R.*, lxxiii (1958), 583–613.

2. Davies, p. 64.

3. The events of the next three years are very complicated. For a full discussion, see J.R. Lander, 'Henry VI and the Duke of York's Second Protectorate, 1455–1456', *Bulletin of the John Rylands Library*, xliii (1960), 46–69, and C.A.J. Armstrong, 'Politics and the Battle of St. Albans, 1455', *B.I.H.R.*, xxxiii, 2–3.

4. See J.S. Roskell, 'The Problem of the Attendance of the Lords in Medieval Parliaments', *B.I.H.R.*, xxxix (1956), especially p. 189ff.

5. See Armstrong, *B.I.H.R.*, xxxiii, 2–3.

6. See G.L. Harriss, 'The Struggle for Calais: An Aspect of the Rivalry Between Lancaster and York', *E.H.R*, lxxv (1960), 34–47.

TWO

The Fight for the Throne

York and Lord Clinton fled from Ludlow, breaking down the bridges as they went to frustrate pursuit, and made their way to Ireland. Salisbury, Warwick and the young Earl of March rode wildly into Devon where a squire, John Dinham, paid £73 for a small ship in which they sailed to Calais, Warwick himself, according to Waurin, acting as their steersman as none of their crew was skilled enough to do so. Well received at Calais by Warwick's brother, Lord Fauconberg, they arrived just in time to prevent the Duke of Somerset* taking over the town. On the Lancastrian side incompetent episodes and misfortunes followed each other in rapid succession. Lord Ryvers and his son, Anthony Wydeville were sent to command a fleet at Sandwich but Warwick, in a daring raid, captured them and their entire fleet, except for one vessel, the *Grace Dieu* 'which might not be had away because she was broke in the bottom', and bore them off to Calais.

On 28 January 1460, William Paston, writing from London, told his mother the news from Calais:

As for tidings, my Lord Ryvers was brought to Calais, and before the lords with eight score torches, and there my Lord of Salisbury rated him, calling him knave's son, that he should be so rude to call him and these other lords traitors, for they shall be found the king's true liege men, when he should be found a traitor, etc. And my Lord of Warwick rated him, and said that his father was but a squire, and brought up with King Henry the Vte, and sithen himself made by marriage, and also made Lord, and that it was not his part to have such language of lords, being of the king's blood. And my Lord of March† rated him in like

*The son of the duke slain at St Albans I (1455).
†Ironically enough, after this in 1464 'my Lord of March' (Edward IV) married Lord Ryvers' daughter, Elizabeth.

wise. And Sir Anthony was rated for his language of all three lords in like wise.(1)

A Devonshire knight, Sir Baldwin Fulford, undertook to clear the seas of Warwick and his men for 1,000 marks but achieved nothing. Then the Lord Admiral, the Duke of Exeter, although according to *Davies' Chronicle* he commanded 'a great navy', had to disperse his men owing to lack of money and victuals and failed to prevent Warwick returning from Ireland (where he had been conferring with the Duke of York) to Calais. Warwick, on the other hand, frustrated Somerset's return from Guisnes to England.

Davies' Chronicle went on:

... In the meantime the Earl of Wiltshire Treasurer of England, the Lord Scales, and the Lord Hungerford, having the king's commission went to the town of Newbury, the which longed to the Duke of York, and there made inquisition of all them that in any wise had shewed any favour or benevolence or friendship to the said duke, or to any of his; whereof some were found guilty and were drawn, hanged and quartered, and all other inhabitants of the foresaid town were spoiled of all their goods.

When this was done the Earl of Wiltshire went to Southampton, and there under colour for to take the Earl of Warwick, but specially for to steal privily out of the realm as it proved afterwards, he armed and victualled five great carracks of Genoa that were at that time in the port of the said town, and stuffed them with soldiers of Englishmen, taking victual of the king's price without payment, as he should have made a voyage for the king, and put a great part of his treasure into the said carracks; and soon after he passed out of the port and sailed about in the sea, dreading alway the coming of the foresaid Earls of Warwick and Salisbury, and at last arrived in Dutchland, and sent his soldiers into England again.(2)

As treasurer Wiltshire had assessed men for loans to the king and had promised repayment from the property of York and his followers:

Furthermore, the commons of Kent, dreading the malice and the tyranny of the foresaid Earl of Wiltshire and of other, lest he would exercise his vengeance upon them, as he had done upon them at Newbury, and sent privily messagers and letters to Calais to the foresaid earls, beseeching them that they would in all haste possible come and succour them fro their enemies, promising that they would assist them with all their power.

The said earls would not anon give credence to their writing and words, but sent over into Kent the Lord Fauconberg, to know whether their promise and their deeds should accord: and anon the people of Kent and of other shires about resorted to the said Lord Fauconberg in great number abiding the coming of the earls.(3)

Francesco Coppini, Bishop of Terni, the papal legate, crossed the Channel with the earls. Besides being papal legate he was also the emissary of Francesco Sforza, Duke of Milan, who had instructed the bishop to arrange a series of alliances which would prevent France from giving active support to Angevin claims in Naples. John of Calabria, the Angevin claimant to the throne of Naples, was Margaret of Anjou's brother. If Angevin power in England could be neutralized and France isolated, the King of France would be unable to assist John of Calabria to make good his claims in southern Italy. Coppini most improperly used his position as legate to advance Francesco Sforza's affairs. Therefore, at a critical moment, he gave valuable support to the English rebels, hoping that if they were successful they would declare war on France. International events thus began to tangle with English domestic politics. On 4 July 1460 Coppini wrote an open letter to Henry VI which he also published at St Paul's Cross:

. . . on coming to Calais, owing to recent events I found almost everything in turmoil, and those nobles all ready to cross to England, declaring that they could not wait any longer in the existing state of affairs. Nevertheless, after I had conferred with them and exhorted them to peace and obedience, they gave me a written pledge that they were disposed to devotion and obedience to your Majesty, and to do all in their power for the conservation and augmentation of your honour and the good of your realm. But they desired to come to your Majesty and to be received into their former state and favour, from which they declare they have been ousted by the craft of their opponents, and begged me to cross the sea with them to interpose my efforts and prevent bloodshed, assuring me that they would do anything honourable and just that I should approve for the honour and estate of your Highness and the welfare of your realm, especially certain things contained in documents under their own seals and oaths, which they handed over, and which I am confident your Serenity would approve after viewing them with a tranquil and open mind . . .(4)

Davies again tells the story:

. . . then the noble Earls of March, Warwick, and Salisbury, having wind and weather at their pleasance, arrived graciously at Sandwich; where met with them Master Thomas Bourchier Archbishop of Canterbury, and a great multitude of people with him; and with his cross before him, [he] went forth with the said earls and their people toward London, and sent an herald to the city to know how they were disposed, and whether they would stand with them in their just quarrel, and grant them leave for to pass through the city. They that were not friendly to the earls, couselled the mayor and the commonalty for to lay guns at the bridge for to keep them out, and so a little division there was among the citizens, but it was soon ceased.*

Then sent they of the city to the said earls twelve worshipful and discreet aldermen, the which, in the name of all the city, granted them free entry with such service as they could and might do to their worship and honour. This done, the aldermen returned to the city, and the said herald again to the lords.

And the second day of July they entered into London. And with them came the pope's legate, that not long before had been in England; the which had authority by the pope's bulls for to entreat peace between the king and the earls, if need were; but, how it were, he usurped and took upon him more power than he had, as it was known afterward.

___

*The London records show that there was more than 'a little division'. The city authorities had no wish to support either side. Their main concern was to prevent destruction within the city. See M.I. Peake, 'London and the Wars of the Roses', (Unpubl. M.A. thesis, London, 1925), summarized *B.I.H.R.*, iv (1926–7), 45–47.

Then was a convocation of the clergy holden at Paul's in London, and thither came the said earls: and the Earl of Warwick there purposed, and recited before all the convocation, and innumerable people standing about, the causes of their coming in to this land; and misrule and mischieves thereof; and how with great violence they had be repelled and put from the king's presence, that they might not come to his highness for to excuse them of such false accusations as were laid against them; and now were come again, by God's mercy, accompanied with people for to come to his presence, there to declare and excuse their innocence, or else to die in the field; and there [they] made an open oath upon the cross of Canterbury that they had ever bore true faith and liegance to the king's person, willing no more hurt to him than to their own persons; whereof they took God and his mother and all the saints of heaven to witness.

The king, that held a council at Coventry, hearing of the coming of the earls, went to Northampton.

The Earl of Salisbury by common assent of the city was made ruler and governor of London, in absence of the foresaid earls. And the said Earls of March and Warwick and other lords, that is to say the Lord Fauconberg,† Lord Clinton, Lord Bourchier, Prior of St John's, Lord Audley,‡ Lord Bergavenny,§ Lord Say, Lord Scrope, th'Archbishop of Canterbury the pope's legate, the Bishop of Exeter,¶ the Bishops of Ely, Salisbury, and Rochester, dressed them forth to the King at Northampton.

The Lord Scales and the Lord Hungerford that before the coming of the earls were in the City of London, would have had the rule and governance thereof, but they of the city would not suffer them, for they said that they were sufficient for to rule the city themself; whereof the lords having indignation went in to the Tower of London, and many other great men with them. . . . And the Tower was besieged by land and water, that no victual might come to them that were within.

†Warwick's brother, John Neville.
‡See p. 77. By this time he had gone over to the Yorkists.
§Warwick's uncle, Edward Neville.
¶Warwick's brother, George Neville.

When the earls and lords were gone to Northampton they that were within the Tower cast wild fire into the city, and shot in small guns, and brend and hurt men and women and children in the streets. And they of London laid great bombards on the further side of the Thames against the Tower and crazed the walls thereof in divers places; nathless they hoped daily forto have be rescued, but all was in vain.

The king at Northampton lay at Friars and had ordained there a strong and a mighty field, in the meadows beside the nunnery,* armed and arrayed with guns, having the river at his back.

The earls with the number of 60,000, as it was said, came to Northampton, and sent certain bishops to the king beseeching him that in eschewing of effusion of Christian blood he would admit and suffer the earls for to come to his presence to declare them self as they were. The Duke of Buckingham that stood beside the king, said unto them, 'Ye come not as bishops for to treat for peace, but as men of arms'; because they brought with them a notable company of men of arms. They answered and said, 'We come thus for surety of our persons, for they that be-eth about the king be-eth not our friends.' 'Forsooth,' said the duke, 'the Earl of Warwick shall not come to the king's presence, and if he come he shall die.' The messengers returned again, and told this to the earls.

Then the Earl of Warwick sent an herald of arms to the king, beseeching that he might have hostages of safe going and coming, and he would come naked to his presence, but he might not be heard. And the third time he sent to the king and said that at two hours after noon, he would speak with him, or else die in the field.

The Archbishop of Canterbury sent a bishop of this land to the king with an instruction, the which did not his message indifferently, but exhorted and couraged the king's part for to fight, as they said that were there. And another time he was sent to the king by the commons, and then he came not again, but privily departed away. The Bishop of Hereford, a White Friar, the king's confessor, did the same; wherefore after the battle he was committed to the castle of Warwick, where he was long in prison.

*Delapré Abbey.

Then on the Thursday the 10th of July, the year of Our Lord 1460, at two hours after noon, the said Earls of March and Warwick let cry through the field, that no man should lay hand upon the king ne on the common people, but only on the lords, knights and squires: then the trumpets blew up, and both hosts countered and fought together half an hour. The Lord Grey, that was the king's vaward, brake the field and came to the earl's party, which caused sauvation of many a man's life: many were slain, and many were fled, and were drowned in the river.

The Duke of Buckingham, the Earl of Shrewsbury, the Lord Beaumont, the Lord Egremeont were slain by the Kentishmen beside the king's tent, and many other knights and squires. The ordnance of the king's guns availed not, for that day was so great rain, that the guns lay deep in the water, and so were queynt* and might not be shot.

When the field was do, and the earls through mercy and help had the victory, they came to the king in his tent, and said in this wise:

'Most Noble Prince, displease you not, though it have pleased God of His Grace to grant us the victory of our mortal enemies, the which by their venomous malice have untruly stirred and moved your highness to exile us out of your land, and would us have put to final shame and confusion. We come not to that intent for to inquiet ne grieve your said highness, but for to please your most noble person, desiring most tenderly the high welfare and prosperity thereof, and of all your realm, and for to be your true liegemen, while our lives shall endure.'(5)

Lord Grey of Ruthyn's spectacular desertion of the king at the battle of Northampton was ominous of the changes now taking place. Until after the flight from Ludford the nobility as a whole stood remarkably aloof from York's ambitions. Salisbury and Warwick apart, only four peers† are known who were prepared to fight for him, though others may have regarded him as hardly used. Only during the last months of his life, for reasons now

---

*i.e. quenched.
†The Earl of Devonshire and Lord Cobham in 1452, Lord Clinton at St Albans I (1455) and Lord Clinton and Lord Grey of Powys at Ludford.

obscure, did York receive any considerable support from his fellow nobles. Between the flight from Ludford in October 1459 and Edward IV's accession in 1461 the Yorkist fighting strength rose to seventeen peers – out of a titled aristocracy of about sixty. However, this group seems far less impressive if the small number of the higher ranks is taken into account: it included, apart from Salisbury and Warwick, only two dukes, one earl and one viscount.

York delayed suspiciously long in Ireland. Precarious as this new venture was, needing every available man for its success, the duke made no attempt to co-ordinate his arrival in England with the invasion which his friends mounted from Calais. He came to England only when the Nevilles had won his victory for him at Northampton. No one was certain of his intentions and he made his way slowly across the country, timing his entry into London and into the Parliament Chamber so as to avoid any discussion with his allies. He now sprang upon his fellow rebels plans which left them aghast and dismayed; plans to revive the dormant title of the house of Mortimer and claim the throne. If we can believe the Burgundian chronicler, Jehan de Waurin, York, besotted by his own dreams, had even fixed the day for his coronation. Abbot Whethamstede of St Albans, who may have been present, described the scene in parliament:

> While, however, the people were tossed with doubt in this way, and the lord king with the prelates, magnates and commons continued in the parliament assembled at Westminster for the good government of his kingdom, shortly, and as if for the opening of parliament the said lord Duke of York suddenly arrived, with great pomp and splendour, and in no little exaltation of spirit, since [he was accompanied] by trumpets and horns, and with men-at-arms, and a very large retinue; and there entering the palace he went straight through the great hall until he came to the usual room, where the king, with the commons, was accustomed to hold his parliament. And coming there he walked straight on, until he came to the king's throne, upon the covering or cushion of laying his hand, in this very act like a man about to take possession of his right, he held it upon it for a short time. But at length withdrawing it,* he turned

---

*i.e. his hand.

his face to the people, [and] standing quietly under the canopy of royal state, he looked eagerly for their applause.

While, however, he was standing thus and turning his face to the people and while he was judging their applause, Master Thomas Bourchier, Archbishop of Canterbury, rose up and having exchanged greetings asked if he would come and see the king. He, as if stung in soul by this question, replied shortly, 'I do not recall that I know anyone within the kingdom whom it would not befit to come sooner to me and see me rather than I should go and visit him.'

The archbishop, having heard this reply, quickly withdrew, and reported to the king, the answer which he had heard from the duke's mouth. While the archbishop was thus withdrawing, he too retired (the king lying in the queen's rooms) to the principal apartments of the whole palace. Having smashed the bolts and thrown open the doors, he lodged there for no little time more like a king than a duke. After such high-handed conduct on the part of the duke had been noised about amongst the vulgar and also how he had made his entry in this way on the strength of his own unlawful judgment and by no means as a result of considered and weighed resolve, forthwith [people on all estates and ranks, age, sex, order and condition began to murmur vehemently against him and to say by way of reproach . . .*(6)

The Burgundian chronicler, Waurin, who probably obtained his information several years later from English acquaintances who had taken part in these events, claimed that the reactions of York's friends were extremely hostile for he had acted completely in isolation without informing them of his intentions. When Salisbury discussed these events with his son, the Earl of Warwick, Warwick was furious at the deception and because he already knew of the discontent which they had provoked in London. Warwick went to see York:

. . . and there were angry words (*grosses parolles*) for the earl showed the duke how the lords and the people were ill content against him because he wished to strip the king of his crown.(7)

*A long imaginary speech follows at this point.

Obstinate and headstrong, dead to reason, York pressed his claims in parliament. However, even in a house empty of Henry VI's staunchest supporters, it is obvious from their prolonged debates, that everybody involved wished to avoid responsibility, that finally only York's dogged tenacity forced the Lords to compromise. The Parliament Roll tells the story:

'Memorand', that the 16th day of October, the 9th day of this present Parliament, the counsel of the right high and mighty Prince Richard Duke of York brought into the Parliament chamber a writing, containing the claim and title of the right, that the said duke pretended unto the crowns of England and of France, and Lordship of Ireland, and the same writing delivered to the Right Reverend Father in God George Bishop of Exeter, Chancellor of England, desiring him that the same writing might be opened to the Lords Spiritual and Temporal assembled in this present Parliament, and that the said duke might have brief and expedient answer thereof. Whereupon the said Chancellor opened and shewed the said desire to the Lords Spiritual and Temporal, asking the question of them, whether they would the said writing should be openly read before them or no. To the which question it was answered and agreed by all the said Lords: In asmuch as every person high and low, suing to this high Court of Parliament, of right must be heard, and his desire and petition understand, that the said writing should be read and heard, not to be answered without the King's commandment, for so much as the matter is so high, and of so great weight and poise . . .*

Everybody concerned was absolutely dismayed, and tried to shift responsibility to the others. Pressed by the Chancellor the Lords went to the king who asked them to find evidence to refute York's claim to the throne. The Lords then consulted the king's justices in the Parliament Chamber. The justices replied that:

. . . the matter was so high and touched the king's high estate and regalie, which is above the law and passed their learning, whereof they durst not enter into any communication thereof . . .

*A long and technical exposition of York's descent and claim follows at this point.

and that such matters were the responsibility of the peers. Baffled by the judges the Lords resorted to the lesser luminaries of the legal profession, the king's sergeants and attorney who gave more or less the same reply. The Lords then debated the matter again. In the end they could do nothing but allege that prescriptive right, the House of Lancaster's long tenure of the throne, their own oaths to the king and various acts of parliament stood in the way of York's claim. Then:

> ... the said Richard Plantagenet answereth and saith, that in truth there been none such acts and tailles* made by any Parliament here before, as it is surmised; but only in the 6th year of King Henry the Fourth, a certain act and ordinance was made in a Parliament by him called, wherein he made the realms of England and France amongst other, to be unto him and to the heirs of his body coming, and to his four sons and the heirs of their bodies coming, in the manner and form as it appeareth in the same act. And if he might have obtained and rejoiced the said crowns, etc. by title of inheritance, descent or succession, he neither needed nor would have desired or made them to be granted to him in such wise, as they be by the said act: the which taketh no place, neither is of any force or effect against him that is right inheritor of the said crowns, as it accordeth with God's law, and all natural laws ...
>
> ... for though right for a time rest and be put to silence, yet it rotteth not nor shall not perish ... (8)

In the end the Lords decided that Henry's title could not 'be defeated' and arranged a compromise – the so-called Act of Accord under which it was agreed that Henry should remain king, but York and his heirs should succeed him. The Act of Accord also allotted York and his family an income of 10,000 marks a year, a large slice of the royal revenue – a proceeding hardly consistent with the duke's former support of Acts of Resumption. It was, of course, customary to endow the heir presumptive from the royal revenues, but he was generally penniless except for what the king gave him, whereas Richard of York was probably the richest man in England. The London chronicler, Gregory, wrote of Margaret of Anjou's preparations to continue the fight:

* i.e. entails.

And that night the king removed* unto London against his will, to the
bishop's palace of London, and the Duke of York come unto him that
same night by the torchlight and took upon him as king, and said in
many places that this is ours by very right. And then the queen hearing
this she voided unto Wales, but she was met with beside the castle of
Malepas,‡ and a servant of her own that she had made both yeoman
and gentleman, and after appointed for to be in office with her son the
prince, spoiled her and robbed her, and put her so in doubt of her life
and son's life also. And then she come to the castle of Harlech in Wales,
and she had many great gifts and greatly comforted, for she had need
thereof, for she had a full easy meinie§ about her, the number of four
persons. And most commonly she rode behind a young poor
gentleman of fourteen year age, his name was John Combe, i-born at
Amesbury in Wiltshire. And there hence she removed full privily unto
the Lord Jasper, Lord and Earl of Pembroke, for she durst not abide in
no place that [was] open but in private. The cause was that counterfeit
tokens were sent unto her as though that they had come from her most
dread lord the King Harry the VI; but it was not of his sending, neither
of [his] doing, but forged things, for they that brought the tokens were
of the king's house, and some of the prince's house, and some of her
own house, and bade her beware of the tokens, that she gave no
credence thereto; for at the king's departing fro Coventry toward the
field of Northampton, he kissed her and blessed the prince, and
commanded her that she should not come unto him till that [he] sent a
special token unto her that no man knew but the king and she. For the
lords would fain had her unto London, for they knew well that all the
workings that were done grew by her, for she was more wittier than
the king, and that appeareth by his deeds, etc.

Then the queen having knowledge of this praty† while she sent unto
the Duke of Somerset, at that time being in Dorsetshire at the castle of
Corfe, and for the Earl of Devonshire, and for Alexander Hody, and
prayed them to come to her as hastily as they might, with their tenants

*from Westminster.
‡Malepas in Cheshire.
§i.e. insignificant.
†i.e. cunning.

as strong in their harness as men of war, for the Lord Roos, the Lord Clifford, the Baron of Greystock, the Lord Neville, the Lord Latimer, were waiting upon the Duke of Exeter to meet with her at Hull. And this matter was not tarried but full privily i-wrought; and she sent letters unto all her chief officers that they would do the same, and that they should warn all tho servants that loved her or purposed to keep and rejoice their office, to wait upon her at Hull by that day as it appointed by her. All these people were gathered and conveyed so privily that they were whole in number of 15,000 ere any man would believe it; in so much if any man said, or told, or talked of such gathering, he should be schende,* and some were in great danger, for the common people said by thoo that told the truth, 'Ye talk right ye would it were', and gave no credence of their saying. But the last the lords purposed to know the truth.(9)

Davies can once again take up the tale of the Yorkist counter-preparations:

. . . and anon after the said Duke of York, the Earl of Rutland his son, and the Earl of Salisbury, a little before Christmas, with a few persons went in to the north also, for to repress the malice of the northern men the which loved not the said Duke of York ne the Earl of Salisbury, and were lodged at the castle of Sandal and at Wakefield.

Then the Lord Neville, brother to the Earl of Westmorland, under a false colour went to the said Duke of York, desiring a commission of him for to raise a people for to chastise the rebels of the country; and the duke it granted, deeming that he had be true and on his part. When he had his commission he raised to the number of 8,000 men, and brought them to the lords of the country; that is to say, the Earl of Northumberland, Lord Clifford, and Duke of Somerset, that were adversaries and enemies to Duke Richard. And when they saw a convenient time† for to fill their cruel intent, the last day of December they fell upon the said Duke Richard, and him killed, and his son

---

*i.e. disgraced.

†The *Annales* formerly attributed to William Worcester (Stevenson, ii, Pt. ii, 775), state that York's men were wandering about tne countryside in search of victuals.

th'Earl of Rutland, and many other knights and squires; that is to say, the Lord Harrington a young man, Thomas Harrington Knight, Sir Thomas Neville son to th'Earl of Salisbury, and Sir Harry Radford knight; and of other people to the number of 2,200. The Earl of Salisbury was taken alive, and led by the said Duke of Somerset to the castle of Pomfret, and for a great sum of money that he should have paid had grant of his life. But the common people of the country, which loved him not, took him out of the castle by violence and smote off his head.(10)

Margaret's forces, drunk with victory at what is known as the battle of Wakefield, but unpaid and promised plunder in lieu of their wages, swept down through the North and the Midlands, looting the countryside for several miles either side of their line of march. The faint-hearted Prior of Croyland wailed over their descent, displaying an exaggerated vocabulary of terror:

The duke being thus removed from this world, the northmen, being sensible that the only impediment was now withdrawn, and that there was no one now who would care to resist their inroads, again swept onwards like a whirlwind from the north, and in the impulse of their fury attempted to overrun the whole of England. At this period too, fancying that every thing tended to insure them freedom from molestation, paupers and beggars flocked forth from those quarters in infinite numbers, just like so many mice rushing forth from their holes, and universally devoted themselves to spoil and rapine, without regard of place or person. For, besides the vast quantities of property which they collected outside, they also irreverently rushed, in their unbridled and frantic rage, into churches and the other sanctuaries of God, and most nefariously plundered them of their chalices, books, and vestments, and, unutterable crime! broke open the pixes in which were kept the body of Christ and shook out the sacred elements therefrom. When the priests and the other faithful of Christ in any way offered to make resistance, like so many abandoned wretches as they were, they cruelly slaughtered them in the very churches or church yards. Thus did they proceed with impunity, spreading in vast multitudes over a space of thirty miles in breadth and, covering the whole surface of the earth

just like so many locusts, made their way almost to the very walls of
London; all the moveables which they could possibly collect in every
quarter being placed on beasts of burden and carried off. With such
avidity for spoil did they press on, that they dug up the precious vessels
which, through fear of them, had been concealed in the earth, and with
threats of death compelled the people to produce the treasures which
they had hidden in remote and obscure spots.

What do you suppose must have been our fears dwelling here in this
island, when every day rumours of this sad nature were reaching our
ears, and we were in the utmost dread that we should have to
experience similar hardships to those which had been inflicted by them
upon our neighbours? This fact too, in especial gave us additional
grounds for apprehension, that numbers of persons who lived in the
country, being desirous to provide for the safety of themselves and their
sacred things, had fled with the utmost speed to this island, as their sole
place of refuge. The consequence was that by bringing with them
whatever treasures they considered of especial value, they rendered the
place a still greater object of suspicion to the enemy. In the meantime
our precious vestments were put out of the way, while our jewels, and
silver vessels, together with our charters and muniments were, all of
them, hidden and secured within the walls. Besides this, daily
processions were formed in the convent, and every night, after matin
lauds, prayers and tears were most devoutly poured forth in a spirit of
humility and with a contrite heart, at the tomb of Guthlac our most
holy father and protector, in order through his intervention to obtain
the Divine mercy. In the meantime, at each gate of the monastery, and
in the vill adjoining, both at the rivers as well as on dry land watch was
continually kept; and all the waters of the streams and weirs that
surrounded the vill, by means of which a passage might by any
possibility be made, were rendered impassable by stakes and palisades of
exceeding strength; so much so, that those within could on no account
go forth without leave first given, nor yet could those without in any
way effect an entrance. Our causeways also and dykes, along which
there is a wide and even road for foot passengers, were covered with
obstacles, and trees, spread along them and laid across, caused no small
impediment to those who approached in an opposite direction. For
really we were in straits, when word came to us that this army, so

execrable and so abominable, had approached to within six miles of our boundaries. But blessed be God, who did not give us for a prey unto their teeth! For, after the adjoining counties had been given up to dreadful pillage and spoil (that we may here confess the praises of God, in that at the time of His mercy, He regarded the prayers of the contrite, and in His clemency determined to save us from the yoke of this calamity) our Croyland became as though another little Zoar,★ in which we might be saved; and, by the Divine grace and clemency, it was preserved.(11)

Queen Margaret now realized, too late, the harm which these depredations were doing her cause and, on her way to London, sent two letters trying to still the fears of the terrified city fathers. Meanwhile, they heard the news that Edward, Earl of March, had won a victory in the west at Mortimer's Cross. Gregory relates:

Edward, Earl of March, the Duke of York's son and heir, had a gre★★ journey at Mortimer's Cross in Wales the second day of February next so following, and there he put to flight the Earl of Pembroke, the Earl of Wiltshire. And there he took and slew of knights and squires and of the,† to the number of 3,000 etc.

And in that journey was Owen Tudor i-take and brought unto Haverford-west, and he was beheaded at the market place, and his head set upon the highest grice of the market cross, and a mad woman combed his hair and washed away the blood of his face, and she got candles and set about him brenning, moo than a hundred. This Owen Tudor was father unto the Earl of Pembroke, and had wedded Queen Katherine, King Harry the VI's mother, weening and trusting all away that he should not be headed till he saw the axe and the block, and when that he was in his doublet he trusted on pardon and grace till the collar of his red velvet doublet was ripped off. Then he said, 'That head shall lie on the stock that was wont to lie on Queen Katherine's lap', and put his heart and mind wholly unto God, and fully meekly took his death.(12)

★*Genesis*, xix, 20.
★★i.e. favourable.
†So in MS.

Meanwhile, the Earl of Warwick had marched out of London, taking the king with him, to halt the queen's advance. As Gregory again relates they came to battle at St Albans:

And the 17th day* next following King Harry rode to St Albans, and the Duke of Norfolk with him, the Earl of Warwick, the Earl of Arundel, the Lord Bourchier, the Lord Bonvile, with many great lords, knights, and squires, and commons of an 100,000 men.† And there they had a great battle with the queen, for she come ever on fro the journey of Wakefield till she come to St Albans, with all the lords aforesaid; and her meinie and every lord's men bare their lord's livery, that every man might know his own fellowship by his livery. And beside all that, every man and lord bare the prince's livery, that was a bend of crimson and black with ostrich's feathers. The substance that gate that field were household men and feed men. I ween there were not 5,000 men that fought in the queen's party, for the most part of Northern men fled away, and some were take and spoiled out of their harness by the way as they fled. And some of them robbed ever as they yede,‡ a pitiful thing it is to hear it. But the day before that battle there was a journey at Dunstable; but the king's meinie lacked good guiding, for some were but new men of war, for the chiefest captain was a butcher of the same town; and there were the king's meinie overthrew only by the Northern men. And soon after the butcher, for shame of his simple guiding and loss of the men, the number of 800, for very sorrow as it is said, hung himself; and some men said that it was for loss of his good, but dead he is – God knoweth the truth.

And in the midst of the battle King Harry went unto his queen and forsook all his lords,** and trust better to her party than unto his own lords. And then through great labour the Duke of Norfolk and the Earl of Warwick escaped away; the Bishop of Exeter, that time Chancellor of

---

*i.e. of February.
†This figure is wildly exaggerated.
‡i.e. went.
**It was reported in France that Henry sat under a tree a mile away and laughed and sang while the battle raged. *C.S.P.M.*, i, 55.

England, and brother unto the Earl of Warwick, the Lord Bourchier, with many other knights, squires, and commons fled, and many men slain in both parties. And the Lord Bonvile was beheaded, the common saying that his longage* caused him to die. The prince was judge his own self. And there was slain that manly knight Sir Thomas Kyriel. The number of dead men was 3,500 and moo that were slain. The lords in King Harry's party pitched a field and fortified it full strong, and like unwise men brake their [ar-]ray and took another, and ere that they were all sette a-buskyd‡ to battle, the queen's party was at hand with them in town of St Albans, and then all thing was to seek and out of order, for their prickers come not home to bring no tiding how nigh that the queen was, save one come and said that she was nine mile off. And ere the gunners and borgeners§ could level their guns they were busily fighting, and many a gynne¶ of war was ordained that stood in little avail or nought; for the borgeners had such instruments that would shoot both pellets of lead and arrows of an ell of length with six feathers, three in midst and three at the other end, with a great mighty head of iron at the other end, and wild fire with all. All these three things they might shoot well and easily at once, but in time of need they could shoot not one of these, but the fire turned back upon them that would shoot these three things. Also they had nets made of great cords of four fathom of length and of four foot broad, like unto a haye,** and at every two knot there was a nail standing up right, that there could no man pass over it by likelihood but he should be hurt. Also they had pavysse†† bore as a door i-made with a staff folding up and down to set the pavysse where they liked, and loops with shooting windows to shoot out at, they standing behind the pavysse, and the pavysse as full of 3d. nail after order as they might stand. And when their shot was spend and done they cast the pavysse before them, then

---

*i e. language (?), the words he used to the prince.
‡i.e. set in order.
§i.e. Burgundians. Warwick was employing foreign mercenaries.
¶i.e. engines..
**i.e. a net for catching rabbits.
††i.e. shields.

there might no man come unto them over the pavysse for the nails that stood upright, but if he would mischief himself. Also they had a thing made like unto a lattice full of nails as the net was, but it would be moved as a man would; a man might bryse* it together that the length would be more than two yards long, and if he would he might hale it abroad, then it would be four square. And that served to lie at gaps there at horsemen would enter in, and many a caltrap.† And as the substance of men of worship that will not glose‡ nor curry favour (favyl) for no partiality, they could not understand that all this ordnance did any good or harm but if it were among us in our part with King Harry. Therefore it is much left, and men take them to mallys§ of lead, bows, swords, *glaives*¶ and axes. As for spearmen they been good to ride before the footmen and eat and drink up their victual, and many moo such pretty things they do, hold me excused though I say the best, for in the footmen is all the trust.(13)

London now lived in terror that Margaret's northern troops would enter and sack the city. The authorities sent envoys accompanied by the Dowager Duchesses of Buckingham and Bedford. An eye-witness, an Italian, G. Gigli, in letters written to Michele Arnolfini at Bruges described the results:

They returned on the 20th, and reported that the king and queen had no mind to pillage the chief city and chamber of their realm, and so they promised; but at the same time they did not mean that they would not punish the evildoers. On the receipt of this reply by the magistrates a proclamation was issued that everyone should keep fast to his house and should live at peace, in order that the king and his forces might enter and behave peacefully. But less than an hour later all the people ran to arms and reports circulated that York** with 60,000 Irish

---

*i.e. draw.
†a trap or obstacle for cavalry.
‡i.e. flatter.
§i.e. clubs.
¶i e. spears and lances.
**Gigli apparently did not know of York's death at the battle of Wakefield.

and March with 40,000 Welsh had hastened to the neighbourhood and would guard their place for them; and they said that the mayor must give them the keys of the gates. They called for a brewer as their leader, and that day this place was in an uproar, so that I was never more afraid than then that everything would be at hazard. But, by the grace of God and the excellent arrangements of the mayor and aldermen and of the notables who were at the council, they decided last Saturday to send to the king and queen four aldermen with some others, including the same ladies, and they were to fetch four cavaliers in whom the king and queen had perfect confidence, and treat here with the magistrates in the presence of the people, and come to an arrangement that they might enter, that is the king, queen, prince and all the nobles with their leaders without the body of the army. They have started once more this morning to fetch these four, and so the people have quieted down, and one sees no arms except with the mayor and sheriffs, who keep guard with a great company throughout the place as well as at the gates, where they keep good guard, and no one takes arms except those who are ordered, and they behave prudently ...(14)

Finally the negotiations broke down and Margaret, to her eternal credit, threw away her chances of success and retreated northwards rather than risk the sack of London. After his defeat at St Albans, Warwick fled westward and joined the Earl of March, advancing towards London after his victory at Mortimer's Cross, at Burford in the Cotswolds. They continued their journey together and entered London on 27 February, ten days after Warwick's defeat at St Albans. *The Great Chronicle of London* written by the City draper, Robert Fabyan, tells of their audacity – and of the danger of their position:

And upon the Thursday following th'Earls of March and of Warwick with a great power of men, *but few of name*,* entered into the City of London, the which was of the citizens joyously received, and upon the Sunday following the said earl caused to be mustered his people in St John's Field, where unto that host were proclaimed and shewed certain

*My italics.

articles and points that King Henry had offended in, whereupon it was demanded of the said people whether the said Henry were worthy to reign as king any longer or no. Whereunto the people cried hugely and said, Nay, Nay. And after it was asked of them whether they would have th'Earl of March for their king and they cried with one voice, Yea, Yea. After the which admission thus by the commons assented, certain captains were assigned to bear report thereof unto the said Earl of March, then being lodged at his place called Baynard's Castle. Of the which when he was by them ascertained he thanked God and them. And how be it that like a wise prince he shewed by a convenient style that he was insufficient to occupy that great charge for sundry considerations by him then shewed, yet he lastly by the exhortation of the Archbishop of Canterbury and the Bishop of Exeter and other noble men then present took upon him that charge, and granted to their petition. . . . Then th'Earl of March thus as is abovesaid being elected and admitted for king upon the morrow next ensuing rode unto Paul's and there rode in procession and offered, and there had *Te Deum* sungen with all solemnity. After which solemnisation finished he was with great royalty conveyed unto Westminster and there in the hall set in the king's see* with St Edward's sceptre in his hand. Where he so being set and his lords spiritual and temporal standing about him and the hall being full of people, anon after that silence was commanded, it was there showed the rightful inheritance of this prince by two manner of ways, as first by the right and title of the Duke of York his father, and secondarily by the forfeiture made by King Henry, which he committed contrary to the ordinances made and stablished in the parliament holden at Westminster at All Hallowentide last past. In consideration whereof it was then again asked of the people, if they would have th'Earl of March to be their king. And it was answered Yea. Yea. Whereafter, certain homages by him received, he was with procession received into th'abbey of Westminster and there set in the choir in a place ordained for all kings, where he sat the while that *Te Deum* was sungen, and that done he offered at St Edward's shrine, and then returned by water unto Paul's and then was lodged within the bishop's palace. And thus took this noble prince possession of this realm of England upon a Tuesday being the 4th day of March.(15)

*i.e. seat.

The vital decision to make Edward king was taken at the meeting at Baynard's Castle:

The 3rd March the Archbishop of Canterbury, the Bishops of Salisbury (Beauchamp) and Exeter (namely the reverend George Neville), and John Duke of Norfolk, Richard Earl of Warwick, Lord Fitzwalter, William Herbert, Lord Ferrers of Chartley, and many others, held a council at Baynard's Castle, where they agreed and concluded, that Edward, Duke of York, should then be king. And the 4th March the said Lord Edward, Duke of York, with the said lords straightway (aperte) going over to Westminster, was received in procession. After his title was declared he was seized of the crown and sceptre of the holy King Edward and had himself proclaimed King Edward IV.(16)

In spite of the propaganda put out by the Yorkists shortly afterwards, Coppini, for once almost brutally frank, spoke the truth when he wrote a few weeks later to Francesco Sforza, 'Just now, although matters in England have undergone several fluctuations, yet in the end my lord of Warwick has come off the best and has made a new king of the son of the Duke of York.'[1] Edward's position was still precarious in the extreme. All kinds of fantastic rumours about events in England were crossing the Channel. Prospero di Camulio, the Milanese ambassador to the court of France, sent many of them home, though to do him justice, he was extremely sceptical about some of the wilder tales. On 15 March he wrote from Brussels:

They say here that the Queen of England, after the king had abdicated in favour of his son, gave the king poison. At least he has known how to die, if he did not know what to do else. It is said that the queen will unite with the Duke of Somerset. However these are rumours in which I do not repose much confidence. The sea between here and England has been stormy and unnavigable since the 10th.(17)

Twelve days later he wrote home his assessment of the situation in England. In spite of some inaccurate information it was shrewd enough.

Commenting on Edward's acceptance of the throne he remarked:

... By the last letters they say that his lordship accepted the royal sceptre and staff and all the other ceremonies except the unction and the crown,* which they have postponed until he has annihilated the other king† and reduced the island and the realm to a stable peace, and among other things, exacted the vengeance due for the slaughter of his father and of so many knights and lords, who have been slain of late ...

... As is usual in common and great matters, opinions vary in accordance with men's passions. Those who support the claims of Edward and Warwick say that the chances in favour of Edward are great, both on account of the great lordship which he has in the island and in Ireland, and owing to the cruel wrongs done to him by the queen's side, as well as through Warwick and London, which is entirely inclined to side with the new king and Warwick, and as it is very rich and the most wealthy city of Christendom, this enormously increases the chances of the side that it favours. To these must be added the good opinion of the temper and moderation of Edward and Warwick. Some, on the other hand, say that the queen is exceedingly prudent, and by remaining on the defensive, as they say she is well content to do, she will bring things into subjection and will tear to pieces these attacks of the people, who, when they perceive that they are not on the road to peace, will easily be induced to change sides, such being the very nature of the people, especially when free, and never to let things go so far that they cannot turn But, however this may be, as I have written before to your Excellency, York, through having been long and ardent is reduced to a few moves, and must of necessity move soon one way or the other.(18)

---

*In spite of these rapid decisions the ceremonies, with a shrewd eye to their propaganda effect, were organized with great magnificence, even to the extent of a deliberately antiquarian revival of *Laudes Regiae*, ritual adoration of the ruler, unknown in England for nearly a century and probably longer. See C.A.J. Armstrong, 'The Inauguration Ceremonies of the Yorkist Kings', in *T.R. Hist. S.*, 4 Ser., xxx (1948), 51–73.

†One reason may have been that there was no time to adjudicate on claims to office at the coronation. On the other hand Edward may have desired confirmation of his claim by the judgment of God in battle. The Croyland writer states: 'However, he would not at present allow himself to be crowned, but immediately, like unto Gideon or another of the judges, acting faithfully in the Lord, girded himself with the sword of battle.'

After his secular enthronement in Westminster Hall, Edward set out in pursuit of the retreating Lancastrians, whom he defeated in the greatest and most bloody battle of the Wars of the Roses – the battle of Towton, on Palm Sunday, 1461. George Neville, Bishop of Exeter and the Earl of Warwick's brother, described the pursuit and the battle in a letter written to Coppini:

The king, the valiant Duke of Norfolk, my brother aforesaid and my uncle, Lord Fauconberg, travelling by different routes, finally united with all their companies and armies near the country round York. The armies having been re-formed and marshalled separately, they set forth against the enemy, and at length on Palm Sunday, near a town called Feurbirga,* about sixteen miles from the city, our enemies were routed and broken in pieces. Our adversaries had broken the bridge which was our way across, and were strongly posted on the other side, so that our men could only cross by a narrow way which they had made themselves after the bridge was broken. But our men forced a way by the sword, and many were slain on both sides. Finally the enemy took to flight, and very many of them were slain as they fled.

That day there was a great conflict, which began with the rising of the sun, and lasted until the tenth hour of the night, so great was the pertinacity and boldness of the men, who never heeded the possibility of a miserable death. Of the enemy who fled, great numbers were drowned in the river near the town of Tadcaster, eight miles from York, because they themselves had broken the bridge to cut our passage that way, so that none could pass, and a great part of the rest who got away who gathered in the said town and city, were slain and so many dead bodies were seen as to cover an area six miles long by three broad and about four furlongs. In this battle eleven lords of the enemy fell, including the Earl of Devon, the Earl of Northumberland, Lord Clifford and Neville with some cavaliers; and from what we hear from persons worthy of confidence, some 28,000 persons perished on one side and the other. O miserable and luckless race and powerful people, would you have no spark of pity for our own blood, of which we have lost so much of fine quality by the civil war, even if you had no compassion for the French!

*i.e. Ferrybridge.

If it had been fought under some capable and experienced captain against the Turks, the enemies of the Christian name, it would have been a great stroke and blow. But to tell the truth, owing to these civil discords, our riches are beginning to give out, and we are shedding our own blood copiously among ourselves, while we were unwilling to give help in men and money to the army of his Holiness against the infidel Turks, despite all the instances of his Holiness and your Reverence. But the limitations of writing do not permit me to state my mind on all these things.(19)

George Neville added that it was rumoured* that Henry, the queen, the Prince of Wales, the Duke of Somerset and some others had been captured and the certain news that the new King Edward had entered York. Various foreign observers sent their impressions home. An unknown correspondent wrote from London on 14 April to Pigello Portinari:

Their side is practically destroyed and King Edward has become master and governor of the whole realm. Words fail me to relate how well the commons love and adore him, as if he were their God. The entire kingdom keeps holiday for the event, which seems a boon from above. Thus far he appears to be a just prince who intends to amend and organise matters otherwise than has been done hitherto, so all comfort themselves with hopes of future well-being.(20)

Prospero di Camulio's assessment of events, four days later, was far less favourable:

The reputation of Edward and Warwick is great owing to their good conduct, and their popularity from having conquered is enormous ...
... I think it my duty to make the following remarks:
Firstly, if the King and Queen of England with the other fugitives mentioned above are not taken, it seems certain that in time fresh disturbances will arise, nor are the people disinclined to these, since the storm falls equally on the heads of princes as on their own, and the less nobles there are the better they are pleased, and think that they are

*The rumour was false.

nearer a chance for liberty; and from what I have been told the people of London have great aspirations.

If, however, they are taken, then that kingdom may be considered settled and quiet under King Edward and the earl of Warwick; and then, as they are well affected to the Dauphin and the Duke of Burgundy, it seems likely, both from the unexpected things that the King of France has done to the Duke of Burgundy, as well as out of respect for the Dauphin, who considers that things cannot continue thus, that they will pursue the plan to pass to France,* especially if the Dauphin did not happen to be in accord with the King of France ...

... I have observed the great importance that the Duke of Burgundy attaches to England. Thus he has kept in with the Earl of Warwick, and his son with the Queen of England, so that whatever happens England will have friendship in the house of the Duke of Burgundy ...

...We have news of English affairs hour by hour. Two days ago letters arrived here from English merchants of repute, and we have also heard by way of Calais, that it is true that King Henry, the queen, the Prince of Wales, their son, the Duke of Somerset, Lord Roos, his brother,† the Duke of Exeter were taken, and of these the Duke of Somerset and his brother were immediately beheaded. When the same fate was about to befall the Duke of Exeter, there came a message to let him off, and they say he escaped because he is related to King Edward, whose sister he married. However as he is fierce and cruel, it is thought that they will put him to a more honourable death. I postponed writing about this to see if it would be confirmed;‡ if it is, then before long grievances and recrimination will break out between King Edward and Warwick, King Henry and the queen will be victorious, and he who seemed to have the world at his feet will provide a remarkable example of what prudent men, in excuse for human errors, have called Fortune.

---

*A reference to Francesco Sforza's plan to diminish French influence in Italy by promoting an Anglo-Burgundian attack on France.
†His step-brother. The widowed Duchess of Somerset had married Lord Roos.
‡He added a postscript saying that it was not.

Any one who reflects at all upon the wretchedness of that queen and the ruins of those killed and considers the ferocity of the country, and the state of mind of the victors, should indeed, it seems to me, pray to God for the dead, and not less for the living.

With respect to what will follow, there are many considerations for those who have studied that kingdom, deprived of so many of its natural princes, and left with only two who have name and reputation as princes, both by their prudence and good behaviour and by the courage with which they have recovered from such great persecution and have overcome everything. However as it does not become my feebleness to square the circle of such great matters, I shall wait to hear what happens, and shall keep your Excellency advised of all that occurs.(21)

NOTE

1. *C.S.P.M.*, i, 69.

THREE

Edward of York and
Warwick the Kingmaker

Prospero di Camulio was not alone in his doubts about the new king's future. In May 1461 even Coppini remarked that Edward and Warwick needed advice and comfort 'at this time when their position is not very solid'. By 2 June Camulio was writing home with alarming news of the prospect of a French invasion with a force of 20,000 men but at the same time he stressed the strong leadership of King Edward and the Earl of Warwick.

Having been prorogued in June owing to danger in the north from the Scots, parliament met at last on 4 November. After the speaker, Sir John Strangeways, a connection of the Nevilles, had delivered a fulsome speech praising Edward's personal beauty and his recent 'Redemption and Salvation' of his subjects the king and his advisers issued a viciously worded propaganda pamphlet disguised as an Act of Parliament* declaring his title to the throne. The act did not defend the Yorkist title: it assumed argument on the point to be impossible. Edward had merely claimed his just inheritance, and had decided at last to exercise his family's long-ignored rights. As the Duke of York had asserted 'though right for a time rest and be put to silence, yet it rotteth not nor shall not perish.' In vehement tones the act proclaimed that:

> . . . Henry late Earl of Derby, son of the said John of Gaunt . . . temerously against rightwiseness and justice, by force and arms, against his faith and liegance, reared war at Flint in Wales against the said King

*The act was an almost verbatim reproduction of a speech made at the time of Edward's secular enthronement in March. See C.A.J. Armstrong, 'The Inauguration Ceremonies of the Yorkist Kings and their Title to the Throne', in *T.R Hist. S.*, e Ser., XXX (1948).

Richard, him took and imprisoned in the Tower of London of great violence; and the same King Richard so being in prison and living, usurped and intruded upon the royal power, estate, dignity, pre-eminence, possessions and lordship aforesaid, taking upon him usurpously the crown and name of king and lord of the same realm and lordship; and not therewith satisfied or content, but more grievous thing attempting, wickedly of unnatural, unmanly and cruel tyranny, the same King Richard, king anointed, crowned and consecrate, and his liege and most high lord in the earth, against God's law, man's liegance and oath of fidelity, with uttermost punicion a-tormenting, murdered and destroyed, with most vile, heinous and lamentable death; whereof the heavy exclamation in the doom of every Christian man soundeth into God's hearing in heaven, not forgouen in the earth, specially in this realm of England, which therefore hath suffered the charge of intolerable persecution, punicion and tribulation, whereof the like hath not been seen or heard in any other Christian realm, by any memory or record; then being on live the said Edmund Mortimer Earl of March, son and heir of the said Roger, son and heir of the said Philippa, daughter and heir to the said Lionel, the third son of the said King Edward the third: To the which Edmund, after the decease of the said King Richard, the right and title of the same crown and lordship, then by law, custom and conscience, descended and belonged; and of right belongeth at this time unto our said Liege and Sovereign Lord King Edward the fourth, as cousin and heir to the said King Richard, in manner and form abovesaid. Our said Sovereign and Liege Lord King Edward the fourth, according to his right and title of the said crown and lordship, after the decease of the said right noble and famous Prince Richard Duke of York his father, in the name of Jesu, to his pleasure and loving, the fourth day of the month of March last past, *took upon him to use his right and title** to the said realm of England and lordship, and entered into th'exercise of the royal estate, dignity, pre-eminence and power of the same crown, and to the reign and governance of the said realm of England and lordship; and the same fourth day of March, a-moved Henry, late called King Henry the sixth, son to Henry, son to the said Henry late Earl of Derby; son to the said

*My italics.

John of Gaunt, from the occupation, usurpation, intrusion, reign and governance of the same realm of England and lordship, to the universal comfort and consolation of all his subjects and liegemen, plenteously joyed to be a-moved and departed from the obeisance and governance of the unrightwise usurper, in whose time not plenty, peace, justice, good governance, policy, and virtuous conversation, but unrest, inward war and trouble, unrightwiseness, shedding and effusion of innocent blood, abusion of the laws, partiality, riot, extortion, murder, rape and vicious living, have been the guiders and leaders of the noble realm of England . . .(1)

The victorious Yorkists now passed an Act of Attainder imposing the penalties of treason on one hundred and thirteen of their opponents. Corruption, the curse of political and social relationships everywhere now crept in thus early. Sir John Scudamore, one of Henry VI's former supporters, later claimed that some of the new government's adherents placed their own interests before the king's solemn promise of pardons, implying a greedy desire for grants from forfeited estates. Scudamore himself, according to his own account, was thus victimized by what he called 'sinister labour' and 'marvellous private labour'.

Edward was not left in peace for long. Early in 1462 the Earl of Oxford's conspiracy was discovered. Real though they were, rumours wildly exaggerated its dangers. Francesco della Torre, an envoy whom Edward and Warwick sent to Coppini, wrote the following account from Bruges:

Eleven days before the king's departure they discovered a great conspiracy, at the head of which was the Earl of Oxford, and he, his eldest son and many other knights and esquires lost their heads. Before the king left the treason was discovered in this manner, *quidquid fortassis dicatur*. The said earl, with his accomplices, sent letters to King Henry and the queen in Scotland by a servant of his, who, after having been to York, returned to King Edward and presented the leners, which were read as well as copied and then sealed upn again and sent by this same messenger to King Henry with a promise that he would return with the reply. He did so and it was done very secretly. After the reply had been read the Earl of Worcester, who has been made Constable of England, was sent to take the said earl and others.

Their plan was as follows: to follow the king as his servants towards the north, as his Majesty was not going to take more than a thousand horse and their two thousand or more, and once among the enemy they were to attack the king and murder him and all his followers. In the meantime the Duke of Somerset, who was at Bruges and is still there, was to descend upon England, and King Henry was also to come with the Scots, and the Earl of Pembroke from Brittany. Some priests and others also have been taken, because so they say, they wrote some notices over the doors of the churches in which they stated that the supreme pontiff had revoked all that your lordship had done in this kingdom, that he gave plenary absolution to all those who would be with King Henry and excommunicated those who were with our king. I believe they will be punished as they deserve.*(2)

The Paston circle heard even more alarming stories. Some time in February 1462 Thomas Howes wrote to John Paston:

Item, sir, please your mastership it was letten me weet in right secret wise that a puissance is ready to arrive in three parties of this land, by the mean of King Harry and the queen that was, and by the Duke of Somerset and others, of 120,000 men; and here they, if wind and weather had served them, should a' been here soon upon Candlemass; at Trent to London wards they should a' been by Candlemass or soon after, one party of them, and another party coming from Wales, and the third from Jersey and Guernsey. Wherefore it is well done ye inform mine Lord Warwick, that he may speak to the king that good provision be had for withstanding their malicious purpose and evil will . . .(3)

The conspiracy was suppressed and Oxford executed. Even then Edward's troubles were by no means over. As events have already shown the Wars of the Roses were far from being a purely domestic matter. For the next seventeen years the politics of north-western Europe revolved about the suspicions of the rulers of England, France and Burgundy. Each was prepared to intrigue in the lands of the others whenever it served his purpose to do

*The abbot and monks of Bury St Edmunds were placed under arrest at this time and although they soon received a general pardon the abbot was fined 500 marks.

so. In April 1462 Margaret of Anjou journeyed from Scotland to France and soon, from Boulogne, was trying to suborn the garrison of Calais. Louis XI, for his own purposes, decided to support her cause, but later in the year, owing to changes in the diplomatic situation, lost interest. Nevertheless, he allowed Pierre de Brezé, the Grand Seneschal of Normandy, to lead a small force of men to England – a disappointingly small force after Margaret's earlier hopes. One of the London chronicles describes the expedition:

In this year, the third day of November, Queen Margaret came out of France into Scotland with a strength of people; and so entered into England and made open war. Then the king went northward with a great people; and the 13th day of November the queen, hearing of his coming with his great host, anon brake her field and fled. And in a carvel, wherein was the substance of her goods, she fled; and as she sailed there came upon her such a tempest that she was fain to leave the carvel and take a fisher's boat, and so went a-land to Berwick; and the said carvel and goods were drowned. And the same day four hundred of Frenchmen or there about, being of her host, were driven a-land about Bamborough; where as when they saw they might not have away their ships for the tempest, they set fire in them and brent them, and so went into an island of Northumberland, where they were encountered with one Maners, a squire, and the Bastard of Ogle with two hundred men, which slew and took prisoners the said four hundred Frenchmen. And when the king had knowledge of her departure, he intended to have pursued to have taken her; but then it fortuned him to be visited with the sickness of measles, where through his purpose was letted. And upon the 12th day in Christmas the Scots came to rescue the castle of Alnwick, but it was yolden to the king ere they came. And about the same season the castles of Bamborough and Dunstanborough were yolden to the king also. And the Duke of Somerset and Sir Ralph Percy submitted them to the king's grace, whom the king admitted to his grace. And about Shrovetide the king came southward.(4)

Success in the north proved to be delusive after all. *Gregory's Chronicle* describes the events of the last part of 1463 and the early months of 1464:

And then the foresaid Ralph Percy returned again into Northumberland, and had the keeping of the said two castles according unto the pointment.* And the said Sir Harry Beaufort† abode still with the king, and rode with him to London. And the king made full much of him; in so much that he lodged with the king in his own bed many nights, and some time rode a-huntingi behind the king, the king having about him not passing six horse at the most, and yet three were of the duke's men of Somerset. The king loved him well, but the duke thought treason under fair cheer and words, as it appeared. And for a great love the king made a great jousts at Westminster, that he should see some manner sport of chivalry after his great labour and heaviness. And with great instance the king made him to take harness upon him, and rode in the place, but he would never cope with no man and no man might not cope with him, till the king prayed him to be merry and sent him a token, and then he ran full justly and merrily, and his helm was a sorry hat of straw. And then every man marked him well.

But within short time after the said Sir Ralph Percy by false collusion (colysyon) and treason he let the French men take the castle of Bamborough fro him *nolens volo*. As for the castle of Alnwick all the men of war that were of worship brake out of the castle by force and war and rescued Sir Perys de Brasylle‡ on twelve day by the morn, and they that were within the castle gave it up by appointment, etc. And then King Edward made Sir John Astley, the knight that fought so manly in Smithfield with an alien that challenged, he was made captain of the castle, and Sir Ralph Grey Constable of the said castle of Alnwick. And within three or four months after that false knight and traitor, Sir Ralph Grey, by false treason took the said Sir John Astley prisoner, and delivered him to Queen Margaret, and then delivered the castle to the Lord Hungerford and unto the French men accompanied with him; and by this mean he put the king our sovereign lord out of

*Under the terms of surrender in December 1462 Percy had been given the command of Bamborough and Dunstanborough.
†i.e. the Duke of Somerset. He had been taken prisoner at the surrender of the northern castles in December 1462.
‡i.e. Pierre de Brezé.

possession. And then after that come King Harry that was, and the queen to the King of Scots, Sir Perys de Brasylle, with four score thousand Scots, and laid a siege unto the castle of Norham, and lay there eighteen days. And then my Lord of Warwick and his brother the Lord Montagu put them in devoir to rescue the said castle of Norham, and so they did, and put both King Harry and the King of Scots to flight. And Queen Margaret with all her counsel, and Sir Perys de Brasylle with the French men, fled away by water with four balingers; and they landed at the Scluse in Flanders, and left King Harry that was behind them, and all their horse and their harness, they were so hasted by my Lord of Warwick, and his brother the Lord Montagu, and by their fellowship with them accompanied. And at the departing of Sir Perys de Brasylle and his fellowship was one manly man that purposed to meet with my Lord of Warwick, that was a taboret, for he stood upon an hill with his tabor and his pipe, taboring and piping as merrily as any man might, standing by himself, till my lord come unto him he would not lesse his ground; and there he become my lord's man; and yet he is with him full good and to his lord.

Then the King Edward the IV purposed to make an army into Scotland by land and by water, that the great rebellious Harry and the Queen Margaret should not pass a way by water. And the king made the Earl of Worcester captain by water. And then there was ordained a great navy and a great army both by water and by land. And all was lost and in vain, and came to no purpose, neither by water ne by land.

Also the king soon after disposed him, and was purposed to ride into Yorkshire and to the country about, to see and understand the disposition of the people of the north. And took with him the Duke of Somerset, and two hundred of his men well horsed and well i-harnessed. And the said duke, Harry of Somerset, and his men were made the king's guard, for the king had that duke in much favour and trusted him well. But the guard of him was as men should put a lamb among wolves of malicious beasts; but Almighty God was the shepherd. and when the king departed from London he took his way to Northampton, and thither the king come a Saint James day the Apostle, and that false duke with him. And the commons of the town of Northampton and of the shire about saw that the false duke and traitor was so nigh the king's presence and was made his guard. The commons arose upon that false traitor the Duke of Somerset, and would have slain him within the king's palace. And then the king with fair speech and great difficulty saved his life for that time, and that was pity, for the saving of his life at that time caused many man's deaths soon after, as ye shall hear. And then the king sent that false Duke of Somerset into a castle of his own full secretly, for safeguard of his the duke's life, and the duke's men unto Newcastle, to keep the town, and gave them good wages full truly paid. And the king full lovingly gave the commons of Northampton a tun of wine that they should drink and make merry. And the wine was drunken merrily in the market place, for they had many fair pieces of silver. I dare say there is no tavern that hath not so much of stuff as they occupied in hys [sic] their taverns. For some fette wine in basins, and some in cauldrons, and some in bowls (bollys), and some in pans and some in dishes. Lor, the great treasure that they schenyd* that time ...

And this same year about Christmas that false Duke of Somerset, without any leave of the king, stale out of Wales with a privy meinie toward the Newcastle, and he and his men were confedered for to have betrayed the said Newcastle. And in the way thitherward he was aspied, and like to have been taken beside Durham in his bed. Notwithstanding he escaped away in his shirt and barefoot, and two of his men were take. And they took with them that false duke's casket and his harness. And when that his men knew that he was escaped, and his false treason aspied, his men stale from the Newcastle as very false traitors, and some of them were take and lost their heads for their labour, etc.

And then the king, our sovereign lord Edward the IV, had knowledge of his false disposition of this false Duke Harry of Somerset. The king sent a great fellowship of his household men to keep the town of Newcastle, and made the Lord Scrope of Bolton captain of the town; and so they kept it surely all that winter. And about Easter next after the Scots sued unto our sovereign lord the king for peace. And the king ordained commissioners to meet with the Scots . . .† The

---

*i.e. obtained.
†I have omitted the names of the commissioners.

pointment was that they Scots and they should meet at York. And then was my Lord of Montagu assigned to fetch in the Scots peaceably, for he was Warden of the Marches. And then my Lord of Montagu took his journey towards Newcastle. And by the way was full falsely i-purveyed* that false Duke Harry of Somerset and Percy, with their fellowship associate unto them, that there was laid by the way, a little from the Newcastle, in a wood, that false traitor Sir Humphrey Neville,‡ with four score spears, and the bows thereto. And they should have fall on the Lord Montagu suddenly, and slain him suddenly, but, God be thanked, their false treason was aspied and known. And then the Lord Montagu took another way, and made to be gathered a great fellowship, and went to the Newcastle, and so took his journey unto Norham ward. And in the way thitherward there met with him that false Duke of Somerset, Sir Ralph Percy, the Lord Hungerford, and the Lord Roos, with all their company, to the number of 5,000§ men of arms. And this meeting was upon St Mark's day; and that same day was Sir Ralph Percy slain. And when that he was dead all the party was [dis]-comforted and put to rebuke. And every man avoided and took his way with full sorry hearts. And then my lord of Montagu took his horse and rode to Norham, and fetched in the Scots, and brought them unto the Lords Commissioners. And there was concluded a peace for fifteen year with the Scots. And the Scots been true it must needs continue so long, but it is hard for to trust unto them, for they been ever found full of guile and deceit.

And the 14th day of May next after, my Lord of Montagu took his journey toward Hexham from Newcastle. And there he took that false Duke Harry Beaufort of Somerset, the Lord Roos, the Lord Hungerford, Sir Philip Wentworth, Sir Thomas Findern, with many other; lo, so manly a man is this good Earl Montagu, for he spared not their malice, nor their falseness, nor guile, nor treason, and took many of men and slew many one in that journey . . .

*i e. purveyed, provided.
‡Sir Humphrey Neville of Brancepeth, who had been attainted in 1461. He escaped from imprisonment in the Tower of London, was later pardoned, but in spite of this fled to join Henry VI during the winter of 1463–4.
§Probably a gross exaggeration.

And beside Newcastle, the same month, there was i-take Tailbois* in a coal pit, and he had much money with him, both gold and silver, that should have gone unto King Harry: and if [it] had come to Harry, late King of England, it would have caused much sorry sorrow, for he had ordained harness and ordnance i-nowe, but the men would not go one foot with him till they had money. And they waited daily and hourly for money that this Tailbois should have sent unto them or brought it; the sum was 3,000 mark. And the lord's meinie of Montagu were sore hurt and sick, and many of him men were slain before (by for) in the great journeys, but this money was departed among them, and was a very wholesome salve for them. And in the day following Tailbois lost his head at Newcastle.(5)

On his way to the north, Edward secretly married Elizabeth Wydeville, the widow of a Lancastrian, Sir John Grey of Groby and daughter of Sir Richard Wydeville, Lord Ryvers, and Jacquetta of Luxembourg, Dowager Duchess of Bedford. Fabyan, the London draper, many years later set down the story:

In such pass time, in most secret manner, upon the first day of May, King Edward spoused Elizabeth, late the wife of Sir John Grey, knight, which before time was slain at Towton or York field, which spousals were solemnised early in the morning at a town named Grafton, near Stony Stratford; at which marriage was no persons present but the spouse, the spousess, the Duchess of Bedford her mother, the priest, two gentlewomen, and a young man to help the priest sing. After which spousals ended, he went to bed, and so tarried there upon three or four hours, and after departed and rode again to Stony Stratford, and came in manner as though he had been on hunting, and there went to bed again.†(6)

The marriage was revealed in a Great Council at Reading in September. Warwick, who had been carrying on negotiations for a French marriage for

*Sir William Tailboys of Kyme.
†It was said then, and later, that Elizabeth, thinking herself too base to be the king's wife but too good to be his harlot, was one of the few women who ever denied Edward Plantagenet her bed.

Edward, was outraged at his loss of face abroad. The rise of the new queen's family, natural enough but too rapid for discretion, alienated him still more – though the rise and its political consequences were by no means as great as some historians have claimed, and Warwick, for a long time, dissembled his anger. These events are described, very much from the point of view of one of Warwick's partisans, in a meagre anonymous chronicle formerly attributed to William Worcester:

> . . . And on Michelmas Day at Reading the said Lady Elizabeth was there admitted into the abbey chapel, led by the Duke of Clarence and the Earl of Warwick, and honoured as queen by the lords and all the people. . . . The same month[†] a marriage was arranged at Reading between Lord Maltravers, the son and heir of the Earl of Arundel, and Margaret, sister of Queen Elizabeth.
>
> . . . In the month of January,[‡] Catherine, Duchess of Norfolk, a slip of a girl of about eighty years old,[§] was married to John Wydeville, the queen's brother, aged twenty years; a diabolical marriage . . .
>
> . . . The king caused Henry, Duke of Buckingham, to marry a sister of Queen Elizabeth to the secret displeasure of the Earl of Warwick. And the son and heir of the Earl of Essex married — (blank in MS) another sister of the queen. And Grey Ruthyn, son and heir of the Earl of Kent, married another sister of the queen.
>
> In the month of March[*] the lord king in his secret council at Westminster relieved Walter Blount, Lord Mountjoy, of the office of Treasurer of England, and caused Richard, Lord Ryvers, to be put in his place, to the secret displeasure of the Earl of Warwick and the magnates of England.
>
> The king kept Whitsun[†] at Windsor, where he created Lord Ryvers Earl Ryvers, to the honour of the queen and the displeasure of the whole kingdom (*communis regni*).
>
> In September[‡] a marriage was made at Windsor between the son and heir of Lord Herbert and Mary, sister of Queen Elizabeth, and

†October 1464.
‡January 1465.
§She could not in fact have been more than sixty-seven.
*1466.

between the young Lord Lisle and the daughter of this Lord Herbert. And the lord king knighted Herbert's heir and created him Lord Dunster, to the secret displeasure of the Earl of Warwick and the magnates of the land.

. . . In the month of October at Greenwich the king arranged a wedding between Thomas Grey, knight, the queen's son, and Lady Anne, heiress of the Duke of Exeter, the king's niece, to the great and secret displeasure of the Earl of Warwick, for a marriage was previously bespoken between the said Lady Anne and the son of the Earl of Northumberland, the Earl of Warwick's brother, and the queen paid the said duchess 4,000 marks for the aforesaid: marriage . . .*(7)

After her defeat in the north in 1463** Margaret of Anjou heard to her: dismay of a diplomatic conference between England, France and Burgundy to be held at St Omer. In the hope of frustrating any agreement between them she set out for the Burgundian court. Georges Chastellain, the Duke of Burgundy's official historiographer, described her arrival:

. . . recalling how she was daughter of a King of Sicily, niece of a King of France and her husband [his] nephew, there where blood and natural love could not fail her, to the point of giving up her life for him†† resolved to cross the sea. And certainly knowing her husband King Henry to be in a safe enough place for some time, took her son Edward, named Prince of Wales; and embarking on the sea for the first and most accessible port and haven with the advice and consent of the valiant knight, Sir Pierre de Brezé, upholder of her quarrel, took him with her, not only with the principal intention of coming to sojourn in France with her relations and friends, as of set purpose to come and sojourn in the lands and territories of the Duke of Burgundy. So a tranquil breeze brought her to Sluys with all the number of her people that she had with her, which was not great, towards the end of July,

---

*See my article 'Marriage and Politics in the Fifteenth Century' in *B.I.H.R.*, xxxvi (1963), 129–45, reprinted J.R. Lander, *Crown and Nobility*, 1450–1509 (London, 1976), 94–126.

**See above p. 108.

††i.e. Henry VI.

there coming to port, [she] gave all hearts cause for wonder, for to everyone it was known and recognised that she had been the duke's mortal enemy in the days of her prosperity, and she above all in England the most hostile in action and in spirit. Wherefore were heard divers murmurs against her in many mouths, and many savage comments on the nature of her misfortune. For [she] arrived there poor and alone, destitute of goods and all desolate; [she] had neither credence, nor money, nor goods, nor jewels to pledge. [She] had her son, no royal robes, nor estate;* and her person without adornment befitting a queen. Her body was clad in one single robe, with no change of clothing. [She] had no more than seven women for her retinue, and whose apparel was like that of their mistress, formerly one of the most splendid women of the world and now the poorest; and finally she had no other provision not even bread to eat, except from the purse of her knight, Sir Pierre de Brezé, of his good-will, who himself was in extreme poverty; for he had disbursed and spent everything in serving her and in carrying on the war against her enemies, to the point of having nothing left himself, nor anything to help [with], notwithstanding, as he told me, he had spent up to 50,000 crowns of his own.

It was a thing piteous to see, truly, this high princess so cast down and laid low in such great danger, dying of hunger and hardship, become forced to throw herself on the mercy of the one in all the world whose fame ran, as is known, as being most set against her and hard towards her. All ways, hoping to obtain grace for herself by excuses, and that her noble and high courage by nature of her estate would engender pity for her in her ill fortune, [she] neither delayed nor feared to put herself in his hands . . .

. . . Which, when the duke knew her will and that he could in no way turn her from it therefore agreed and said: that since it must be, he would see and receive her kindly, as circumstances prescribed, and turn it to account. But because the countryside through which she came was full of danger for her, and that he had already heard that the English in Calais were looking out for her and would try to capture her

*i.e. surroundings or possessions befitting her rank.

and throw her down as she came towards him he sent to her at once to inform her that she should remain in the first good town in which she found herself after these tidings were received, as he, as soon as he could, in all haste would come to her, without more ado. So did the English queen and by the duke's advice stayed at St Pol until his coming, which was on the last Tuesday in August. And this noble princess had come there from Bruges in a country cart covered over with canvas and harnessed with four mares like a poor woman going unknown. She had no more than three women with her, Sir Pierre de Brezé and a few others small in number, to say no more. [She] had spoken with the Count of Charolois in Bruges who had lent her five hundred crowns, with which she had come there. It was a thing most piteous and distressing to see her high royal magnificence of former days come to such lowliness and abasement. [She] had left her son the Prince of Wales in Bruges, partly from necessity and lack of means to provide for him, partly not wishing to put his person in any danger. And not knowing what to do, nor what to say until she had spoken to the duke (so unworthy she called herself), left all her poor retinue at Bruges, dressed herself like a village woman in the garb of a chambermaid to come and seek him out. And so it was that she came to Béthune, and there as she lay the English came out upon her with about two hundred horse, thinking to capture her as she came to Boulogne; but she came safe and sound to St Pol, there where the duke came towards her, and ordered her not to move, as indeed she did; for he himself disregarded [the danger] and came to see her in magnificent and seemly manner . . .(8)

The Duke of Burgundy, though polite and sympathetic enough towards a distressed princess, refused to change his policy. After this rebuff Margaret moved on to her father's lands and for the next few years lived with her poverty-stricken little court at St Michel-sur-Bar.

Early in 1465 she once again tried to obtain help from Louis XI of France. Albrico Malleta, the Milanese ambassador in France, wrote home:

The queen, wife of King Henry, has written to the king here that she is advised that King Edward and the Earl of Warwick have come to very great division and war together. She begs the king here to be pleased to give her help so that she may be able to recover her kingdom or at least allow her to receive assistance from the lords of this kingdom who are willing to afford this, and if he will not take any one of these courses, she writes that she will take the best course that she can. The king remarked, 'Look how proudly she writes . . .'(9)

John Warkworth, Master of Peterhouse, Cambridge (1473–1500), some time between 1474 and his death wrote or commissioned a chronicle dealing with the events of the first thirteen years of Edward IV's reign. He tells of the next disastrous blow to the Lancastrian cause:

Also the same year, King Harry was taken beside a house of religion in Lancashire, by the mean of a black monk of Abingdon, in a wood called Cletherwood, beside Bungerly Hippingstones, by Thomas Talbot, son and heir to Sir Edmund Talbot of Basshalle, and John Talbot his cousin of Colebry, with other moo; which deceived, being at his dinner at Waddington Hall, and carried to London on horseback, and his leg bound to the stirrup, and so brought through London to the Tower, where he was kept long time by two squires and two yeomen of the crown, and their men; and every man suffered to come and speak with him, by licence of the keepers.(10)

By the early part of 1467 both Burgundy and France were eager for an English marriage alliance. King Edward favoured Burgundy: Warwick was determined on an agreement with France. Louis XI, was as usual, in case of failure, prepared to consider even the most apparently fantastic ideas. In February Giovanni Pietro Panicharola sent to the Duke and Duchess of Milan the details of an acrimonious dinner party between Louis and Margaret of Anjou's brother, John of Calabria:

The king has recently been on a pilgrimage to our Lady of Bourges. There he happened to be at table with Duke John, who accompanied him on the journey. After discussing falcons and hunting they spoke to the Marshal of Burgundy, ambassador of M. de Charolais* to his

*The son of Duke Philip the Good of Burgundy, from 1467 Charles the Bold.

Majesty, who said the duke had caused him to lose that friendship. The duke said he was very glad if that was the case. When his Majesty spoke highly of the marshal, the duke vilified him to the extent of his powers.

When they went on to speak of the Earl of Warwick, the first noble of England, the duke angrily rejoined that he was a traitor; he would not say or suffer any good to be said of him; he only studied to deceive, he was the enemy and the cause of the fall of King Henry and his sister the Queen of England. His Majesty would do better to help his sister to recover her kingdom than to favour the Earl of Warwick, and many other exaggerated and opprobrious words.

His Majesty replied that he had more reason to speak well of the Earl of Warwick than of many others, not excepting his own relations, as the earl had always been a friend to his crown and had advised against making war on this realm. King Henry, on the other hand, had been a mortal enemy and had waged many wars against him, and therefore this friendship is worth preserving.

As the king persisted in his praise of the Earl of Warwick, the duke said that as he was so fond of him he ought to try and restore his sister in that kingdom, when he would make sure of it as much as he was sure at present and even more so.

The king asked what security they would give or if they would offer the queen's son as a hostage. This boy, though only thirteen years of age, already talks of nothing but of cutting off heads or making war, as if he had everything in his hands or was the god of battle or the peaceful occupant of that throne. The king also asked, supposing they promised, if the security would be observed. At this the duke in a fume said that if his nephew promised at his instance and did not keep his word, he would have to reckon with him and with others, and they would fly at him and tear out his eyes.

After some further discussion the duke began to complain about his Majesty without any respect, saying he had never loved their house; to which the king retorted that the House of Anjou had given him reason for this. Thus, half joking they said very sharp things to each other during the dinner.(11)

By May the Milanese ambassadors were reporting:

It is asserted that the Earl of Warwick will come here and soon. His Majesty will go to Rouen to meet him. There is a fresh report that M. Charolais has again opened secret negotiations to take King Edward's sister to wife, confirming once more the old league with the English. If this takes place, they have talked of treating with the Earl of Warwick to restore King Henry in England, and the ambassador of the old Queen of England is already here.(12)

By the beginning of 1468 diplomatic affairs between Burgundy, England and France were thick with suspicion. In England, Warwick, seeing Edward more and more determined on the Burgundian marriage alliance, may already have been disgruntled enough to plan treason. On 16 January, Sir William Monypenny, one of the French ambassadors in England, wrote this letter to Louis XI:

Sire, Master Robert Neville* and I landed at Sandwich in England the Thursday before Christmas, for the wind was so strongly contrary to us that we could not go by sea to the place where my Lord of Warwick was; and from there we took our way to London, where we found the council of my said Lord of Warwick. . . . They asked me if it was true that an embassy from Burgundy had gone to you and your brother. I said yes, that I had seen at Honfleur Monsieur Olivier de la Marche and others of the council of the said Duke of Burgundy. They replied that it was the best news they could have for the good of my said Lord of Warwick. . . . Also they said they had heard that there was much talk of a marriage between one of my ladies your daughters and the Prince of Wales:† about which everybody here was alarmed as people could be; saying in all the London taverns and throughout the country that those traitors ought to be beheaded who had advised their king to neglect to make any arrangement with you and to ally with the Duke of Burgundy.

Also, Sire, by their advice, I went to the place where the king was: who, immediately I arrived, sent to ask me to speak with him, and

*A cousin of Warwick's who had carried letters to the King of France.
†Edward, the son of Henry VI and Margaret of Anjou.

asked me for news of you, enquiring if I had any letters addressed to him.

With regard to news, I answered that, thanks be to God, the king was in great prosperity . . . and that I had left you as well accompanied with lords and men-at-arms as ever a king of France was.

As regards letters, I answered that none had been sent addressed to him . . . He enquired if any had been sent addressed to my Lord of Warwick: I said yes. He asked me if anything was known of their contents: I said that I thought nothing, except that you were greatly surprised that he had not sent to you concerning the answer that he ought to give upon the proposal of your last embassy, seeing that he had sent you word by your ambassadors and also by letters that he would speedily send an embassy to you to answer you upon that proposal. He answered that it was his intention to send someone to you soon, with the advice of his council and of my said Lord of Warwick, to treat with you . . . he told me . . . in the presence of his chamberlain and Lord Scales* and five or six others, that he would aid you against your brother . . . As far as I can hear, it seems to me that he is not very sure of any of the promises made to him by lords of your kingdom, the more so since my said Lord of Burgundy has informed him by a secretary of his who came after I arrived that, concerning the conclusion of the marriage of the said Duke of Burgundy and the sister of the said king, he would give him a full answer at the end of the present month, when his embassy to the Pope should have returned, saying that he was greatly harmed touching the dispensation at the court of Rome.

Sire, if any way can be found with the Pope to defer the said dispensation for the said marriage, I have no doubt at all that, with God's will, you will set the whole of this Kingdom of England against the said Duke of Burgundy; for they will think that all that he does is only dissimulation, and in this way you will destroy all those here who have held to his party. Sire, it seems to me, under correction, that you should, by such means as seem good to you, carry on negotiations with my said Lord of Burgundy, without concluding anything . . .

*Anthony Wydeville, the eldest son of Earl Ryvers and brother of the queen.

Also, Sire, on the morrow of the Three Kings,* the King of England sent a messenger to my said Lord of Warwick and commanded him to come to him, to which, after long deliberation of his council, he replied shortly that he would not go . . .

Also, Sire, on New Year's Day, a party of the commons of Kent rose and went to a place which the treasurer, father of the queen, holds in the said county of Kent, and threw down his parks and killed the deer that he had there . . . Also, in another county, named 'Surforchier',** there have risen full three hundred archers and have made a captain like Robin† and have sent to my Lord of Warwick to know if it is time to act and that all their neighbours were ready. He has commanded them to return home and that is not yet time to act but that he will let them know when there is need of it.

Also, Sire, my Lord of Warwick keeps Master Robert Neville with him until he has spoken and arranged with his brother the Earl of Northumberland . . . and afterwards he will send him to you in all haste . . . but do not cease to negotiate with my Lord of Burgundy and to hinder the marriage as far as you can. And when that is broken off, there will not be a woman or child in England who will not attack him . . .

Also, Sire, the Duke of Brittany has lately sent here to the King of England, offering him fourteen or fifteen places which he said he had taken from you in the Duchy of Normandy, on condition, however, that three thousand archers should be sent to him to aid him and defend the said places and his country.

Also, Sire, my Lord of Warwick leaves tomorrow . . . for the Scottish frontier, where his brother the Earl of Northumberland and all the men of the frontier will come to him and he intends, if the king comes northward, to defend himself against him. It is a question of who is to be master and who servant . . . and upon my soul I think there is no man in this world more loyal to you than he has been.(13)

---

*i.e. 7 January.

**i.e. South Yorkshire?

†The meaning is obscure. It is too early to be a reference to Robin of Redesdale's rising.

Despite Warwick's vehement opposition, Edward went on with his plans for the Burgundian alliance. In July the Duke of Burgundy and Margaret of York were married with ceremonies of the greatest splendour, but according to Panicharolo the occasion was marred by malicious gossip. He wrote that because the duke was:

> . . . informed of what more and more people know, to wit that his future consort in the past has been somewhat devoted to love affairs, indeed in the opinion of many she even has a son, he has issued a public edict and ordinance, that no one in his country, in the presence of his lordship or elsewhere in private or public shall be so bold as to make mention or speak of such a thing, under pain of being thrown into the river forthwith, when he is found in such error . . .(14)

At home, the pseudo-William Worcester described the rumours, suspicions and plots that created an atmosphere of panic-stricken terror during the years 1467–8, before and after the Burgundian marriage:

> Secret displeasure continued between the lord king and the lord Earl of Warwick about the marriage between the Duke of Clarence and the said earl's daughter which marriage the king ever suspected them of making.*
>
> Master [William] Lacy was sent to the court of Rome for a licence, on account of consanguinity, to allow the said marriage, but he could not be heard by the Pope. A certain person was captured in Wales bearing letters from Queen Margaret to Harlech Castle, and, sent to London to the king by Lord Herbert. He accused many men of treason against the king and amongst others accused the Earl of Warwick for he [had] heard suspicious words overseas that the earl favoured Queen Margaret's party. So the king because the earl would not come sent the said (—)† under guard to the lord earl at Middleham, so that he might be examined there. In the end the matter was pronounced paltry. The lord king appointed two hundred valets, trusty and stout English

*From early in 1467 Warwick was conspiring to marry Clarence to his eldest daughter, Isabel. They were married at Calais on 11 July 1469.
†Blank in MS.

archers, ordering that each of them should have eightpence a day for riding and attending upon his own proper person, and so he rode to Coventry ...

... The king with the queen and many other lords, held the feast of our Lord's Nativity at Coventry in the abbey there, where for six days the Duke of Clarence behaved in a friendly way. And soon after Epiphany, by means of secret friends, the Archbishop of York and Lord Ryvers were brought together at Nottingham, and they were so agreed that the archbishop brought the Earl of Warwick to the king at Coventry to a council in the month of January, where the Earl of Warwick, Lords Herbert, Stafford and Audley were reconciled (*concordati sunt*). And there the king restored to the archbishop the lands of Penely and Widestone before taken from him by resumption.

... on (—)* October certain letters from the Pope dated (—)* September ... were delivered to the king at Brainford in which the lord Pope created the lord Thomas Bourchier, Archbishop of Canterbury, cardinal presbyter in the title of Saint Ciriacus and the lord king jestingly handed over the said letters to the Lord George, Archbishop of York, to show what was written in them ...

... Parliament was dissolved the third day after the feast of Whitsun. And in the said week, a certain Cornelius, a shoemaker serving Robert Whittingham who was with Queen Margaret, was captured, secretly bringing divers letters into England from Queen Margaret's party, upon which one was discovered from the said Robert Whittingham to Thomas Danvers, on account of which the said Thomas Danvers about midnight on the eve of Holy Trinity, drawn by guile out of the hospice of the Temple in London, was arrested and brought to the king at Stratford Langthorn, was three days later committed to the Tower of London, to his great fear and sorrow. And in like manner Hugh Mille was dragged from the Fleet to the Tower of London on suspicion of treason. There the said Cornelius was tortured by burning in the feet until he confessed many things. He then accused Peter Alfrey, draper of London, John Plummer, Genase Clifton, knight, Hugh Pakenham, Nicholas Huse, Thomas Portaleyn, William Belknap, Robert Knollys,

*Blank in MS.

squires, John Fisher of the Temple, John Hawkins, a servant of Lord Wenlock's and many others of the receipt of letters from the said Queen Margaret. And the said Hawkins when arrested accused Thomas Cook, knight, of misprision of treason with Hugh Mille, and he said a good deal against his own lord, Wenlock. (15)

The *Great Chronicle of London* relates that Hawkins was also tortured and under torture accused Sir Thomas Cook who was brought to trial on a charge of treason but a jury found him guilty only of misprision. He was heavily fined. The chronicle alleged that the accusation against him was due to the malice of Sir John Fogge and the Wydevilles, especially the queen's mother, the Duchess of Bedford, to whom Cook had refused to sell an especially splendid tapestry at a low price. The hostility between the factions ran higher and higher:

. . . And in this mayor's time many murmurous tales ran in the city atween th'Earl of Warwick and the queen's blood, the which earl was ever had in great favour of the commons of this land, by reason of the exceeding household which he daily kept in all countries wherever he sojourned or lay, and when he came to London he held such an house that six oxen were eaten at a breakfast, and every tavern was full of his meat, for who that had any acquaintance in that house, he should have had as much sodden and roast as he might carry upon a long dagger which those days were much used as now they use murderers . . .*

. . . Then the spark of envy before spoken of in the time of the mayoralty of Matthew Philip began to kindle among the lords that parties were made, and the commons in the north began to stir. About this time one Woodhouse a sage dyzour being in good favour of the King's Grace for his mannerly railing and honest disports which he often exercised in the court, came upon a day of the hot and dry summer into the king's chamber clad in a short coat cut by the points and a pair of boots upon his legs as long as they might be tied to his points of his hoses, and in his hand a long marys† pyke. When the king

*i.e. another type of dagger.
†i.e. marsh.

had beholden his apparel, he frayned of him what was the cause of his long boots and of his long staff. Upon my faith, Sir, said he, I have passed through many countries* of your realm, and in places that I have passed the 'Ryvers' have been so high that I could hardly scrape through them, but as I was fain to search the depth with this long staff. The king knew that he meant it by the great rule which the Lord Ryvers and his blood bare that time within his realm, and made thereof a disport. But this was an ill prenostication as ye shall shortly hear after.(16)

On 11 July Clarence married Warwick's daughter Isabel Neville at Calais. From Calais, the duke and earl denounced the king's advisers and crossed to Kent to raise rebellion. At the same time the mysterious north-country rebel, Robin of Redesdale, was marching south. He encountered and defeated the royal forces under the Earl of Devonshire and Sir William Herbert at Edgecott, six miles north-east of Banbury. Writing in 1486, the Second Anonymous Croyland Continuator, generally thought to have been one of Edward's councillors, or closely connected with one of them, gave his interpretation of the events of these years – and also described the Earl of Warwick's first, and premature successes against Edward. He wrote:

At this marriage,§ Richard Neville, Earl of Warwick, who had for some years appeared to favour the party of the French against the Burgundians, conceived great indignation. For he would greatly have preferred to have sought an alliance for the said Lady Margaret in the Kingdom of France, by means of which a favourable understanding might have arisen between the monarchs of those two kingdoms; it being much against his wish, that the views of Charles, now Duke of Burgundy, should be in anyway promoted by means of an alliance with England. The fact is, that he pursued that man with a most deadly hatred.

This, in my opinion, was really the cause of the dissensions between the king and the earl, and not the one which has been previously mentioned† – the marriage of the king with Queen Elizabeth.

*i.e. counties.
§i.e. the marriage of Margaret of York and the Duke of Burgundy.
†By an earlier continuator of *The Croyland Chronicle* whom this writer regarded as prejudiced and ill-informed.

. . . In the meantime, King Edward was taken prisoner at a certain village near Coventry, and, all his attendants being dismissed, was led thence to Warwick Castle, where he was detained in captivity. This calamity was caused by his own brother, George, Duke of Clarence, Richard, Earl of Warwick, and his brother George, Archbishop of York: and befell him in the summer of the ninth year of his reign, being the year of our Lord, 1469.

Lest it should come to pass that the faithful subjects of the said king, in the southern parts of the kingdom, should attempt to avenge the commission of so great an injury, and liberate him from his captivity in the said castle, they now transferred him to Middleham Castle, in the north; from which place, however, in a manner almost miraculous, and beyond all expectation, he did not so much make his escape, as find himself released by the express consent of the Earl of Warwick himself. For there was now a rising in England, in the vicinity of the Scottish border, of many persons who formed the remains of Henry's party, and who had chosen for their captain one Sir Humphrey Neville. The Earl of Warwick found himself unable to offer an effectual resistance to these, without first making public proclamation in the king's name that all the king's liege subjects must rise to defend him against the rebels. For the people, seeing their king detained as a prisoner, refused to take any notice of proclamations to this effect, until, having been entirely set at liberty, he had made his appearance in the city of York; after which, the enemy were most valiantly routed by the said earl, and the king, seizing the opportunity, in the full enjoyment of his liberty came to London.

From this day, as already stated, there were repeated messages and embassies passing to and fro between the king and the dissatisfied nobles. In the end, a great council of all the peers of the kingdom was summoned, and on a certain day, which had been previously named there appeared in the great chamber of parliament, the Duke of Clarence, the Earl of Warwick, and the rest of their confederates; upon which, peace and entire oblivion of all grievances upon both sides was agreed to. Still, however, there probably remained, on the one side, deeply seated in his mind, the injuries he had received and the contempt which had been shown to majesty, and on the other: 'A mind too conscious of a daring deed.'(17)

Warwick's first *coup d'état* thus collapsed before the country's passive resistance. His deep personal rancour, bred on excessive greed and lust for power, proved too narrow an emotion to unite even his own family circle behind him in a career of active treason, still less the mass of the nobility. Force of circumstances had led the nobility to acquiesce in Henry VI's deposition in 1461. Now, they were too wary to follow Warwick again. So far only two peers, his brothers-in-law, the Earl of Oxford and Lord Fitzhugh, had given him active support. Nevertheless, he soon made another attempt, equally ill-supported.* An anonymous chronicle, inspired by the Yorkist court, describes the 1470 rebellion in Lincolnshire:

. . . when he (the king) was commen unto Waltham the 6th day of March, on the morrow after, the 7th day of March, there was brought unto him word that Robert Welles, calling himself great captain of the Commons of Lincolnshire, had do made proclamations in all the churches of that shire the Sunday the 4th day of March in the king's name, the duke, earl† and his own name, every man to come to come to Ranby Hawe upon the Tuesday the 6th day of March, upon pain of death, to resist the king in coming down into the said shire, saying that his coming thither was to destroy the commons of the same shire, as appeareth by the copy of the same. And thereupon, the 7th day of March, the king sent to London for the late Lord Welles, Sir Thomas Dymmoke, and other, which were come thither by the king's privy seals.**

Upon the Thursday the 8th day of March, the king, riding betwixt Buntingford and Royston, took in the way a child which was sent from John Morling, steward to the Lord Cromwell. Whereby appeared clearly the gathering of the said commons, and part of their intents, which letters purporteth that by the time they came to Stamford there

---

*Only two peers now supported him: Lord Willoughby and Welles and Lord Scrope of Bolton.

†i.e. Clarence and Warwick.

**The rebellion began in a quarrel between Lord Willoughby and Welles and Sir Thomas Burgh, a member of the royal household. Edward had summoned Lord Willoughby and Welles to court to deal with the matter. Robert Welles was Lord Willoughby and Welles' son.

should be of them and of Yorkshire and other countries that would fall to them 100,000 men. And the same letter was written at Tatteshall, the 6th day of March, and is ready to be shewed.

The same Thursday the king come to Royston, whither come to him a servant of the Duke of Clarence with a letter letting his highness weet that, notwithstanding that he had taken his leave of him at London, to have gone westward, yet, for to do him service in this his journey, he would a-ready himself to come towards his highness at such time and place appointed as th'Earl of Warwick should also come, as he had promised the king at London. Whereunto the king then answered, that he was glad, and wrote him a letter of thank of his own hand; which message so sent by the duke was false dissimulation, as by the works after it appeared. Nevertheless the king, not understanding no such doubleness, but trusting that they meant truly as they shewed, sent unto the said duke and earl incontinent his several commissions for to arraise the people in divers shires, and to bring them unto the king to do him service against his rebels. And so on the Friday the 9th day of March the king come to Huntingdon.

The king being at Huntingdon did the said Lord Welles to be examined, and Sir Thomas Dymmoke and other severally, in which examination it was knowledged that in the Lord Welles all such counsels and conspirations were taken and made betwixt his son, the said Sir Thomas Dymmoke, the commons, and other; and that he and the said Sir Thomas Dymmoke were privy and knowing of their communications, and they might have let it and did not, but very provokers and causers of the same, with other circumstances touching it. Whereupon the king gave him an injunction that he should send to his son, commanding him to leave his fellowship, and humbly submit him, or else they for their said treasons should have death, as they had deserved. The king there being, come eftsoons tidings that the said Robert Welles and commons were in great number, and passed Lincoln towards Grantham.

Upon the Sunday the 6th day of March,* the king come to Fotheringay, where he had new knowledge that his rebels were passed Grantham towards him, but somewhat they began to change their way

*This should obviously be '11th'.

towards Leicester; which, as it was after clearly confessed, was done by the stirring and message sent from the Duke of Clarence and Earl of Warwick unto the said late Sir Robert Welles and other petty captains, desiring them to have [been] by the Monday at Leicester, where they promised to have joined with them with 20,000 men, as it appeared after in effect and by several confessions of the said captains . . .*

. . . on the morrow after the king departed out of London the said duke [Clarence], the Lord Welles, the Prior of St John's and other divers persons, kept their counsel secretly at St John's, and forthwith he departed towards Warwick, contrary to his saying afore to the king; and upon the way sent the king a pleasant letter as above, which letter his highness received at Royston, where he wrote again, thanking and trusting verily he would so have done; and so divers other times they both sent to the king such pleasant messages, ever weening the king their writing and messages had been faithful and true, to the 14th day of March, which day the king came to Grantham; which all notwithstanding, falsely and subtly dissimiled with his highness; for under this they sent their messages daily to the king's rebels, bidding them to be of good cheer and comfort, and hold forth their way towards Leicester, where they promised to have joined with them and utterly to have taken their part, whereby their unnatural and false double treason appeareth.

And if God ne had put in the king's mind at Huntingdon to put the Lord Welles in certainty of his death for his false conspirations and concealments as is afore shewed, unless then his son would have left his fellowship, and submitted as above, and thereupon a message sent to the said Sir Robert from his father, they had be certainly joined with the said duke and earl ere the king might have had to do with them; but as God of his grace provided for the king's weal, the same late Sir Robert Welles being onwards on his way towards Leicester, understanding his father life to be in jeopardy, by a message brought him from his father, knowing also that the king was that Sunday at night at Fotheringay, and deeming that he would now have passed Stamford the same Monday, not intending to make any submission ne beyng† in his fellowship, but

*A paragraph commenting on Clarence's dissimulation is omitted.
†Bowing, submission.

disposing him to make his part good against the king, and traitorly to levy was against his highness, arredied him and his fellowship that day to have set upon the king in Stamford the Monday night, and so to have distressed him and his host, and so rescued his father life; and for that intent turned with his whole host out of Leicester way and took his way towards Stamford upon that same purpose.

The king, not understanding these false dissimulations but, of his most noble and rightwise courage, with all speed purposing to go upon his said rebels, early on the Monday afore day drew him to field and addressed him towards Stamford; and at his thither coming set forth his forward* towards his said rebellion, and baited himself and his fellowship in the town, whither come eftsoons a message from the said duke and earl by a priest called Sir Richard (—),† and Thomas Woodhille, which brought letters from them, certifying the king that they were coming towards him in aid against his rebels, and that night they were at Coventry, and on the Monday night they would be at Leicester; whereof the king delivered them with letters of thanks of his own hand, and incontinent took the field, where he understood the said Sir Robert Welles to be in arms with banners displayed against him, disposed to fight; thought it not according with his honour ne surtied‡ that he should jeopard his most royal person upon the same to leave the father and the said Sir Thomas Dymmoke of live that such treason had conspired and wrought, as so it was thought to all the lords, noblemen and other that time being in his host; wherefore his highness in the field under his banner displayed commanded the said Lord Welles and Sir Thomas Dymmoke to be executed; and so forthwith proceeding against his said rebels, by the help of Almighty God, achieved the victory and distressed mo than 30,000 men, using therewith plenteously his mercy in saving of the lives of his poor and wretched commons.

Where it is so to be remembered that, at such time as the battles were towards joining, the king with [his] host setting upon [the rebels],

---

*i.e. vanguard.

†Blank in the MS.

‡J.G. Nichols suggests 'suretyhood'.

and they avauncing themself, their cry war, *A Clarence! a Clarence! a Warwick!* that time being in the field divers persons in the Duke of Clarence livery, and especially Sir Robert Welles himself, and a man of the duke's own, that after were slain in the chase, and his casket taken, wherein were founden many marvellous bills, containing matter of the great seduction, and the very subversion of the king and the common weal of all this land, with the most abominable treason that ever were seen or attempted within the same, as they be ready to be shewed; and in the same chase was taken the late Sir Thomas Delalande. This victory thus had, the king returned to Stamford late in the night, giving laud and praising to Almighty God.

Upon the Tuesday the 13th day of March, the king, yet no thing mistrusting the said duke and earl, sent from Stamford towards them John Donne,* one of the sewers for his body, with two letters of his own hand, signifying unto them the victory that God had sent him, and desired them to come toward him with convenient number for their estates, commanding them to depart the people of the shires that were a-raised by them by virtue of his commission, for him seemed full necessary to set good directions in Lincolnshire, for he was therein, wherein the advises were to him right behovefull, the king supposing verily that they had been that Monday night at Leicester, as they afore so had written to his highness that they would have been. And it is to deem so they should have been, or at least upon Tuesday, ne had be the king's victory on the Monday, and that they had no such number of people as they looked after, which caused them to staker§ and to tarry still at Coventry, where the said John Donne found them ...

Upon the Wednesday and Thursday the 14th and 15th day of March, the king being at Grantham, were taken and brought thither unto him all the captains in substance, as the said late Sir Robert Welles, Richard Warren, and other, severally examined of their free wills uncompelled, not for fear of death ne otherwise stirred, knowledged and confessed the said duke and earl to be partners and chief provokers of all their treasons. And this plainly, their purpose was to destroy the king, and to

---

*Donne commissioned from Memlinc the famous Donne Triptych, formerly at Chatsworth, now in the National Gallery.
§i.e. waver.

have made the said duke king, as they, at the time that they should take their deaths, openly before the multitude of the king's host affirmed to be true.

And what time the said John Donne had delivered the king's letters to them* at Coventry, they said and promised to him plainly they would in all haste come towards the king, leaving their footmen, with a thousand or at the most fifteen hundred men; which notwithstanding, the said John Donne being present, they departed, with all their fellowship, towards Burton-upon-Trent; and when the said John Donne remembered them that him seemed they took not the right way towards the king, their answer was, that they took that way for certain footmen were before them, with whom they would speak, and courteously departed from thence, to th'intent they should be the more ready and better-well willed to do him service hereafter; and under colour thereof they went to Burton, and sithen to Derby, for to gather more people unto them, to enforce themself against the king in all that they could or might so ever, continually using their accustomed false dissimulation.(18)

Clarence and Warwick persisted in their attempts to outwit the king. By the time they reached Chesterfield Edward had sent a herald to inform them of Sir Robert Welles' revelations. Negotiations followed, but as the king refused to give the rebellious pair guarantees for their personal safety they withdrew to Lancashire hoping for support from Lord Stanley. Edward pursued them as far as Rotherham. He dared not advance further as the rebel forces had swept the countryside clean of victuals. The royal army went on to York hoping to cut off the insurgents from any help from the north. Thus frustrated, Clarence and Warwick fled south, seized a ship at Dartmouth in Devonshire and made for Calais.

Philippe de Commynes, at this time still one of the Duke of Burgundy's councillors, wrote of a game of deceit and double-dealing:

Lord Wenlock, Warwick's Lieutenant of Calais, instead of receiving the earl 'fired his great guns upon him' . . . [but] being a person of great

*Clarence and Warwick.

prudence secretly sent him word, that if he entered he was a lost man for all England and the Duke of Burgundy would be against him; besides, the inhabitants of the town would be his enemies, as well as a great part of the garrison, as Monsieur de Duras, who was the King of England's marshal, and several others, who had great interest in the place, were hostile to him. Wherefore he advised him, as the best thing he could do, to retire into France, and not to concern himself for Calais, for of that he would give him a fair account upon the first opportunity. He did his captain good service by giving him that counsel, but none at all to his king. Certainly no man ever showed such great loyalty as Lord Wenlock,* considering the King of England had made him Governor in Chief of Calais, and the Duke of Burgundy settled a large pension upon him.‡(19)

Much to Louis XI's embarrassment Clarence and Warwick had landed in Normandy. They were anything but welcome for Warwick's ill-judged piracy had enraged Charles the Bold to such an extent that Louis became afraid of a joint attack on France by Burgundy and Brittany. After some doubts and hesitation he once again made one of his sudden twists of policy, received Warwick and promised Charles the Bold compensation. As early as 1468 Sir John Fortescue had sent from St Michel-sur-Bar several memoranda suggesting an alliance between Warwick and the exiled Lancastrians.[2] Louis now decided to go on with this plan and hastily sent for Margaret of Anjou. John Stow, the sixteenth-century London tailor and antiquarian, transcribed many fifteenth-century documents which otherwise would have been lost to us. One of these – its authorship is unknown – is an account of the meeting between Margaret and Warwick at Angers in July 1470:

First, by the mean of the King of France, the said Earl of Warwick purchased a pardon of the Queen Margaret and of her son. Secondly, by the said mean was treated the marriage of the said queen's son called Prince of Wales, and th'Earl of Warwick's second daughter. Thirdly,

---

*That is to the Earl of Warwick. I have amended the translation at this point following the suggestions made by Calmette and Périnelle. (*Mémoires* i, 196, n 2).
‡Following his apparent betrayal of Warwick.

there was appointed upon his passage over the sea into England with a puissance.

Touching the first point, the said queen was right difficile, and showed to the King of France, being present the Duke of Guienne and many other, that with the honour of her and her son, he ne she might not, nor could not pardon the said earl, which hath been the greatest causes of the fall of King Henry, of her, and of their son, and that never of her own courage she ne might be contented with him, ne pardon him.

Item, the said queen shewed to the king and other aforesaid, that it should be thing greatly hurting and prejudicial to the King Henry, her, and her son, to pardon the said Earl of Warwick, ne to take party with him. And over this, that the King Henry, she, and her son had certain parties and friends which they might lightly lese by this mean, and that should be a thing that greatly might grieve them, and do them more harm and hindrance than the said earl and his allies might bring or bear unto them profit or advantage. Wherefore she besought the king that it would please him to leave off, or further to speak or labour for the said pardon, amity, or alliance aforesaid.

Th'Earl of Warwick, all these things heard, said unto the queen that he confessed well that by his conduct and mean the King Henry and she were put out of the realm of England; but, for an excuse and justification thereof, he shewed that the King Henry and she by their false counsel had enterprised the destruction of him and his friends in body and in goods, which he never had deserved against them. And him seemed that for such causes, and the great evil will that they have showed him he had a rightwise cause to labour their undoing and destruction, and that therein he had not done but that a nobleman outrayed and disperred* ought to have done. Also he said over that, and well confessed that he was causer of the upsetting of the King of England that now is, but now, seeing the evil terms that the king hath kept him, and cast him out of the realm and, as much as he hath been with him in times passed, now he will be as far contrary and enemy unto him hereafter; beseeching there the queen and the said prince that so they would take and repute him, and forgive him that in time passed

---

*i.e. disparaged.

he had done and attempted against them: offering himself to be bounden, by all manner wise, to be their true and faithful subject in time to come, and upon that he would set for surety the King of France. Whereunto the said king then being present agreed himself to be surety for all the premises with good will, praying the said queen that at his request she would pardon the said Earl of Warwick, showing the great love that she had unto him, and that he was bounded and beholden to the said earl more than to any other man, and therefore he would do as much and more for him than for any man living.

And so the queen, thus required by the king, as it is said, counselled also by the servants of the King of Sicily her father, after many treaties and meetings, pardoned th'Earl of Warwick, and so did her son also. And after that they pardoned th'Earl of Oxford being with th'Earl of Warwick; to whom the queen said that his pardon was easy to purchase, for she knew well that he and his friends had suffered much thing for King Henry's quarrels.

Touching the second point, that is of marriage, true it is that the queen would not in any wise consent thereunto for offer shewing, or any manner request that the King of France might make her. Some time she said that she saw never honour ne profit for her, ne for her son the prince. In other she [al]-ledged that and she would, she should find a more profitable party, and of a more advantage with the King of England. And indeed, she shewed unto the King of France a letter which she said was sent her out of England the last week, by the which was offered to her son my lady the princess; and so the queen persevered fifteen days ere she would anything intend to the said treaty of marriage, the which finally, by the mean and conduct of the King of France and the counsellors of the King of Sicily being at Angers, the said marriage was agreed and promised . . .

. . . Item, in treating the foresaid marriage, it was promitted and accorded that after the recovery of the realm of England for and in the name of the said King Henry, he holden and avouched for king, and the prince for regent and governor of the said realm, my Lord of Clarence shall have all the lands that he had when he departed out of England, and the Duchy of York, and many other, and th'Earl of Warwick his, and other named in th'appointment.

Item, that from thenceforth the said daughter to th'Earl of Warwick shall be put and remain in the hands and keeping of Queen Margaret, and also that the said marriage shall not be perfected to th'Earl of Warwick had been with an army over the sea into England, and that he had recovered the realm of England in the most party thereof, for the King Henry. Many other points were spoken of in the said treaty of marriage which were over long to put in writing.

. . . Touching the point concerning th'Earl of Warwick's passage, truth it is that th'earl every day gave to understand, and yet doth to the King of France, that he hath letters often from lords of England containing that as soon as he shall be landed there, he shall have moo than 50,000 fighters at his commandment; wherefore the said earl promised the king that if he would help him with a few folk, ships, and money, he shall pass over the sea without any delay, and upon this his words and promises to the king, he hath spended and daily spendeth great sums of money for entertaining the state of him and his, and beside that hath helpen in victual for his ships of 66,000 scuts,* content of 2,000 frank archers, etc.(20)

This agreement being made, *Warkworth's Chronicle* describes their successful invasion of England:

And in the same tenth year aforesaid, a little before Michaelmas, the Duke of Clarence and the Earl of Warwick landed in the west country,† and gathered there a great people. The Lord Marquess Montagu had gathered 6,000 men, by King Edward's commission and commandment, to the intent to have resisted the said Duke of Clarence and the Earl of Warwick. Never the latter, the said Marquess Montagu hated the king, and purposed to have taken him; and when he was within a mile of King Edward, he declared to the people that was there gathered with him, how King Edward had first given to him the earldom of Northumberland, and how he took it from him and gave it Herry Percy, whose father was slain at York field; and how of late time

*Louis, in fact, promised, 30,000.
†Their men were landed on 13 September, partly at Dartmouth, partly at Plymouth.

had he made him Marquess of Montagu, and gave a pye's nest to maintain his estate with* wherefore he gave knowledge to his people that he would hold with the Earl of Warwick, his brother, and take King Edward if he might, and all tho that would hold with him. But anon one of the host went out from the fellowship, and told King Edward all manner of thing, and bade him avoid, for he was not strong enough to give battle to Marquess Montagu; and then anon King Edward hasted him in all that he might to the town of Lynn, and there he took shipping one Michaelmas day, in the tenth year of his reign, with Lord Hastings, that was the king's chamberlain, Lord Say, with divers other knights and squires, passed and sailed over the sea into Flanders, to his brother-in-law the Duke of Burgundy, for succour and help, etc.

Here is to know, that in the beginning of the month of October, the year of Our Lord a 1470, the Bishop of Winchester, by the assent of the Duke of Clarence and the Earl of Warwick, went to the Tower of London where King Herry was in prison by King Edward's commandment, and there took him from his keepers, which was not worshipfully arrayed as a prince, and not so cleanly kept as should seem such a prince; they had him out, and new arrayed him, and did to him great reverence, and brought him to the palace of Westminster, and so he was restored to the crown again ...(21)

The chronicler continued that the Lancastrians, the Duke of Exeter, the Duke of Somerset, the Earl of Pembroke Jasper Tudor) and many others returned to England and took possession of their lands again, that a parliament reversed all the Yorkist attainders and that Queen Elizabeth fled to the Westminster Sanctuary where she gave birth to her first son.

The Duke of Burgundy, by no means pleased to hear of his brother-in-law's arrival near Alkmaar, was at first inclined to ignore him as far as he possibly could. Louis XI had supported Warwick's recent invasion of England because he had been afraid at least since 1468 of an Anglo-Burgundian

---

* It is true that John Neville had been made to surrender the Percy title and estates in exchange for a marquessate, but record evidence shows that Edward had already begun to endow him with considerable estates.

combination against him. An English attack on Burgundy was the price of Louis' support. Louis himself had declared war early in 1471 and on 12 February Warwick commanded the Calais garrison to join forces with him. Duke Charles' last hesitations vanished. He assisted Edward to mount an expedition against England. His force was certainly no larger than 2,000 men, probably no more than 1,200. The story of his return is told in a narrative known as the *Arrivall of Edward IV* written, a very short time after, 'by a servant of the king's that presently saw in effect a great part of his exploits, and the residue knew by true relation of them that were present at every time.' Once again one version of this narrative is preserved in John Stow's collections.* A considerable part of the Stow manuscript now follows. Edward set sail from Flushing on 11 March:

> . . . The same night following, upon the morn, Wednesday, and Thursday the 14th day of March, fell great storms, winds and tempests upon the sea, so that the said 14th day, in great torment, he came to Humberhead, where the other ships were disseevered from him, and every from other, so that, of necessity, they were driven to land, every far from other. The king, with his ship alone, wherein was the Lord Hastings, his Chamberlain and other to the number of 500 well chosen men, landed within Humber, on Holderness side, at a place called Ravenersporne,† even in the same place where sometime the usurper Henry of Derby, after called King Henry the IV, landed, after his exile . . . The king's brother Richard, Duke of Gloucester, and, in his company, 300 men, landed at another place four mile from thence. The Earl Ryvers, and the fellowship being in his company, to the number of 200, landed at a place called Paull, fourteen mile from there the king landed, and the remnant of the fellowship where they might best get land. That night the king was lodged at a poor village, two mile from his landing, with a few with him; but that night, and in the morning, the residue that were comen in his ship, the rage of the tempest somewhat appeased, landed and alway drew towards the king. And on the morn, the 15th day of March, from every landing place the

*Another, sent abroad at the time, in Dijon.
† Ravenser, a port at the mouth of the Humber, now engulfed by the sea.

fellowship came whole toward him. As to the folks of the country there came but right few to him, or almost none, for, by the scuringe* of such persons as for that cause were, by his said rebels, sent afore into those parts for to move them to be against his highness, the people were sore induced to be contrary to him, and not to receive, ne accept him, as for their king; notvvithstanding, for the love and favour that before they had borne to the prince of full noble memory, his father, Duke of York, the people bare him right great favour to be also Duke of York, and to have that of right appertained unto him, by the right of the said noble prince his father. And, upon this opinion, the people of the country, which in great number, and in divers places, were gathered, and in harness, ready to resist him in challenging of the realm and the crown, were disposed to content them self, and in no wise to annoy him, ne his fellowship, they affirming that to such intent were [they] comen, and none other. Whereupon, the whole fellowship of the king's comen and assembled together, he took advice what was best to do, and concluded briefly that, all be it his enemies and chief rebels were in the south parts, at London and there about, and that the next way towards them had be by Lincolnshire, yet, inasmuch as, if they should have taken that way, they must have gone eftsoons to the water again, and passed over Humber, which they abhorred for to do; and also, for that, if they so did it would have be thought that they had withdraw them for fear, which note of slander they were right loth to suffer; for these, and other good considerations, they determined in themselves not to go again to the water, but to hold the right way to his city of York. The king determined also, that, for as long as he should be in passing through and by the country, and to the time that he might, by th'assistance of his true servants, subjects and lovers, which he trusted verily in his progress should come unto him, be of such might and puissance as that were likely to make a sufficient party, he, and all those of his fellowship, should noise, and say openly, where so ever they came, that his intent and purpose was only to claim to be Duke of York, and to have and enjoy th'inheritance that he was born unto, by the right of the full noble prince his father and none other . . .

---

*i.e. to ride rapidly through and search a place.

The first insurgent force he met with therefore let him pass. Beverley admitted him; Hull refused. His own personal courage gained him admission to York:

Truth it is that aforn the king came at the city, by three miles, came unto him one called Thomas Coniers, recorder of the city, which had not been afore that named true to the king's party. He told him that it was not good for him to come to the city, for either he should not be suffered to enter, or else, in case he entered, he was lost, and undone, and all his. The king, seeing so far-forthly he was in his journey that in no wise he might go back with that he had begun, and that no good might follow but only of hardies, decreed in himself constantly to pursue that he had begun, and rather to abide what God and good fortune would give him, though it were to him uncertain, rather than by laches,* or default of courage, to sustain reproach, that of likelihood thereby should have ensued; and so, therefore, notwithstanding the discouraging words of the recorder, which had be afore suspect to him and his party, he kept boldly forth his journey, straight towards the city. And, within a while, came to him, out of the city, Robert Clifford and Richard Burgh, which gave him and his fellowship better comfort, affirming, that in the quarrel aforesaid of his father the Duke of York, he should be received and suffered to pass; whereby, better somewhat encouraged, he kept his way; natheless eftsoons came the said Coniers, and put him in like discomfort as afore. And so, sometime conforted and sometime discomforted, he came to the gates afore the city, where his fellowship made a stop, and himself and sixteen or seventeen persons, in the leading of the said Clifford and Richard Burgh, passed even in at the gates, and came to the worshipful folks which were assembled a little within the gates, and shewed them th'intent and purpose of his coming, in such for, and with such manner language, that the people contented them therewith, and so received him, and all his fellowship, that night, when he and all his fellowship abode and were refreshed well to they had dined on the morn, and then departed out of the city to Tadcaster, a town of th'Earl's of Northumberland, ten

*i.e. laziness, negligence.

mile southwards. And, on the morrow after that, he took his way towards Wakefield and Sandal, a great lordship appertaining to the Duke of York, leaving the castle of Pomfret on his left hand, where abode, and was, the Marquess Montagu, that in no wise troubled him, ne none of his fellowship, but suffered him to pass in peaceable wise, were it with good will, or no, men may judge at their pleasure; I deem ye; but truth it is, that he ne had not, ne could not have gathered, ne made, a fellowship of number sufficient to have openly resisted him in his great quarrel, ne in King Henry's quarrel; and one great cause was, for the great party of the people in those parties loved the king's person well, and could not be encouraged directly to do again him in that quarrel of the Duke of York, which in all manner language of all his fellowship was covertly pretended, and none other. Another great cause was, for the great party of [the] noble men and commons in those parties were towards th'Earl of Northumberland, and would not stir with any lord or noble man other than with the said earl, or at least by his commandment. And, for so much as he sat still, in such wise that if the Marquess would have done his business to have assembled them in any manner quarrel, neither for his love, which they bare him none, ne for any commandment of higher authority, they ne would in no cause, ne quarrel, have assisted him. Wherein it may right well appear, that the said earl, in this behalf, did the king right good and notable service . . .

Edward went on through Wakefield to Nottingham. On hearing of his approach the Duke of Exeter and the Earl of Oxford fled from Newark, and Warwick himself, uncertain of the loyalty of some of his recruits, withdrew behind the walls of Coventry. The *Arrivall* continues:

At Leicester came to the king right-a-fair fellowship of folks, to the number of three thousand men, well abled for the wars, such as were verily to be trusted, as those that would unerly impart with him at best and worst in his quarrel, with all their force and might do him their true service. And, in substance, they were such as were towards the Lord Hastings, the King's Chamberlain, and, for that intent abovesaid, came to him, stirred by his messages sent unto them, and by his servants, friends, and lovers, such as were in the country.

And so, better accompanied than he had been at any time aforn, he departed from Leicester, and came before the town of Coventry, the 29th day of March. And when he understood the said earl within the town [was] closed, and with him great people, to the number of six or seven thousand men, the king desired him to come out, with all his people, into the field, to determine his quarrel in plain field, which the same earl refused to do at that time, and so he did three days after-ensuing continually. The king, seeing this, drew him and all his host straight to Warwick, eight small miles from thence, where he was received as king, and so made his proclamations from that time forth wards; where he took his lodgings, weening thereby to have given the said earl greater courage to have issued out of the town of Coventry, and to have taken the field, but he ne would so do. Natheless daily came certain persons on the said earl's behalf to the king, and made great moynes,* and desired him to treat with him, for some good and expedient appointment. And, howbeit the king, by the advice of his counsellors, granted the said earl his life, and all his people being there at that time, and divers other fair offers made him, consyther** his great and heinous offences; which seemed reasonable, and that for the weal of peace and tranquillity of the realm of England, and for thereby to avoid th'effusion of Christian blood, yet he ne would accept the said offers, ne accord thereunto, but if he might have had such appointment unreasonable as might not in any wise stand with the king's honour and surety.

By this time Edward's treacherous brother, George, Duke of Clarence, was taking stock of his position and little comfort he found therein. Inordinate ambition and disloyalty were obviously not paying off. The current situation was advantageous to Warwick and deleterious to him:

. . . And in especial, he considered well, that himself was had in great suspicion, despite, distain, and hatred, with all the lords, noblemen, and other, that were adherents and full partakers with Henry, the Usurper, Margaret his wife, and his son Edward, called Prince; he saw also that

*i.e. means, steps to find ways.
**i e considering.

they daily laboured amongst them, breaking their appointments made with him, and, of likelihood, after that, should continually more and more fervently intend, conspire, and procure the destruction of him, and of all his blood, wherethrough it appeared also, that the realm and regalie should remain to such as thereunto might not in any wise have any rightwise title . . .

Inducements were held out by the other side. Clarence's mother, his sisters, the Duchesses of Exeter and Suffolk and the Duchess of Burgundy, the Archbishop of Canterbury and Edward's close friend and chamberlain, William, Lord Hastings were all working through messengers on his fickle and unstable mind and he went over to the king with a force of more than 4,000 men. The king and Clarence met and were finally reconciled at a meeting three miles outside Warwick on the road to Banbury. Clarence then attempted to reconcile his brother and Warwick, but the earl utterly rejected his advances:

. . . In this mean season of the king's being at Warwick, came to the Earl of Warwick, to Coventry, the Duke of Exeter, the Marquess Montagu, th'Earl of Oxford, with many other in great number, by whose then coming daily grew and increased the fellowship of that party. The king, with his brethren, this considering, and that in no wise he could provoke him to come out of the town, ne thinking it behoveful to assail, ne to tarry for the a-sieging thereof; as well for avoidance of great slaughters that should thereby ensure, and for that it was thought more expedient to them to draw towards London, and there, with help of God, and th'assistance of his true lords, lovers, and servants, which were there, in those parts, in great number; knowing also, that his principal adversary, Henry, with many of his partakers, were at London, there usurping and using the authority royal, which barred and letted the king of many aids and assistances, that he should and might have had, in divers parties, if he might once show himself of power to break their authority; wherefore, by th'advice of his said brethren, and other of his counsel, he took his purpose to London wards, and so departed fro Warwick; yet, eftsoons, shewing him, and his host, before Coventry, and desiring the said earl, and his fellowship, to come out, and for to determine his quarrel by battle, which he and they utterly refused, wherefore the king and his brethren kept forth their purpose southwards. And this was the 5th day of April the Friday.

And on the Saturday, the king, with all his host, came to a town called Daventry, where the king, with great devotion, heard all divine service upon the morn, Palm Sunday, in the parish church, where God, and Saint Anne, shewed a fair miracle; a good pronostique of good aventure that after should befall unto the king by the hand of God, and mediation of that holy matron Saint Anne. For so it was that, afore that time the king, being out of his realm, in great trouble, thought, and heaviness, for the infortune and adversity that was fallen him, full often and, specially upon the sea, he prayed to God, Our Lady, and Saint George and, amongst other saints, he specially prayed Saint Anne to help him, where that he promised that at the next time that it should hap him to see any image of Saint Anne, he should thereto make his prayers, and give his offering, in the honour and worship of that blessed saint. So it fell that, the same Palm Sunday, the king went in procession, and all the people after, in good devotion, as the service of that day asketh and, when the procession was comen into the church and, by order of the service, were comen to that place where the veil should be drawn up afore the Rood, that all the people shall honour the Rood, with the anthem, *Ave*, three times begun, in a pillar of the church, directly aforn the place where the king kneeled, and devoutly honoured the Rood, was a little image of Saint Anne, made of alabaster, standing fixed to the pillar, closed and clasped together, with four boards, small, painted, and going round about the image, in manner of a compass, like as it is to see commonly, and all about, where as such images be wont to be made for to be sold and set up in churches, chapels, crosses, and oratories, in many places. And this image was thus shut, closed, and clasped, according to the rules that, in all the churches of England, be observed, all images to be hid from Ash Wednesday to Easter Day in the morning. And so the said image had been from Ash Wednesday to that time. And even suddenly, at that season of the service, the boards compassing the image about gave a great crack, and a little opened, which the king well perceived and all the people about him. And anon, after, the boards drew and closed together again, without any man's hand, or touching and, as though it had been a thing done with a violence, with a greater might it opened all abroad, and so the image stood, open and discovered, in sight of all the people there being. The king, this seeing, thanked and honoured God, and Saint Anne, taking it for a good sign, and token of good and prosperous aventure that God would send him in that he had to do. . . (22)

The royal army went on towards London. *The Great Chronicle* tells what was happening in the city:

Then at London by the means of Sir Thomas Cook and few other was means of provision made to keep King Edward out of the city which by this time drew fast thitherward. And for to cause the citizens to bear their more favour unto King Henry, the said King Henry was conveyed from the palace of Paul's through Cheap and Cornhill, and so about to his said lodging again by Candlewick Street and Wading Street, being accompanied with the Archbishop of York which held him all that way by the hand and the Lord Zouche, an old and impotent man, which that day being Sheer Thursday about nine of the clock, bare the king's sword, and so with a small company of gentlemen going on foot before, and one being on horseback and bearing a pole or long shaft with two fox tails* fastened upon the said shaft's end, held with a small company of serving men following, the progress before shewed, the which was more liker a play than the showing of a prince to win men's hearts, for by this mean he lost many and won none or right few, and ever he was shewed in a long blue gown of velvet as though he had no moo to change with. But ere this progress was fully finished King Edward's fore riders were comen to Shoreditch and Newington, wherefore the said archbishop having small confidence in the citizens that they would resist King Edward or his people, shifted for himself and left King Henry in the palace as alone and the remnant that were of any reputation did as the bishop had done.(23)

Philippe de Commynes commented on Edward's entry into London:

---

*Foxes' tails were an insultng symbol of defiance.

As I have been since informed, there were three things especially which contributed to his reception into London. The first was, the persons who were in the sanctuaries, and the birth of a young prince, of whom the queen was there brought to bed. The next was, the great debts which he owed in the town, which obliged all the tradesmen who were his creditors to appear for him. The third was, that the ladies of quality, and rich citizens' wives with whom he had formerly intrigued, forced their husbands and relations to declare themselves on his side.(24)

Warwick now advanced from Coventry – hoping either that London would have kept out the king – or that Edward would not expect an attack on Easter Day. The *Arrivall* continues its account:

> . . . but the king, well advertised of this evil and malicious purpose, did great diligence to recounter him, ere he might come near to the city, as far from it as he goodly might; and, therefore, with a great army, he departed out of the City of London towards him, upon the Saturday, Easter's even, the 13th day of April. And so he took in his company to the field, King Henry; and so, that afternoon, he rode to Barnet, ten miles out of London, where his afore-riders had founden the afore-riders of th'Earl of Warwick's host, and beat them, and chased them out of the town, more some what than an half mile; when, under an hedge-side, were ready assembled a great people, in array, of th'Earl of Warwick. The king, coming after to the said town, and understanding all this, would [ne] suffer one man to abide in the same town, but had them all to the field with him, and drew towards his enemies, without the town. And, for it was right dark, and he might not well see where his enemies were embattled afore him, he lodged him, and all his host, afore them, much neare[r] than he had supposed, but he took not his ground so even in the front afore them as he would have done if he might better have seen them, but somewhat a-sydenhand, where he disposed all his people, in good array, all that night; and so they kept them still, without any manner language, or noise, but as little as they well might. Both parties had guns, and ordnance, the th'Earl of Warwick had many moo than the king, and therefore, on the night, weening gready to have annoyed the king, and his host, with shot of

guns, th'earl's field shot guns almost all the night. But, thanked be God! it so fortuned that they alway overshot the king's host, and hurted them nothing, and the cause was the king's host lay much nearer them than they deemed. And, with that also, the king, and his host, kept passing great silence all night, and made, as who saith, no noise, whereby they might not know the very place where they lay. And, for that they should not know it, the king suffered no guns to be shot on his side, all that night, or else right few, which was to him great advantage, for, thereby, they might have esteemed* the ground that he lay in, and have levelled their guns near.

On the morrow, betimes, the king, understanding that the day approached near, betwixt four and five of the clock, notwithstanding there was a great mist and letted the sight of either other, yet he committed his cause and quarrel to Almighty God, advanced banners, did blow up trumpets, and set upon them, first with shot and, then and soon, they joined and came to hand-strokes, wherein his enemies manly and courageously received them, as well in shot as in hand-strokes when they joined; which joining of their both battles was not directly front to front, as they so should have joined ne had be the mist, which suffered neither party to see other, but for a little space, and that of likelihood caused the battle to be the more cruel and mortal; for, so it was, that the one end of their battle over-reached th'end of the king's battle, and so, at that end, they were much mightier than was the king's battle at the same [end] that joined with them, which was the west end and, therefore, upon that party of the king's battle, they had a greater distress upon the king's party, wherefore many fled towards Barnet, and so forth to London, or ever they left; and they fell in the chase of them, and did much harm. But the other parties, and the residue of neither battle, might see that distress, ne the fleeing, ne the chase, by cause of [the] great mist that was, which would not suffer no man to see but a little from him; and so the king's battle, which saw none of all that, was thereby in nothing discouraged for, save only a few that were near unto them, no man wist thereof; also the other party by the same distress, flight, or chase, were therefore never the greadier couraged. And, in likewise, at the east end, the king's battle, when they came to joining,

*i.e. judged of.

over-reached their battle, and so distressed them there greatly, and so drew near towards the king, who was about the middest of the battle, and sustained all the might and weight thereof. Nethless upon the same litde distress at the west end anon ran to Westminster, and to London, and so forth further to other countries, that the king was distressed, and his field lost, but, the laud be to Almighty God! it was otherwise; for the king, trusting verily in God's help, our Blessed Lady's, and Saint George, took to him great hardies and courage for to suppress the falsehood of all them that so falsely and so traitorously had conspired against him, where-through, with the faithful, well-beloved, and mighty assistance of his fellowship, that in great number dissevered not from his person, and were as well assured unto him as to them was possible, he manly, vigorously, and valiantly assailed them, in the midst and strongest of their battle, where he with great violence, beat and bear down afore him all that stood in his way and then turned to the range, first on that one hand, and then on that other hand, in length, and so beat and bare them down, so that nothing might stand in the sight of him and the well assured fellowship that attended truly upon him; so that, blessed be God! he won the field there, and the perfite victory remained unto him, and to his rebels the discomforture of thirty thousand men, as they numbered themselves . . .

Edward returned in triumph to London where the corpses of Warwick and Marquess Montagu were exposed in St Paul's Cathedral to forestall risings that might follow if rumours spread that they were still alive. After three weeks' delay at Honfleur due to bad weather, Queen Margaret at last set sail, to land at Weymouth the very day of her friends' defeat at Barnet. Edward sent out scouts to observe the movements of her forces and when he learned that they were making for the north-west, hoping to join with supporters in Wales, Cheshire and Lancashire, he set off in pursuit. The great race for the Severn bridges had now begun. A feint towards Yeovil failed to deceive the king, who left Windsor on 24 April, going via Abingdon to Cirencester when on Monday 29 April, the *Arrivall* continues:

. . . he had certain tidings that they would, on Tuesday next, [be] at Bath, as so they were; and that on the morn next, the Wednesday, they would come on straight towards the king's battle. For which cause, and for that he would see and set his people in array, he drove all the people* out of the town, and lodged him, and his host, that night in the field, three mile out of the town. And, on the morrow, he, having no certain tidings of their coming forward, went to Malmesbury, seeking upon them. And there he had knowledge that they, understanding his approaching and marching near to them, had left their purpose of giving battle, and turned asidehand, and went to Bristol, a good and strong walled town, where they were gready refreshed and relieved, by such as were the king's rebels in that town, of money, men, and artillery; where through they took new courage, the Thursday after to take the field, and give the king battle, for which intent they had sent fore-riders to a town nine mile from Bristol, called Sudbury and, a mile towards the king, they appointed a ground for their field at a place called Sudbury Hill. The king, hearing this, the same Thursday, first day of May, with all his host in array and fair ordnance** came towards the place by them appointed for their field Th'enemies also advance them forth, the same day, out of Bristol, making semblance as though they would have comen straight to the place appointed but, having knowledge of the king's approaching, they left that way, albeit their harbingers were come afore them as far as Sudbury town; where they distressed certain of the king's party, five or six, such as negligently pressed so far forwards, dreading no danger, but only intending to have purveyed there their masters' lodgings; and so they changed their said purpose and took their way straight to Berkeley, travelling all that night, and, from thence, towards the town of Gloucester. The king, the same Thursday, soon after noon, came near to the same ground, called Sudbury Hill and, not having any certainty of his enemies, sent his scorars all about in the country, trusting by them to have wist where they had been. About that place was a great and a fair large plain, called a wold, and doubtful it was for to pass further, to† he might hear somewhat of them, supposing that they were right near, as so they might well have been, if they had kept forth the way they took out of

---

*i.e. his army, not the townsfolk.
**i.e. arrangement in ranks or rows.
†i.e. until.

Bristol. And, when he could not hear any certainty of them, he advanced forwards his whole battle, and lodged his vaward beyond the hill, in a valley towards the town of Sudbury, and lodged himself, with the remnant of his host, at the self hill called Sudbury Hill. Early in the morning, soon after three of the clock, the king had certain tidings that they had taken their way by Berkeley toward Gloucester, as so they took indeed. Whereupon he took advice of his counsel of that he had to do for the stopping of their ways, at two passages afore named, by Gloucester, of else by Tewkesbury, and, first, he purveyed for Gloucester, and sent thither certain servants of his own to Richard Beauchamp, son and heir to the Lord Beauchamp, to whom afore he had committed the rule and governance of the town and castle of Gloucester, commanding him to keep the town and castle for the king, and that he, with such help as he might have, should defend the same against them, in case they would in any wise assail them; as it was supposed they so would do that same aforenoon; letting them weet that he would have good espye upon them if they so did. And, if he might know that they so did, he promised to come their rescues, and comfort. With this the king's message they were well received at Gloucester, and the town and castle put in sure and safe keeping of the said Richard, and the said king's servants. Which message was sent and done in right good season, for certain it is the king's enemies were put in sure hope, and determined to have entered the town, and either have kept it against the king, or, at the least, to have passed through the town into other countries, where they thought [to] have been mightily assisted, as well with Welshmen, which they deemed should have fallen to them in those parties, in the company of Jasper, called Earl of Pembroke, as also for to have gotten into their company, by that way-taking, great number of men of Lancashire, and Cheshire, upon whem they much trusted. For which causes they had gready travailled their people all that night and morning, upon the Friday, to the about ten of the clock they were comen afore Gloucester; where their intent was utterly denied them by Richard Beauchamp, and other of the king's servants that, for that cause, the king had sent thither. Notwithstanding, many of the inhabitants of that town were gready disposed towards them, as they had certain knowledge. Of this demeaning they took right great displeasure, and made great menaces, and pretended as though they would have assaulted the town, and won it upon them, but, as well those that kept the town as the said enemies that so pretended, knew well, that the king with a mighty puissance was near to them, and, if any affray had there be made, he might soon have been upon them, and taken upon them right great advantage; wherefore they in the town nothing doubted, and they without durst not for fear begin any such work; and, therefore, they shordy took their conclusion for to go the next way to Tewkesbury, whither they came the same day, about four after noon. By which time they had so travailled their host that night and day that they were right weary for travailling; for by that time they had travailled thirty-six long miles, in a foul country, all in lanes and stony ways, betwixt woods, without any good refreshing. And, for as much as the greater part of their host were footmen, the other party of the host, when they were comen to Tewkesbury, could, ne might, have laboured any further, but if they would wilfully have forsaken and left their footmen behind them, and thereto themselves that were horsemen were right weary of that journey, as so were their horses. So, whether it were of their election and good will, or no, but that they were verily compelled to bide by two causes; one was, for weariness of their people, which they supposed not their people would have any longer endured; another, for they knew well that the king ever approached towards them, near and near, ever ready, in good array and ordnance,* to have pursued and fallen upon them, if they would any further have gone and, peradventure, to their most disadvantage. They therefore determined t'abide there th'aventure that God would send them in the quarrel they had taken in hand. And, for that intent, the same night they pight them in a field, in a close even at the town's end; the town, and the abbey, at their backs; afore them, and upon every hand of them, foul lanes, and deep dykes, and many hedges, with hills, and valleys, a right evil place to approach, as could well have been devised.

The king, the same morning, the Friday, early, advanced his banners, and divided his whole host in three batdes, and sent afore him his fore-riders, and scorars, on every side of him, and so, in fair array and

---

*i.e. arrangement in ranks or rows.

ordnance, he took his way through the champaign* country, called
Cotswold, travailling all his people, whereof were mo than three
thousand footmen, that Friday, which was right-an-hot day, thirty mile
and more; which his people might not find, in all the way, horse-meat,
ne mans-meat, ne so much as drink for their horses, save in one little
brook, where was full little relief, it was so soon troubled with the
carriages that had passed it. And all that day was evermore the king's
host within five or six miles of his enemies; he in plain‡ country and
they amongst woods; having alway good espialls upon them. So,
continuing that journey to§ he came, with all his host, to a village called
Cheltenham, but five miles from Tewkesbury, where the king had
certain knowledge that, but little afore his coming thither, his enemies
were comen to Tewkesbury, and there were taking a field, wherein they
purposed to abide, and deliver him battle. Whereupon the king made
no longer tarrying, but a little comforted himself, and his people, with
such meat and drink as he had done to be carried with him, for
victualling of his host; and, incontinent, set forth towards his enemies,
and took the field, and lodged himself, and all his host, within three
mile of them.

Upon the morrow following, Saturday, the 4th day of May, [the king]
apparelled himself, and all his host set in good array; ordained three
wards; displayed his banners; did blow up the trumpets; committed his
cause and quarrel to Almighty God, to our most blessed lady his
mother, Virgin Mary, the glorious martyr Saint George, and all the
saints; and advanced directly upon his enemies; approaching to their
field, which was strongly in a marvellous strong ground pight, full
difficult to be assailed. Netheless the king's ordnance¶ was so
conveniently laid afore them, and his vaward so sore oppressed them,
with shot of arrows, that they gave them right-a-sharp shower. Also
they did again-ward to them, both with shot of arrows and guns,
whereof netheless they ne had not so great plenty as had the king. In
the front of their field were so evil lanes, and deep dykes, so many

---

*i e. open field.

‡i.e. open.

§i.e. until.

¶i.e. in this case 'artillery' – or merely ranks of men?

hedges, trees, and bushes, that it was right hard to approach them near, and come to hands; but Edmund, called Duke of Somerset,* having that day the vaward, whether it were for that he and his fellowship were sore annoyed in the place where they were, as well with guns-shot, as with shot of arrows, which they ne would nor durst abide, or else, of great heart and courage, knightly and manly advanced himself, with his fellowship, somewhat aside-hand the king's vaward, and, by certain paths and ways therefore afore purveyed, and to the king's party unknown, he departed out of the field, passed a lane, and came into a fair place, or close, even afore the king where he was enbattled and, from the hill that was in that one of the closes, he set right fiercely upon th'end of the king's battle. The king, full manly, set forth even upon them, entered and won the dyke, and hedge, upon them, into the close, and, with great violence, put them up towards the hill and, so also, the king's vaward, being in the rule of the Duke of Gloucester.

Here it is to be remembered how that, when the king was comen afore their field, ere he set upon them, he considered that, upon the right hand of their field, there was a park, and therein much wood, and he, thinking to purvey a remedy in case his said enemies had laid any bushment in that wood of horsemen, he chose, out of his fellowship, two hundred spears, and set them in a plomp,† togethers, near a quarter of a mile from the field, giving them charge to have good eye upon that corner of the wood, if case that any need were, and to put them in devoir and, if they saw none such, as they thought most behoveful for time and space, to employ themself in the best wise as they could; which provision came as well to point at this time of the battle as could well have been devised, for the said spears of the king's party, seeing no likeliness of any bushment in the said wood-corner, seeing also good opportunity t'employ themself well, came and brake on, all at once, upon the Duke of Somerset, and his vaward, aside-hand, unadvised, whereof they, seeing the king gave them enough to do afore them, were greatly dismayed and abashed, and so took them to flight into the park, and into the meadow that was near, and into lanes, and dykes, where they best hoped to escape the danger: of whom, netheless, many

*'Called' because his family were attainted.
†i.e. a compact group.

were distressed, taken, and slain; and, even at this point of their flight, the king courageously set upon that other field, where was chief Edward, called Prince, and, in short while, put him to discomforture and flight; and so fell in the chase of them that many of them were slain, and namely, at a mile-end, in the meadow fast by the town, were many drowned; many ran towards the town; many to the church; to the abbey; and else where; as best they might.

In the winning of the field such as abode hand-strokes were slain incontinent; Edward, called Prince,* was taken, fleeing to the town wards, and slain, in the field. There was also slain, Thomas, called th'Earl of Devonshire; John of Somerset, called Marquess Dorset;† Lord Wenlock; with many other in great number.(25)

According to the *Arrivall* Edward granted a free pardon to the refugees in the abbey church, but a local chronicle claims that they were dragged out and executed after a brawl so bloody that the church had to be reconsecrated. The king then started for the north to deal with new risings there, intending to recruit on his way. At Coventry Margaret of Anjou was brought in – captured 'in a poor religious place,‡ where she had hid herself, for the surety of her person' – and the king heard that the remnant of the northern rebels, now leaderless without a Neville, had submitted to the Earl of Northumberland. He therefore changed his plans and marched for London to deal with the Bastard of Fauconberg's attack on the city.

Warkworth now tells the story:

And in the same time that the battle of Tewkesbury was, Sir Walter Wrottesley and Geoffrey Gate, knights of the Earl of Warwick's, were governors of the town of Calais, did send Sir George Broke knight out of Calais, with three hundred of soldiers unto Thomas Bastard Fauconberg, that was on the sea with the Earl of Warwick's navy, that

---

*Most contemporary writers state that he was killed either on the battlefield or in flight. The story that he was captured and the king ordered his death occurs for the first time in *Fabyan's Chronicle* (printed 1496). See Ramsay, *Lancaster and York* (1892), ii, 381, n 3.

† 'Called' because their families were under attainder.

‡ Possibly Deerhurst Nunnery.

he should the navy save, and go into Kent, and to raise all Kent, to that intent to take King Herry out of the Tower and destroy King Edward, if he might; which Bastard came into Kent, to Canterbury, and he, with help of other gentlemen, they raised up all Kent,* and came to London the 5th day of May the year aforesaid. But then the Lord Scales,§ that King Edward had left to keep the city, with the Mayor and Aldermen, would not suffer the said Bastard to come into the city; for they had understanding that Prince Edward was dead, and all his host discomforted: wherefore the Bastard loosed his guns into the city, and brent at Aldgate and at London bridge; for the which brenning, the commons to London were sore wroth, and gready moved against them: for and they had not brent, the commons of the city would have let them in, maugre of the Lord Scales' head, the Mayor and all his brother. Wherefore the Bastard and all his host went over at Kingston bridge, ten mile westward, and had purposed to have destroyed King Edward, or to have drive him out of the land. And if the Bastard had hold forth his way, King Edward by possibility could not by power have resisted the Bastard; for the Bastard had moo than twenty thousand good men well harnessed, and ever as he went the people fell to him. The Lord Scales, and divers other of King Edward's counsel that were in London, saw that the Bastard and his host went westward, and that it should be a greater jeopardy to King Edward than was Barnet field or Tewkesbury field (in so much when the field of Tewkesbury was done, his host was departed from;†) wherefore they promised to the Bastard, and to divers

*The Great Chronicle of London (p. 218) is worth comparison:' . . . and a rover named the Bastard of Fauconberg having a multitude of rovers in his rule landed in Kent and there a-raised much idle people and after coasted toward London, and caused divers of his ships with ordnance to be brought into Thames. Whereof the fame being blown into Essex, the faint husbands cast from them their sharp scythes and armed them with their wives' smocks, cheese cloths and old sheets and weaponed them with heavy and great clubs and long pitchforks and ashen staves, and so in all haste sped them toward London, making their avunt as they went that they would be revenged upon the mayor for setting of so easy pennyworths of their butter, cheese, eggs, pigs, and all other victual, and so joined them unto the Kentish men.'
§Anthony Wydeville, since the death of his father, Earl Ryvers.
†Edward apparently disbanded his exhausted tooops after Tewkesbury, intending to recruit new forces.

other that were about him, and in especial to one Nicholas Faunt, mayor of Canterbury, that he should entreat him to turn homeward again. And for as much as fair words and promises makes fools fain, the Bastard commanded all his host to turn to Blackheath again; which was destruction of himself and many other; for anon after, by the Duke of Gloucester in Yorkshire, the said Bastard was beheaded, notwithstanding he had a charter of pardon; and Nicholas Faunt was afterward hanged, drawn, and quartered in Canterbury. And when the Bastard and all his host were come to Blackheath again, in the next morning he with the soldiers and shipmen of Calais, to the number of six hundred horsemen, stole away from the host and rode to Rochester, and from thence to Sandwich, where the Bastard abode the king's coming, and the soldiers sailed over sea to Calais. And when the host understood that their Captain was stole from them, they kept them together all a day and a night, and then every man departed to his own house. And when King Edward heard thereof, he was glad, etc.

Here is to know that King Edward made out commissions to many shires of England; which in a ten days there came to him, where he was, to the number of thirty thousand and came with the king to London, and there he was worshipfully received. And the same night that King Edward came to London, King Herry, being inward in prison in the Tower of London, was put to death, the 21st day of May, on a Tuesday night, between eleven and twelve of the clock, being then at the Tower the Duke of Gloucester, brother to King Edward, and many other; and on the morrow he was chested and brought to Paul's, and his face was open that every man might see him; and in his lying he bled on the pament there; and afterward at the Black Friars was brought, and there he bled new and fresh; and from thence he was carried to Chertsey Abbey in a boat, and buried there in our Lady Chapel. On the morrow that the king was come to London, for the good service that London had done to him, he made knights of the aldermen, Sir John Stokton, Sir Ralph Verney, Sir Richard Lee, Sir John Yonge, Sir William Taylor, Sir George Irland, Sir John Stokker, Sir Matthew Philip, Sir William Hampton, Sir Thomas Stalbroke, Sir John Crosby, Sir Thomas Urswick, recorder of London. And after that, the king and all his host rode into Kent to Canterbury, where many of the country that were at Blackheath with the Bastard, were arrested and brought before him; and there was hanged, drawn, and quartered, one Faunt of Canterbury, that was loving to the Earl of Warwick; which entreated the Bastard for to depart from his host; and many divers men of the country were hanged and put to death. After that, the king rode unto Sandwich, and beside all the Earl of Warwick's navy there, that the Bastard had rule of, and took the Bastard with him, and returned again to London. And immediately after that was the Lord Dinham and Sir John Fogge and divers other made commissioners, that sat upon all Kent, Sussex, and Essex, that were at the Blackheath, and upon many other that were not there; for some man paid two hundred mark, some a hundred pound, and some more and some less, so that it cost the poorest man seven shillings which was not worth so much, but was fain to sell such clothing as they had, and borrowed the remnant, and laboured for it afterward; and so the king had out of Kent much good and little love. Lo, what mischief grows after insurrection!(26)

NOTES

1. *C.S.P.M.*, i,83.
2. J. Calmette et G. Périnelle, *Louis XI et l'Angleterre, 1461–1483* (1930), p. 104 and Pièces Justificatives, No. 28. This document is undated but from internal evidence it may be attributed to 1468.

FOUR

Peace and Success,
1471–1483

During the first few months following his return Edward spent enormous sums of money on magnificent new clothes. 'Beau prince entre les beaux du monde', as Philippe de Commynes said, the splendour of his apparel, in an age notorious for ostentatious pageantry, became as much a by-word as his physical beauty. Edward never risked the contempt which his solitary, shabby, blue velvet gown had brought upon Henry VI. Splendour was not just another of the world's vanities: it held its place as one of the weapons of politics. A glittering court was a majestic political asset – as long as the king paid his bills punctually. If John Warkworth was right Edward, in 1470, distracted by a decade of rebellion and self-seeking treachery from amending 'all manner of thing that was amiss' was no less discredited than Henry VI had been in 1460. Now freed at last from Warwick's fatal intransigence he carried on more successfully the policies which he had adopted from almost the beginning of his reign.

Too weak to rule successfully through the narrow clique which had set him on the throne, he attracted old opponents to court. Twenty attainders had already been reversed by 1470, another thirty between 1472 and 1475.[1] Even as old and as prominent an enemy as John Morton, Edward promoted to one of the highest offices of state.* Too wary to disturb vested interests by a thorough-going reform of the antiquated taxation system, after 1474† the king ignored it and accumulated a considerable fortune by methods less likely to unite the prosperous classes against him: gathering in treasure by a vigilant care for royal rights, which those who suffered from it condemned as avarice, and making a show of armed might pay a handsome dividend in an annual pension from the King of France, till at last, as the Croyland Chronicler remarked, he 'stood in fear of no one'.

---

*Attainted in 1461 and one of the most prominent supporters of Henry VI in exile.
†There was no further grant of direct taxation by parliament until 1483.

On the eve of Edward's victories, some of his opponents, like the Earl of Oxford, fled, others, like John Paston the Youngest, contrived to obtain pardons.it Louis XI of France, his grandiose plans defeated for the time being, was thinking, in his old way, of stirring up trouble, and yet at the same time opening negotiations. Edward wanted his revenge on Louis but he had not forgotten his far from cordial reception in Burgundy in 1470. For some time Edward, Charles the Bold and Louis kept up a complicated series of negotiations, trying to get the better of each other. None of them could have learned anything from Machiavelli in the arts of insincerity, chicanery and deceit.

In 1472 Warwick's brother, George Neville, Archbishop of York, who had made his peace with Edward the previous year, was suddenly arrested, all his goods, said to be worth the enormous sum of £20,000 seized, and the archbishop himself imprisoned in Calais. The chronicler, Warkworth, describing Neville's immense covetousness in the accumulation of wealth snidely commented 'wherefore such goods as were gathered with sin, were lost with sorrow.'

The king's brothers, the Dukes of Clarence and Gloucester, soon began to quarrel over the division of Warwick the Kingmaker's estates. Sir John Paston reported dissensions between them as early as February 1472. The Croyland Chronicler describes the progress of the affair:

It is my intention here to insert an account of the dissensions which arose during this Michaelmas Term between the two brothers of the king already mentioned, and which were with difficulty quieted. After . . . the son of King Henry, to whom the Lady Anne, the youngest daughter of the Earl of Warwick, had been married, was slain at the battle of Tewkesbury, Richard, Duke of Gloucester, sought the said Anne in marriage. This proposal, however, did not suit the views of his brother, the Duke of Clarence, who had previously married the eldest daughter of the same earl. Such being the case, he caused the damsel to be concealed, in order that it might not be known by his brother where she was; as he was afraid of a division of the earl's property,*

---

*This quarrel had a considerable influence on the politics of the early 1470s. See J.R. Lander, *The Historical Journal*, iv (1961), 128–130, reprinted in *Crown and Nobility 1450–1509* (1976), pp. 138–9.

which he wished to come to himself alone in right of his wife, and not be obliged to share it with any other person. Still, however, the craftiness of the Duke of Gloucester so far prevailed, that he discovered the young lady in the City of London disguised in the habit of a cookmaid; upon which he had her removed to the sanctuary of St Martin's. In consequence of this, such violent dissensions arose between the brothers, and so many arguments were, with the greatest acuteness, put forward on either side, in the king's presence, who sat in judgment in the council chamber, that all present, and the lawyers even, were quite surprised that these princes should find arguments in such abundance by means of which to support their respective causes. In fact, these three brothers, the king and the two dukes, were possessed of such surpassing talents, that, if they had been able to live without dissensions, such a threefold cord could never have been broken without the utmost difficulty ... (1)

Clarence quickly forgot the lesson of 1470–1 and vague rumours over the next two years again linked his name with plottings and sedition. In 1473 the Earl of Oxford attempted an invasion. Warkworth's Chronicle tells of his movements:

Also in the 13th year of [the] reign of King Edward, Sir John Vere, Earl of Oxford, that withdrew him from Barnet field, and rode into Scotland, and from thence into France a-sailed, and there he was worshipfully received. And in the same year he was in the sea with certain ships, and gate great good and riches, and afterward came into west-country, and, with a subtle point of war, gate and entered Saint Michael's Mount in Cornwall, a strong place and a mighty, and cannot be got if it be well victualled with a few men to keep it; for twenty men may keep it again all the world. So the said earl, with twenty score men save three, the last day of September the year afore said entered first into [the] said mount, and he and his men came down into county of Cornwall, and had right good cheer of the commons, etc. The king and his counsel saw that thereof much harm might grow, etc.; commanded Bodrugan, sheriff ruler of Cornwall, to besiege the said mount. And so he did; and every day the Earl of Oxford's men came down under truce, spake with Bodrugan and his men; and at the last

162   THE WARS OF THE ROSES

the said earl lacked victual, and the said Bodrugan suffered him to be victualled; and anon the king was put in knowledge thereof; wherefore the said Bodrugan was discharged, and Richard Fortescue, squire for the body, by authority of the king, took upon hand to lay siege to the foresaid mount, etc. And so great division (dyversione) rose betwixt Bodrugan and Fortescue, which Fortescue was sheriff of Cornwell, etc.; and the said Fortescue laid siege, etc, the 23rd day of December the year aforesaid; and for the most party every day each of them fought with other, and the said earl's men killed divers of Fortescue's men; and some time when they had well i-fought, they would take a truce for one day and a night, and some time spake and communed with other. The king and his counsel sent unto divers that were with the Earl of Oxford privily their pardons, and promised to them great gifts and lands and goods, by the which divers of them were turned to the king against the earl; and so in conclusion the earl had not passing an eight or nine men that would hold with him; the which was the undoing of the earl. For there is a proverb and a saying, that *a castle that speaketh, and a woman that will hear, they will be gotten both*: for men that been in a castle of war, that will speak and entreat with their enemies, the conclusion thereof [is] the losing of the castle; and a woman that will hear folly spoken unto her, if she assent not at one time, she will at another. And so this proverb was proved true by the said Earl of Oxford, which was fain to yield up the said mount, and put him in the king's grace; if he had not do so, his own men would have brought him out. And so Fortescue entered into the said mount, the 15th day of February the year aforesaid,* in the which was victual enough till midsummer after. And so was the earl aforesaid, the Lord Beaumont, two brothers of the said earl's and Thomas Clifford, brought as a prisoner to the king; and all was done by their own folly, etc.(2)

On 25 November 1473, the papal envoy, Pietro Aliprando, who had been somewhat roughly handled when he had earlier crossed to England from the safety of Flanders relieved his feelings about the English, in a spiteful letter to Galeazzo Maria Sforza, Duke of Milan:

*i.e. 1474.

... In the morning they are as devout as angels, but after dinner they are like devils, seeking to throw the Pope's messengers into the sea ...

... Two ambassadors from the King of France are there, with those from Brittany, and four from Burgundy. They solicit some distemper, offering Normandy and wonderful things. I think the duke has approved them, and if the English are not friends of the Flemish or Burgundians, yet he will now promise them many things, in order to induce them to make a landing, but perhaps they will cheat again.

The king can do no more as he is a tavern bush ...

He added that the people did not love the king, that there were rumours that another Warwick would arise to overthrow him, rumours of a war with France that the king would be deposed by Clarence. In other words the whole situation was totally confused. Aliprando himself seems to have been equally confused for he then added, contradicting an earlier remark in the same letter:

... The king is indeed a most handsome, worthy and royal prince, the country is good, the people bad and perverse ...(3)

By the time Pietro Aliprando wrote this letter Edward had been making his preparations to invade France for over a year. He had circulated 'a declaration in writing' amongst the members of the Commons urging them to approve his policy of war with France. In November 1472 parliament granted a special tax of one-tenth of all incomes from land to pay for 13,000 archers. The Rolls of Parliament tell of Edward's humiliating efforts to levy this and other war taxes, and the resulting state of chaos:

... And how be it that great part of the said 10th part in every shire, city, town and borough, is levied by the collectors thereof, it is so, that some of the collectors have not delivered the sums by them received to the place limited and appointed by the said commissioners, but have converted it to their own use, and some that have received it, and not so delivered it, be now dead, and some of the said 10th part hath be delivered by the collectors thereof to the place limited by the said commissioners, and the governors of the same place have converted it to their own use, and some of the said commissioners have received parcel of the said 10th part, and will not deliver it to the king's commissioner, ordained by the king to be receiver thereof, and some persons to whom parcel of the said 10th part have be delivered by the collectors thereof, safely to be kept to the king's use, will not make payment thereof to the receiver of the same, and some persons that with strong hand have taken parcel of the said 10th part out of the place where it was put to be kept by the said collectors, according to the said grant; through the which defaults, the receivers of the said 10th part, deputed and assigned thereunto by our said Sovereign Lord, have not ne cannot levy the whole of the said 10th part, being within their charge, so as our said Sovereign Lord, in default thereof, lacketh a great part of such sums of money as he should pay at this time to the lords, knights, squires, and other retained with his Highness to attend upon the same in his said voyage and army, to the great let and hurt of his said lords, knights, squires, and other so retained, and to the great displeasure of our said Sovereign Lord: wherefore the same our Sovereign Lord, for the more hasty and ready payment to be made of the said 10th part, in discharge of the generalty of his said commons in this party, by th'advice, assent and authority abovesaid, ordaineth and enacteth, that every person, as well collector of the said 10th part, keeper of it after the gathering of the same, as he that hath received or taken any of the said 10th part, and hath not paid it, that he or they do bring it, or do it to be brought to the Receipt of the King's Exchequer, afore the feast of the ascension of Our Lord next coming, and there deliver it to the Treasurer and Chamberlains of the said Exchequer, upon pain of forfeiture of the treble of so much as he so hath received or taken, and not paid . . . .(4)

The prospects of raising enough money through parliament became so obviously hopeless that Edward, taking immense personal trouble, begged, cajoled, flattered and bullied contributions from his richer subjects – the notorious 'Benevolence'. According to *The Great Chronicle of London*:

The king intending his royal voyage into France, considering that late days he had charged as in the xiith year of his reign, his subjects with notable sums of money used a policy to fore days, by none of his noble

progenitors put in ure.* For after he had known the good minds of his
lords and nobles of his land he called before him the mayor, and shewed
to him his royal purpose with sundry other circumstances, and finally
demanded of him what he would of his free will depart with him
toward his said voyage. The which granted unto him with a glad
semblaunt† £30. The which grant his grace well and thankfully
accepted, and after the mayor's good will thus to him known, he grace
sent for the aldermen one by one, so that some granted £20 and
twenty mark and some £10. And when he had thus perused‡ the
aldermen, he then sent for the head commoners, of the which for the
more party he had granted the wages of half a soldier for a year,
whereof the charge was £4 11s. 3d. And that done he rode into Essex,
Suffolk and Norfolk and other countries of this land and entreated the
people so favourably that he had more money by those means than he
should have had by two fifteens. It was reported that as he passed by a
town in Suffok and called before him among other a rich widow and
frayned§ of her what her good will should be toward his great charge,
and she liberally had granted to him £10, he thanked her and after
took her till him and kissed her, the which kiss she accepted so kindly,
that for that great bounty and kind deed, he should have £20 for his
£10. And thus by his own labour and other solicitors that he assigned
in his stead as the Bishop of Ely [then] Dr Morton and other he
gathered notable sums of money with the which all provision was
made in all goodly haste for the said voyage . . .(5)

During 1475 Margaret Paston claimed that the king's demands had been
great enough to depress the price of farm products.

Christofforo de Bollato told Galeazzo Maria Sforza of Louis XI's
reactions:

I think your lordship will have taken note of the words spoken by the
very lips of the King of France, which I enclose herewith. I inform

*i.e. use.
†i.e. show, pretence.
‡i.e. gone through, dealt with.
§i.e. asked.

your lordship that his Majesty has had positive information that the English are preparing a very large force to invade Normandy at once, and the King of England is coming in person with a good number of men.

His Majesty is more discomposed than words can describe, and has almost lost his wits. In his desperation and bitterness he uttered the following precise words, among others. Ah, Holy Mary, even now when I have given thee 1,400 crowns, thou dost not help me one whit . . .(6)

In June the transport of the army at last began. Edward himself crossed from Dover to Calais on 4 July. Philippe de Commynes, now one of Louis' councillors, noted in his *Mémoires* that his army was 'the most numerous, the best disciplined, the best mounted, and the best armed that ever any king of that nation invaded France with.'[2] Charles the Bold of Burgundy wantonly ignored his treaty obligations and instead of marching his forces to assist the English continued the siege of the Swiss town of Nuz which he had begun some time before. Disappointed of his help Edward listened readily to peace proposals from the frightened and cunning King of France.

Ignoring the furious taunts of the Duke of Burgundy Edward agreed, before his army had even struck a blow, to leave France on payment of 75,000 crowns, on an arrangement for the future marriage of his eldest daughter with the Dauphin of France and an annual pension of 50,000 crowns. Louis XI also paid him 50,000 crowns to surrender Margaret of Anjou. Commercial agreements followed – agreements so fruitful that the Treaty of Pécquigny, as these arrangements were collectively called, became known in Bordeaux as 'the merchants' treaty'. When the agreement had been made Louis lavishly entertained the English army and the two kings arranged a personal interview at Pécquigny. Philippe de Commynes wrote of these events:

In order to bring the peace to a conclusion, the King of England advanced within half a league of Amiens, and the King of France being upon one of the gates, saw his army marching at a great distance. To speak impartially, his troops seemed but raw and unused to action in the field; for they were in very ill order, and observed no manner of discipline. Our king sent the King of England three hundred cart-loads of the best wines in France as a present; and I think the carts made as great an appearance as the whole English army. Upon the strength of the truce, numbers of the English came into the town, where they behaved themselves very imprudently, and without the least regard to their prince's honour; for they entered the town all armed, and in great companies, so that if the King of France could have dispensed with his oath, never was there so handsome an opportunity of cutting off a considerable number of them; but his majesty's design was only to entertain them nobly, and to settle a firm and lasting peace, that might continue during his reign. The king had ordered two large tables to be placed on each side of the street, at the entrance of the town gate, which were covered with a variety of good dishes of all sorts of food most proper to relish their wine, of which there was great plenty, and of the richest that France could produce; and abundance of servants to wait on them, but not a drop of water was drunk. At each of the tables the king had placed five or six boon companions, persons of rank and condition, to entertain those that had a mind to take a hearty glass; amongst these were the Lord of Craon, the Lord of Briquebec, the Lord of Bressure, the Lord de Villiers, and several others. Those English who were within sight of the gate, saw the entertainment, and there were persons appointed on purpose to take their horses by the bridles, and lead them to the tables, where every man was treated handsomely as he came, in his turn, to their very great satisfaction. When they had once entered the town, wherever they went, or whatever they called for, nothing was to be paid; there were nine or ten taverns liberally furnished with all that they wanted, where they had whatever they had a mind to call for, without paying for it, according to the King of France's orders, who bore all the expense of that entertainment, which lasted three or four days . . .

The orgy which followed this lavish provision of drink caused considerable anxiety to some of the French. Commynes and others warned the king that there were 9,000 of the English, all armed, in the town and the situation had reached crisis point. Commynes, then, on the king's orders, asked three or four of the English commanders to get their troops out. They were unsuccessful but Commynes, going round the town observing the drunken state of the English as early as nine o'clock in the morning concluded that there was no real danger. Edward, by this time thoroughly ashamed of the behaviour of his troops, ordered them to evacuate the town:

> . . . And then, in order to bring the whole affair to a conclusion, they consulted what place would be most convenient for the interview of the two kings, and persons were appointed to survey it; the Lord du Bouchage and I were chosen to represent our master; and the Lord Howard, one Chalanger, and a herald, represented the King of England. Upon our taking a view of the river, we agreed the best and securest place was Pécquigny, a strong castle some three leagues from Amiens, belonging to the Vidame of Amiens, which had been burnt not long before by the Duke of Burgundy; the town lies low, the River Somme runs through it, and is not fordable or wide near it. On the one side, by which our king was to come, was a fine champaign* country; and on the other side it was the same, only when the King of England came to the river, he was obliged to pass a causeway about two bow-shots in length, with marshes on both sides, which might have produced very dangerous consequences to the English, if our intentions had not been honourable. And certainly, as I have said before, the English do not manage their treaties and capitulations with so much cunning and policy as the French do, let people say what they will, but proceed more ingenuously, and with greater straightforwardness in their affairs; yet a man must be cautious, and have a care not to affront them, for it is dangerous meddling with them.
>
> After we had fixed upon the place, our next consultation was about a bridge which was ordered to be built, large and strong, for which purpose we furnished our carpenters with materials. In the midst of the bridge there was contrived a strong wooden lattice, such as the lions' cages are made with, the hole between every bar being no wider than to thrust in a man's arm; the top was covered only with boards to keep off the rain, and the body of it was big enough to contain ten or twelve men of a side, with the bars running across to both sides of the bridge, to hinder any person from passing over it either to the one side or the other; and in the river there was only one little boat rowed by two men, to convey over such as had a mind to cross it . . .

*i.e. level and open; unenclosed.

The barrier being finished, and the place fitted for the interview, as you have already heard, on the next day, which was the 29th August, 1475, the two kings appeared. The King of France came first, attended by about eight hundred men-at-arms: on the King of England's side, his whole army was drawn up in order of battle; and though we could not discover their whole force, yet we saw such a vast number both of horse and foot, that the body of troops that were with us seemed very inconsiderable in comparison with them; but indeed the fourth part of our army was not there. It was given out that twelve men of a side were to be with each of the kings at the inteniew, and that they were already chosen from among their greatest and most trusty courtiers. With us we had four of the King of England's party to view what was done among us, and they had as many of ours, on their side, to have an eye over their actions. As I said before, our king came first to the barrier, attended by twelve persons; among whom were John, Duke of Bourbon, and the Cardinal his brother. It was the king's royal pleasure (according to an old and common custom that he had), that I should be dressed like him on that day.

The King of England advanced along the causeway (which I mentioned before) very nobly attended, with the air and presence of a king: there were in his train his brother the Duke of Clarence, the Earl of Northumberland, his chamberlain the Lord Hastings, his chancellor, and other peers of the realm; among whom there were not above three or four dressed in cloth of gold like himself. The King of England wore a black velvet cap upon his head, with a large fleur de lys made of precious stones upon it: he was a prince of a noble and majestic presence, but a little inclining to corpulence. I had seen him before when the Earl of Warwick drove him out of his kingdom; then I thought him much handsomer, and to the best of my remembrance, my eyes had never beheld a more handsome person. When he came within a little distance of the barrier, he pulled off his cap, and bowed himself within half a foot of the ground; and the King of France, who was then leaning against the barrier, received him with abundance of reverence and respect. They embraced through the holes of the grate, and the King of England making him another low bow, the King of France saluted him thus: 'Cousin, you are heartily welcome; there is no person living I was so ambitious of seeing, and God be thanked that this interview is upon so good an occasion.' The King of England returned the compliment in very good French.

Then the Chancellor of England (who was a prelate, and Bishop of Lisle)* began his speech with a prophecy (with which the English are always provided) that at Pécquiguy a memorable peace was to be concluded between the English and French. After he had finished his harangue, the instrument was produced which contained the articles the King of France had sent to the King of England. The chancellor demanded of our king, whether he had dictated the said articles? and whether he agreed to them? The king replied, Yes: and King Edward's letters being produced on our side, he made the same answer. The missal being then brought and opened, both the kings laid one of their hands upon the book, and the other upon the holy true cross, and both of them swore religiously to observe the contents of the truce, which was, that it should stand firm and good for nine years complete; that the allies on both sides should be comprehended; and that the marriage between their children should be consummated, as was stipulated by the said treaty. After the two kings had sworn to observe the treaty, our king (who had always words at command) told the King of England in a jocular way, he should be glad to see his majesty at Paris; and that if he would come and divert himself with the ladies, he would assign him the Cardinal of Bourbon for his confessor, who he knew would willingly absolve him, if he should commit any sin by way of love and gallantry. The King of England was extremely pleased with his raillery, and made his majesty several good repartees, for he knew the cardinal was a jolly companion.

After some discourse to this purpose, our king, to show his authority, commanded us who attended him to withdraw, for he had a mind to have a little private discourse with the King of England. We obeyed, and those who were with the King of England, seeing us retire, did the same, without waiting to be commanded. After the two kings had been alone together for some time, our master called me to him, and asked the King of England if he knew me? The King of England replied he did, and named the places where he had seen me, and told the king that

*Thomas Rotheram, Bishop of Rochester (1468–72); Lincoln (1472–80), Archbishop of York (1480–1500).

formerly I had endeavoured to serve him at Calais, when I was in the Duke of Burgundy's service. The King of France demanded, if the Duke of Burgundy refused to be comprehended in the treaty (as might be expected from his obstinate answer), what the King of England would have him do? The King of England replied, he would offer it him again, and if he refused it then, he would not concern himself any farther, but leave it entirely to themselves. By degrees the king came to mention the Duke of Bretagne (who indeed was the person he aimed at in the question), and made the same demand about him. The King of England desired he would not attempt anything against the Duke of Bretagne, for in his necessity he had never found so true and faithful a friend. The king pressed him no farther, but recalling his retinue, took his leave of the King of England in the handsomest and most civil terms imaginable, and saluted all his attendants in a most particular manner: and both the kings at a time (or very near it) retired from the barrier, and mounting on horseback, the King of France returned to Amiens, and the King of England to his army. The King of England was accommodated by the King of France with whatever he wanted, even to the very torches and candles. The Duke of Gloucester, the King of England's brother, and some other persons of quality, were not present at this interview, as being adverse to the treaty; but they recollected themselves afterwards, and the Duke of Gloucester waited on the king our master at Amiens, where he was splendidly entertained, and nobly presented both with plate and fine horses.

. . . The next day, a great number of English came to Amiens, some of whom reported that the Holy Ghost had made that peace, and prophecies were produced to confirm it; but their greatest argument to support this opinion was that, during the time of their interview, a white pigeon came and sat upon the King of England's tent, and could not be frightened away by any noise they could make in the camp. But some gave another reason, and that was, that a small shower of rain having fallen that day, and soon after the sun shining out very warmly, the poor pigeon, finding that tent higher than the rest, came thither only to dry herself.(7)

War in the Middle Ages was a cooperative enterprise. From the monarch's point of view the Treaty of Pécquigny had been a remarkably profitable end to the French campaign. Many of those who had crossed the Channel cherishing dreams of the lucrative ransom traffic and booty of the early years of the century hardly saw it in the same light. For them the whole incident had been so much wasted effort and bitter disappointment. The Croyland Chronicler describes the army's return home:

Accordingly, our lord the king returned to England, having thus concluded an honourable treaty of peace: for in this light it was regarded by the higher officers of the royal army, although there is nothing so holy or of so high a sanction, that it may not have contempt thrown upon it by being ill spoken of. Indeed, some persons immediately began to cavil at peace being thus concluded, but these soon received condign punishment for their presumption. Others, on their return home, betook themselves to theft and rapine, so that no road throughout England was left in a state of safety for either merchants or pilgrims.

Upon this, our lord the king was compelled, in person, together with his judges, to make a survey of the kingdom; and no one, not even his own domestic, did he spare, but instantly had him hanged, if he was found to be guilty of theft or murder. These rigorous sentences being universally carried into execution, public acts of robbery were soon put a stop to for a considerable time. However, if this prudent prince had not manfully put an end to this commencement of mischief, the number of people complaining of the unfair management of the resources of the kingdom, in consequence of such quantities of treasure being abstracted from the coffers of each and uselessly consumed, would have increased to such a degree that no one could have said whose head, among the king's advisers, was in safety: and the more especially those, who, induced by friendship for the French king, or by his presents, had persuaded the king to make peace in manner previously mentioned.(8)

Edward (or whoever was responsible for his policy in the early months of his reign) had taken to heart the financial lessons of Henry VI's reign – that taxation bred discontent, and the Commons' demand that the king should 'live of his own' by a careful administration of his hereditary revenues. Edward's demands for direct taxation were comparatively few. With an Act of

Resumption in 1461 he immediately transformed the Commons' demands of the 1450s into his official policy. As early as 1462 he began to reorganize the management of the Crown lands, with such success that in January 1468 he made this statement in parliament:

> John Say,* and ye Sirs, comen to this my court of parliament for the common of this my land. The cause why I have called and summoned this my present parliament is, that I purpose to live upon mine own, and not to charge my subjects but in great and urgent causes, concerning more the wealth of them self, and also the defence of them and of this my realm, rather than mine own pleasure, as heretofore by commons of this land hath been done and borne unto my progenitors in time of need; wherein I trust that ye sirs, and all the common of this my land, will be as tender and kind unto me in such cases, as heretofore any commons have been to any of my said progenitors. And for the good wills, kindness, and true hearts that ye have borne, continued and shewed unto me at all times heretofore, I thank you as heartily as I can, as so I trust ye will continue in time coming; for the which by the grace of God, I shall be to you as good and gracious king, and reign as rightwisely upon you, as ever did any of my progenitors upon commons of this my realm in days past; and shall also, in time of need, apply my person for the weal and defence of you and of this my realm, not sparing my body nor life for any jeopardy that might happen to the same.(9)

After his return in 1471 he vigorously continued this policy of financial reform, paying off old debts, building up a financial reserve, insisting on economy in the royal household, tightening up the administration of the customs system, insisting on a stringent administration of the Crown lands and rigidly enforcing his feudal rights of escheat, wardship and marriage. Around 1475 Godfrey Green wrote to his friend and patron Sir William Plumpton about how difficult it had become to obtain lucrative offices on the Crown lands:

> And as for the labour for the bailliships and farms, Sir, your worship understands what labour is to sue therefore; first, to have a bill enclosed

*Sir John Say, Speaker of the Commons.

of the king, then to certain lords of the council, (for there is an act made that nothing shall pass fro the king unto time they have seen it), and so to the privy seal and chancellor; so the labour is so importunate, that I cannot attend it without I should do nothing else, and scarcely in a month speed one matter.(10)

In August 1478 Sir John Paston wrote to his brother John the Youngest on the dangerous subject of the king's feudal rights:

Item, young William Brandon is in ward and arrested for that he should have by force ravished and swived* an old gentlewoman, and yet was not therewith eased, but swived her oldest daughter, and then would have swived the other sister both; wherefore men say foul of him, and that he would eat the hen and all her chickens; and some say that the king intendeth to sit upon him, and men say he is like to be hanged, for he hath wedded a widow.†(11)

Edward's policy of conserving the royal resources, very much in line with Sir John Fortescue's ideas, was not to everybody's taste. The dispossessed captains of the French wars – there were still a good many survivors though their outlook by this time was somewhat passé – dreamed very different dreams. *The Boke of Noblesse*** reveals their opinions.

Moreover, your poor commons, in your antecessour days, not paid wholly their duties† for their loans, prests‡ of victuals and other merchandise, as by open example was oftentimes lent and taken to the behofe of your predecessor Henry sixth, named king, but in sundry wises be delayed and despend§ great part of their good, ere they can

---

*i.e. copulated with.
†Brandon shortly afterwards received a pardon for marrying a widow without royal licence.
***The Boke of Noblesse* was written in the 1450s, then revised and presented to Edward IV just before the French campaign of 1475.
†i e. dues, debts.
‡i.e. advances.
§i.e. spend, lay out.

nigh their duties and payments, and fain to suffer to defalk and release party of their duty to receive the other part, which is the cause of great charge and hindrance of your people. And therefore, to void this inconvenient, right noble king, with the discreet advice of your noble lords, let your rich treasures be spread and put abroad, both jewels, vessel of gold and silver, among your true subjects, and in especially to the help and avancement of your conquest, and to the relief of your indigent and needy people. And in especially to tho that have lost their lands, livelode, and good in the wars, so that the said treasure may be put forth, and let it be set in money to the remedy and succour of this great importunity and necessity, and to the defence of your realm from your adversaries before specified; for it is said that an empire of a realm is better without treasure of gold than without worship, and also better it is to live a poor life in a rich realm in tranquillity and peace than to be rich in a poor realm where debate and strife reigneth. And if ye will do thus, every man then in his degree will do the same. And to example of us all ye so puissant and mighty men of good counsel and stere,* every man help after his degree.(12)

The king ignored their grievances. The Croyland Continuator, not wholeheartedly approving, summed up his financial methods and their results. The chronicler wrote that fearing disastrous political consequences from demands for direct taxation, Edward, by other means made himself far richer than any of his predecessors: by acts of resumption, more stringent administration of the customs system, feudal incidents and dues, the yearly pension from France and trading ventures, ' . . . like a private individual living by trade, exchanged merchandise for merchandise, by means of his factors, among both Italians and Greeks.'

Once again, however, family quarrels disturbed the king's peace. To George, Duke of Clarence, modesty and self-effacement were unknown virtues. Always disgruntled, his discontent grew ever stronger from the time when he had been forced to share the Neville inheritance with his brother Gloucester. By 1477 he had openly shown prolonged and dangerous discontent over resumptions; he had, against the king's determined opposition, considered dangerous and undesirable foreign marriages, had

*i.e. vigorous activity.

procured a judicial murder and was finally, if rather vaguely, accused of plotting to obtain the crown. The fullest, though at key points somewhat evasive, comment is that of the Croyland Chronicler:[3]

In returning to the history of this kingdom, and recalling to memory by what glory and tranquillity King Edward had rendered himself illustrious, after having gathered together treasures innumerable from the French tribute and the other particulars previously mentioned, let us subJoin certain matters that will admit of no denial. A new dissension, which sprang up shortly after, between him and his brother, the Duke of Clarence, very greatly tarnished the glories of this most prudent king. For that duke now seemed gradually more and more to estrange himself from the king's presence, hardly ever to utter a word in council, and not without reluctance to eat or drink in the king's abode. On account of this interrruption of their former friendship, many thought that the duke was extremely sore at heart, because, on the occasion of the general resumption which the king had lately made in parliament,* the duke had lost the noble demesne of Tutbury, and several other lands, which he had formerly obtained by royal grant.

In the meantime, Charles, Duke of Burgundy . . . subjected the whole of Lorraine to his arms. Proceeding onwards, most boldly, not to say rashly, (—)† the third time that he engaged with the people who are at the present day commonly called Switzers, a battle was fought on the day of the Epiphany, in which he was defeated, and met his death; it being in the year of our Lord, according to the Roman computation, 1477. This piece of foreign history I have here inserted, because it was universally mentioned that after the death of Charles, his widow, the Duchess, Lady Margaret, whose affections were fixed on her brother Clarence beyond any of the rest of her kindred, exerted all her strength and energies that Mary, the only daughter and heir of the said Duke Charles deceased, might be united in marriage to that duke, whose wife had recently died. So great a contemplated exaltation as this, however, of his ungrateful brother, displeased the king. He consequently threw all possible impediments in the way, in order that

*In 1473.
†There is a gap in the text here.

the match before-mentioned might not be carried into effect, and exerted all his influence that the heiress might be given in marriage to Maximilian, the son of the Emperor; which was afterwards effected.

The indignation of the duke was probably still further increased by this; and now each began to look upon the other with no very fraternal eyes. You might then have seen (as such men are generally to be found in the courts of all princes), flatterers running to and fro, from the one side to the other, and carrying backwards and forwards the words which had fallen from the two brothers, even if they had happened to be spoken in the most secret closet. The arrest of the duke for the purpose of compelling him to answer the charges brought against him, happened under the following circumstances. One Master John Stacy, a person who was called an astronomer, when in reality he was rather a great sorcerer, formed a plot in conjunction with one Burdet, an esquire, and one of the said duke's household; upon which, he was accused, among numerous other charges, of having made leaden images and other things to procure thereby the death of Richard, Lord Beauchamp, at the request of his adulterous wife. Upon being questioned in a very severe examination as to his practice of damnable arts of this nature, he made confession of many matters, which told both against himself and the said Thomas Burdet. The consequence was, that Thomas was arrested as well; and at last judgment of death was pronounced upon them both, at Westminster, from the Bench of our lord the king, the judges being there seated, together with nearly all the lords temporal of the kingdom. Being drawn to the gallows at Tyburn, they were permitted briefly to say what they thought fit before being put to death; upon which, they protested their innocence, Stacy indeed but faintly; while, on the other hand, Burdet spoke at great length, and with much spirit, and, as his last word, exclaimed with Susanna, 'Behold! I must die; whereas I never did such things as these.'

On the following day, the Duke of Clarence came to the council chamber at Westminster, bringing with him a famous doctor of the order of Minorites, Master William Goddard by name,* in order that he

---

*Not William but John Goddard. A supremely tactless choice as he had preached on Henry VI's right to the throne at St Paul's Cross on 30 September 1470.

might read the confession and declaration of innocence above-
mentioned before the lords in the said council assembled; which he
accordingly did, and then withdrew. The king was then at Windsor, but
when he was informed of this circumstance, he was greatly displeased
thereat, and recalling to mind the information formerly laid against his
brother, and which he had long kept treasured up in his breast, he
summoned the duke to appear on a certain day in the royal palace of
Westminster: upon which, in presence of the mayor and aldermen of
the City of London, the king began, with his own lips, amongst other
matters, to inveigh against the conduct of the before-named duke, as
being derogatory to the laws of the realm, and most dangerous to
judges and jurors throughout the kingdom. But why enlarge? The duke
was placed in custody, and from that day up to the time of his death
never was known to have regained his liberty.

The circumstances that happened in the ensuing parliament my
mind quite shudders to enlarge upon, for then was to be witnessed a
sad strife carried on before these two brethren of such high estate.*
For not a single person uttered a word against the duke, except the
king; not one individual made answer to the king, except the duke.
Some parties were introduced, however, as to whom it was greatly
doubted by many, whether they filled the office of accusers rather, or
of witnesses: these two offices not being exactly suited to the same
person in the same cause. The duke met all the charges made against
him with a denial, and offered, if he could only obtain a hearing, to
defend his cause with his own hand. But why delay in using many
words? Parliament, being of opinion that the informations which
they had heard were established, passed sentence upon him of
condemnation, the same being pronounced by the mouth of Henry,
Duke of Buckingham, who was appointed Seneschal of England for
the occasion. After this, execution was delayed for a considerable
time; until the Speaker of the Commons, coming to the upper house
with his fellows, made a fresh request that the matter might be
brought to a conclusion. In consequence of this, in a few days after,

*Thus Riley translates 'tantae humanitatis' claiming that it can hardly be rendered 'of
such great humanity' when applied to men like these. On the other hand the author's
words may have been ironic.

the execution, whatever its nature may have been,* took place (and would that it had ended these troubles!) in the tower of London . . . (13)

Sir Thomas More and the Croyland Chronicler describe Edward's last peaceful years. More, who was certainly no advocate of loose living, wrote an indulgent, even tender, account of the king's mistress, Jane Shore:

This woman was born in London, worshipfully friended, honestly brought up, and very well married, saving somewhat too soon, her husband an honest citizen, young and goodly and of good substance. But forasmuch as they were coupled ere she were well ripe, she not very fervently loved, for whom she had never longed. Which was haply the thing that the more easily made her incline unto the king's appetite when he required her. Howbeit, the respect of his royalty, the hope of gay apparel, ease, pleasure, and other wanton wealth, was able soon to pierce a soft, tender heart. But when the king had abused her, anon her husband (as he was an honest man and one that could his good,† and not presuming to touch a king's concubine) left her up to him altogether. When the king died, the Lord Chamberlain took her, which in the king's days, albeit he was sore enamoured upon her, yet he forbore her, either for reverence or for a certain friendly faithfulness. Proper she was and fair, nothing in her body that you would have changed, but if you would have wished her somewhat higher. Thus say they that knew her in her youth, albeit some that now see her (for yet she liveth) deem her never to have been well visaged. Whose judgment seemeth me somewhat like as though men should guess the beauty of one long before departed by her scalp** taken out of the charnel house: for now is she old, lean, withered, and dried up, nothing left but rivelled‡ skin and hard bone. And yet, being even such, whoso well advise her visage might guess and devise which parts how filled would

*The legend that Clarence was drowned in a butt of Malmsey is most probably true.
†i.e. knew his advantage.
**i.e. skull.
‡i.e. shrivelled.

make it it a fair face. Yet delighted not men so much in her beauty as in her pleasant behaviour. For a proper wit had she, and could both read well and write, merry in company, ready and quick of answer, neither mute nor full of babble, somtimes taunting without displeasure and not without disport. The king would say that he had three concubines which in three divers properties diversely excelled: one the merriest, another the wiliest, the third the holiest harlot in his realm, as one whom no man could get out of the church lightly to any place, but it were to his bed. The other two were somewhat greater personages, and nevertheless of their humility content to be nameless and to forbear the praise of those properties. But the merriest was this Shore's wife, in whom the king therefore took special pleasure, for many he had, but her he loved, whose favour, to say the truth (for sin it were to belie the devil), she never abused to any man's hurt, but to many a man's comfort and relief. Where the king took displeasure, she would mitigate and appease his mind; where men were out of favour, she would bring them in his grace; for many that had highly offended, she obtained pardon; of great forfeitures she got men remission; and finally, in many weighty suits she stood many men in great stead, either for none or very small rewards, and those rather gay than rich; either for that she was content with the deed self well done, or for that she delighted to be sued unto and to show what she was able to do with the king, or for that wanton women and wealthy be not always covetous. I doubt not some shall think this woman too slight a thing to be written of and set among the remembrances of great matters: which they shall specially think, that haply shall esteem her only by that they now see her. But meseemeth the chance so much the more worthy to be remembered, in how much she is now in the more beggarly condition, unfriended and worn out of acquaintance, after good substance, after as great favour with the prince, after as great suit and seeking to with all those that those days had business to speed, as many other men were in their times, which now be famous only by the infamy of their ill deeds. Her doings were not much less, albeit they be much less remembered because they were not so evil. For men use, if they have an evil turn, to write it in marble; and whoso doth us a good turn, we write it in dust: which is not worse proved by her, for at this day she beggeth of many at this day living, that at this day had begged if she had not been. (14)

Edward died on 9 April 1483:

... neither worn out with old age' (as the Croyland writer said) nor yet seized with any known kind of malady, the cure of which would not have appeared easy in the case of a person of more humble rank, took to his bed.* This happened about the feast of Easter; and, on the ninth day of April, he rendered up his spirit to his Creator, at his palace of Westminster ...

This prince, although in his day he was thought to have indulged his passions and desires too intemperately, was still, in religion, a most devout Catholic, a most unsparing enemy to all heretics, and a most loving encourager of wise and learned men, and of the clergy. He was also a most devout reverer of the Sacraments of the Church, and most sincerely repentant for all his sins. This is testified by those who were present on the occasion of his decease; to whom, and especially to those whom he left as executors of his last will, he declared, in a distinct and Catholic form, that it was his desire that, out of the chattels which he left behind him in such great abundance, satisfaction should be made, either fully, or on a composition made voluntarily, and without extortion on their part, to all those persons to whom he was, by contract extortion, fraud, or any other mode, indebted. Such was the most beseeming end of this worldly prince, a better than which could not be hoped for or conceived, after the manifestation by him of so large a share of the frailties inherent to the lot of mankind. Hence, too, very strong hopes were afforded to all his faithful servants, that he would not fail to receive the reward of eternal salvation. For after like Zaccheus, he had expressed his wish that one half of his goods should be given unto the poor, and that if he had defrauded any one of aught, the same should be returned to him fourfold. I shall be silent upon the circumstance which might have been mentioned above in a more befittingplace that men of every rank, condition, and degree of experience, throughout the kingdom, wondered that a man of such

---

*There has been a good deal of speculation about the cause of Edward's death whether from fever, over-eating, or to chagrin at the failure of his last diplomatic schemes. His latest biographer, Charles Ross, on balance, attributes it to some form of stroke brought on by years of gluttony and excessive high living.

corpulence, and so fond of boon companionship, vanities, debauchery, extravagance, and sensual enjoyments, should have had a memory so retentive, in all respects, that the names and estates used to recur to him, just as though he had been in the habit of seeing them daily, of nearly all the persons dispersed throughout the counties of this kingdom; and this even, if, in the districts in which they lived, they held the rank only of a private gentleman.(15)

To the views of this well-informed English writer, most probably one of Edward's own councillors, or at least closely connected with one of them, we may add those of an Italian visitor, Dominic Mancini:*

Edward was of a gentle nature and cheerful aspect: nevertheless should he assume an angry countenance he could appear very terrible to beholders. He was easy of access to his friends and to others, even the least notable. Frequently he called to his side complete strangers, when he thought that they had come with the intention of addressing or beholding him more closely. He was wont to show himself to those who wished to watch him, and he seized any opportunity that the occasion offered of revealing his fine stature more protractedly and more evidently to on-lookers. He was so genial in his greeting, that if he saw a newcomer bewildered at his appearance and royal magnificence, he would give him courage to speak by laying a kindly hand upon his shoulder. To plaintiffs and to those who complained of injustice he lent a willing ear; charges against himself he contented with an excuse if he did not remove the cause. He was more favourable than other princes to foreigners, who visited his realm for trade or any other reason. He very seldom showed munificence, and only in moderation, still he was very grateful to those from whom he had received a favour. Though not rapacious of other men's goods, he was yet so eager for money, that in pursuing it he acquired a reputation for avarice. He adopted this artifice for piling up wealth: when an assembly from the whole kingdom was convened, he would set forth how he had incurred many expenses, and must unavoidably prepare for much

*For Mancini see below p. 185.

further expenditure by land and sea for the defence of the realm. It was just, he said, that these sums should be repaid by the public in whose benefit they were spent.*

Thus, by appealing to causes, either true or at least with some semblance of truth, he did not appear to extort but almost to beg for subsidies. He behaved similarly with private individuals, but with them at times more imperiously: and so he had gathered great treasures, whose size had not made him more generous or prompt in disbursement than when he was poor, but rather much more stringent and tardy, so that now his avarice was publicly proclaimed. For the same reason he is believed to have abandoned the Flemings, for, had he given them succour against Louis [XI] the King of France, he would have ceased to receive from Louis fifty thousand scuts each year. He knew that he would receive them just as long as he refrained from assisting the Flemings.

In food and drink he was most immoderate: it was his habit, so I have learned, to take an emetic for the delight of gorging his stomach once more. For this reason and for the ease, which was especially dear to him after his recovery of the Crown, he had grown fat in the loins, whereas previously he had been not only tall but rather lean and very active. He was licentious in the extreme: moreover it was said that he had been most insolent to numerous women after he had seduced them, for, as soon as he grew weary of dalliance, he gave up the ladies much against their will to the other courtiers. He pursued with no discrimination the married and unmarried, the noble and lowly: however he took none by force. He overcame all by money and promises, and having conquered them, he dismissed them. Although he had many promoters and companions of his vices, the more important and especial were three of the afore-mentioned relatives of the queen, her two sons and one of her brothers. On the other hand, Lord Ryvers was always considered a kind, serious, and just man, and one tested by every vicissitude of life. Whatever his prosperity he had injured nobody, though benefiting many: and therefore he had entrusted to him the care and direction of the king's eldest son. The other three earned the

---

*This was not so unusual as Mancini implies. It was, in fact, a common technique of raising money in the later Middle Ages. See G.L. Harriss, 'Aids, Loans and Benevolences', *The Historical Journal*, vi (1963), 1–19.

hatred of the populace, on account of their morals, but mostly because of a certain inherent jealousy which arises between those who are equal by birth when there has been a change in their station. They were certainly detested by the nobles, because they, who were ignoble and newly made men, were advanced beyond those who far excelled them in breeding and wisdom. They had to endure the imputation brought against them by all, of causing the death of the Duke of Clarence. There were at the same time three others of no small influence with the king, and ones who must not be omitted from the narrative, because in this revolution they were to play the lesser parts. The first was Thomas Rotheram, Archbishop of York, and at the same time lord chancellor; another was the Bishop of Ely [John Morton], and the third was the king's chamberlain, by name Hastings. Now these men being in age mature, and instructed by long experience of public affairs, helped more than other councillors to form the king's policy, and besides carried it out. But Hastings was not only the author of the sovereign's public policy, as being one that had shared every peril with the king, but was also the accomplice and partner of his privy pleasures. He maintained a deadly feud with the queen's son, whom we said was called the marquess, and that because of the mistresses whom they had abucted, or attempted to entice from one another. The suborned informers of each had threatened a capital charge against the other. An important factor in this revolution appears to have originated in the dissension of these two: and although at the command and entreaty of the king, who loved each of them, they had been reconciled two days before he died, yet, as the event showed, there still survived a latent jealousy.(16)

NOTES

1. See J.R. Lander, 'Attainder and Forfeiture, 1453–1509', *The Historical Journal*, iv (1961), 127–8.

2. *Commynes*, ii, 27, Bohn's translation, i, 251.

3. The best discussion of these events is in C.L. Scofield, *The Life and Reign of Edward the Fourth* (1923), ii, 174–212.

4. C. Ross, *Edward IV* (London, 1974), 414–415.

5. H.A. Kelly, 'The Last Chroniclers of Croyland', *The Richardian*, vii (1985), 142–177.

FIVE

Richard III

The Italian cleric Dominic Mancini,[1] who wrote the account of Edward IV in the last chapter, came to England, most probably with a papal mission, in the late summer of 1482. Here he stayed until shortly after Richard III's coronation on 6 July 1483. His rich and distinguished patron, Angelo Cato, Archbishop of Vienne, planned to write a Latin history of the reign of Louis XI. To Angelo Cato's zeal for gathering information from men well informed about contemporary events we owe two very interesting books. One is the well-known *Mémoires* of Philippe de Commynes written to supply the archbishop with inside information about the French court: the other is Dominic Mancini's *De Occupatione Regni Anglie per Riccardum Tercium*, written by December 1483, preserved in a unique manuscript in the Bibliothèque Municipale at Lille and printed for the first time only in 1936. Written in the new humanist style Mancini's description of affairs is far superior to that of the English authors of his day, still writing in an old-fashioned, and by comparison, rather naive chronicle tradition. Mancini begins the tale of Richard III's usurpation – with the emergence of the 'latent jealousy' which he had already remarked upon:

> At his [i.e. Edward IV's] death his brother Richard was living on the Gloucester estates, two hundred miles distant from the capital.* Edward, the king's son, who was heir to the throne, was also two hundred miles from the capital, for he was residing in the province of Wales, which always falls to the lot of the king's eldest sons, and gives to these princes their appellation . . . The queen, with her second son, the Duke of York, and the rest of her family, were in London, where was also the

---

*Mancini most probably spent all his time in London. His knowledge of English topography was vague and he wrongly assumed that English, like continental, nobles generally resided at the places which provided their titles.

chamberlain Hastings with the Bishops of York and Ely, whom we recently mentioned as friends of the king. The royal, treasure, the weight of which was said to be immense, was kept in the hands of the queen and her people at an impregnable citadel beside the town.* On completion of the royal obsequies, and while many peers of the realm, who had received neighbouring estates, were collecting in the city, a council assembled before the arrival of the young King Edward and Richard Duke of Gloucester. In this meeting the problem of the government during the royal minority was referred to the consideration of the barons. Two opinions were propounded. One was that the Duke of Gloucester should govern, because Edward in his will† had so directed, and because by law the government ought to devolve on him. But this was the losing resolution; the winning was that the government should be carried on by many persons among whom the duke, so far from being excluded, should be accounted the chief. By this means the duke would be given due honour, and the royal authority greater security; because it had been found that no regent ever laid down his office, save reluctantly, and from armed compulsion, whence civil wars had often arisen. Moreover, if the entire government were committed to one man he might easily usurp the sovereignty. All who favoured the queen's family voted for this proposal, as they were afraid that, if Richard took unto himself the crown or even governed alone, they, who bore the blame for Clarence's death, would suffer death or at least be ejected from their high estate. According to common report, the Chamberlain Hastings reported all these deliberations by letter and messengers to the Duke of Gloucester, because he had a friendship of long standing with the duke, and was hostile to the entire kin of the queen on account of the marquess.‡

*The Tower of London. The size of Edward's treasure is unknown. Most authorities merely state that it disappeared after his death. Mancini alone later states (p. 88–9) that it was divided between the queen, the Marquess of Dorset and Sir Edward Wydeville.
†This statement cannot be checked as Edward's final will has not survived. See *Mancini*, p. 131, n 7.
‡Thomas Grey, Marquess of Dorset, the queen's eldest son by her first husband, Sir John Grey of Groby. Hastings and Dorset are said to have competed for the favours of Edward's mistress, Jane Shore.

Besides, it was reported that he advised the duke to hasten to the capital with a strong force, and avenge the insult done him by his enemies. He might easily obtain his revenge if, before reaching the city, he took the young King Edward under his protection and authority, while seizing before they were alive to the danger those of the king's followers, who were not in agreement with this policy. Hastings added that he was alone in the capital and not without great danger, for he could scarcely escape the snares of his enemies since their old hatred was aggravated by his friendship for the Duke of Gloucester. The latter being advised of these things, and with a view to achieving them more easily, wrote to the council in this fashion. He had been loyal to his brother Edward, at home and abroad, in peace and war, and would be, if only permitted, equally loyal to his brother's son, and to all his brother's issue, even female, if perchance, which God forbid, the youth should die. He would expose his life to every danger that the children might endure in their father's realm. He asked the councillors to take his deserts into consideration, when disposing of the government, to which he was entitled by law,* and his brother's ordinance. Further, he asked them to reach that decision which his services to his brother and to the state alike demanded: and he reminded them that nothing contrary to law and his brother's desire could be decreed without harm. This letter had a great effect on the minds of the people, who, as they had previously favoured the duke in their hearts from a belief in his probity, now began to support him openly and aloud; so that it was commonly said by all that the duke deserved the government. However, the lords, who filled the council, voted in a majority for the alternative policy: and they fixed a day for the coronation, and wrote to the young King Edward that he should reach the capital three days before the date appointed for the coronation. There were, however, in the council, those who said that everything ought not thus to be hurried through; rather they should await the young king's uncle, whom this business greatly concerned, so that he might be present both at the making and executionof such important decisions. Because should they act otherwise, the duke could only accede reluctantly, and perhaps might

*There was, in fact, no definite law on the subject.

upset everything. To this the marquess is said to have replied, 'We are so important, that even without the king's uncle we can make and enforce these decisions.'(1)

Sir Thomas More wrote his History of Richard III in about 1513. It was based on the reminiscences of a wide circle of men, some of whom had been active in Yorkist administration, others partisans in exile with Henry of Richmond.[2] Although biased against the king, and despite the fact that More tended to compose speeches for his characters in a manner condemned by present-day historians, his account of Richard's reign (with some exceptions) is plausible enough. He thus described the Duke of Gloucester's first hostile actions:

The queen, being in this wise persuaded,[*] such word sent unto her son, and unto her brother being about the king; and over that the Duke of Gloucester himself and other lords, the chief of his bend, wrote unto the king so reverently, and to the queen's friends there, so lovingly, that they, nothing earthly mistrusting, brought the king up in great haste, not in good speed, with a sober company. Now was the king in his way to London gone from Northampton, when these Dukes of Gloucester and Buckinghan came thither. Where remained behind the Lord Ryvers, the king's uncle, intending on the morrow to follow the king and be with him at Stony Stratford (—)[†] miles thence, early ere he departed. So was there made that night much friendly cheer between these dukes and the Lord Ryvers a great while. But incontinent after that they were openly with great courtesy departed and the Lord Ryvers lodged, the dukes secretly with a few of their most privy friends set them down in council, wherein they spent a great part of the night. And at their rising in the dawning of the day, they sent about privily to their servants in their inns and lodgings about, giving them commandment to make themselves shortly ready, for their lords were

---

[*] i.e. to agree to a limited escort of soldiers for the prince; 2,000 men according to the Croyland Chronicler, according to whom 'The queen most beneficently tried to extinguish every mark of murmuring and disturbance ...'
[†] Blank in MS. The distance from Northampton to Stony Stratford is fourteen miles.

to horsebackward. Upon which messages, many of their folk were attendant when many of the Lord Ryver's servants were unready. Now had these two dukes taken also into their custody the keys of the inn, that none should pass forth without their licence. And over this, in the highway towards Stony Stratford, where the king lay, they had bestowed certain of their folk that should send back again and compel to return any man that were got out of Northampton towards Stony Stratford, till they should give other licence, forasmuch as the dukes themselves intended, for the show of their diligence, to be the first that should that day attend upon the King's Highness out of that town: thus bore they folk in hand.* But when the Lord Ryvers understood the gates closed and the ways on every side beset, neither his servants nor himself suffered to go out, perceiving well so great a thing without his knowledge not begun for naught, comparing this manner present with this last night's cheer, in so few hours so great a change marvellously misliked. Howbeit, since he could not get away, and keep himself close he would not, lest he should seem to hide himself for some secret fear of his own fault, whereof he saw no such cause in himself, he determined upon the surety of his own conscience to go boldly to them and enquire what this matter might mean. Whom, as soon as they saw, they began to quarrel with him and say that he intended to set distance between the king and them and to bring them to confusion; but it should not lie in his power. And when he began (as he was a very well-spoken man) in goodly wise to excuse himself, they tarried not the end of his answer, but shortly took him and put him in ward, and, that done, forthwith went to horseback and took the way to Stony Stratford, where they found the king with his company ready to leap on horseback and depart forward, to leave that lodging for them, because it was too strait for both companies. And as soon as they came in his presence, they lighted adown with all their company about them, to whom the Duke of Buckingham said, 'Go afore, gentlemen and yeomen; keep your rooms.'‡ And thus in a goodly array they came to the king, and on their knees in very humble wise saluted his Grace, which received them in very joyous and amiable manner, nothing

*i.e. deceived people.
‡i.e. places.

earthly knowing nor mistrusting as yet. But even by and by in his presence they picked a quarrel to the Lord Richard Gray, the king's other brother by his mother, saying that he, with the Lord Marquess, his brother, and the Lord Ryvers, his uncle, had compassed to rule the king and the realm, and to set variance among the states,* and to subdue and destroy the noble blood of the realm. Towards the accomplishing whereof, they said that the Lord Marquess had entered into the Tower of London, and thence taken out the king's treasure,† and sent men to the sea. All which things these dukes wist well were done for good purposes and necessary by the whole Council at London, saving that somewhat they must say. Unto which words, the king answered, 'What my brother Marquess hath done, I cannot say; but in good faith, I dare well answer for mine Uncle Ryvers and my brother here, that they be innocent of any such matters.' 'Yea, my liege,' quoth the Duke of Buckingham, 'they have kept their dealings in these matters far from the knowledge of your good grace.' And forthwith they arrested the Lord Richard and Sir Thomas Vaughan, knight,‡ in the king's presence, and brought the king and all back unto Northampton, where they took again further counsel. And there they sent away from the king whom it pleased them, and set new servants about him, such as liked better them than him. At which dealing he wept and was nothing content; but it booted not. And at dinner the Duke of Gloucester sent a dish from his own table to the Lord Ryvers, praying him to be of good cheer, all should be well enough. And he thanked the duke, and prayed the messenger to bear it to his nephew, the Lord Richard, with the same message for his comfort, who he thought had more need of comfort, as one to whom such adversity was strange. But himself had been all his days in ure therewith,§ and therefore could bear it the better. But for all this comfortable courtesy of the Duke of Gloucester, he sent the Lord Ryvers and the Lord Richard, with Sir Thomas Vaughan, into the north

*i.e. lords.
†See above p. 186.
‡Edward IV's Treasurer of the Chamber (1464–83) and a member of the prince's council at Ludlow.
§i.e. experienced therein.

country into divers places to prison, and afterwards all to Pomfret, where they were in conclusion beheaded ...

In this wise the Duke of Gloucester took upon himself the order and governance of the young king, whom with much honour and humble reverence he conveyed upward towards the city. But anon the tidings of this matter came hastily to the queen, a little before the midnight following, and that in the sorest wise, that the king, her son, was taken, her brother, her son and her other friends arrested, and sent no man wist wither, to be done with God wot what. With which tidings the queen, in great flight* and heaviness, bewailing her child's ruin, her friends' mischance, and her own infortune, damning the time that ever she dissuaded the gathering of power about the king, got herself in all the haste possible with her younger son and her daughters out of the Palace of Westminster, in which she then lay, into the Sanctuary, lodging herself and her company there in the Abbot's place.

Now came there one in likewise not long after midnight, from the Lord Chamberlain unto the Archbishop of York, then Chancellor of England, to his place not far from Westminster. And for that he showed his servants that he had tidings of so great importance that his master gave him in charge not to forbear his rest, they letted not to wake him, nor he to admit this messenger in to his bedside, of whom he heard that these dukes were gone back with the King's Grace from Stony Stratford unto Northampton. 'Notwithstanding, Sir,' quoth he, 'my Lord sendeth your Lordship word that there is no fear, for he assureth you that all shall be well.' 'I assure him' quoth the archbishop, 'be it as well as it will, it will never be so well as we have seen it.' And thereupon, by and by, after the messenger departed, he caused in all haste all his servants to be called up and so, with his own household about him, and every man weaponed, he took the great seal with him, and came, yet before day, unto the queen. About whom he found much heaviness, rumble, haste and business, carriage and conveyance of her stuff into Sanctuary, chests, coffers, packs, fardels, trusses, all on men's backs, no man unoccupied, some lading, some going, some discharging, some coming for more, some breaking down the walls to bring in the next†

*i.e. agitation.
†i.e. nearest.

way, and some yet drew to them that helped to carry a wrong way. The queen herself sat alone, alow on the rushes, all desolate and dismayed – whom the archbishop comforted in the best manner he could, showing her that he trusted the matter was nothing so sore as she took it for, and that he was put in good hope and out of fear by the message sent him from the Lord Chamberlain. 'Ah, woe worth him!' quoth she, 'for he is one of them that laboureth to destroy me and my blood.' 'Madam,' quoth he, 'be ye of good cheer. For I assure you if they crown any other king than your son, whom they now have with them, we shall on the morrow crown his brother, whom you have here with you. And here is the great seal, which in likewise as that noble prince, your husband, delivered it unto me, so here I deliver it unto you, to the use and behoof of your son.' And therewith he betook her the great seal, and departed home again, yet in the dawning of the day. By which time he might in his chamber window see all the Thames full of boats of the Duke of Gloucester's servants, watching that no man should go to Sanctuary, nor none could pass unsearched. Then was there great commotion and murmur, as well in other places about as specially in the city, the people diversely divining upon this dealing. And some lords, knights, and gentlemen, either for favour of the queen, or for fear of themselves, assembled in sundry companies and went flockmele* in harness, and many also for they reckoned this demeanour attempted not so specially against other lords as against the king himself in the disturbance of his coronation. But then, by and by, the lords assembled together at (—).‡ Towards which meeting the Archbishop of York, fearing that it would be ascribed (as it was indeed) to his over much lightness that he so suddenly had yielded up the great seal to the queen, to whom the custody thereof nothing pertained, without especial commandment of the king, secretly sent for the seal again, and brought it with him after the customable manner.[3](2)

According to Dominic Mancini sinister rumours were already spreading that the Duke of Gloucester intended to seize the crown. Gloucester, however, wrote to the council and to the Mayor of London that his nephew

†i.e. in groups.
‡Blank in MS.

would be crowned at an early date and a few days later brought the boy to London with a guard of five hundred of his own and Buckingham's adherents. By various devices they attempted to whip up public hostility against the queen's friends and supporters and by (unsuccessfully) accusing some of his opponents of treason. His next aggressive move was to surround the Westminster Sanctuary with troops and terrify the queen into surrendering to him her second son, the Duke of York. He also ordered that the Duke of Clarence's young son should be brought to London. Mancini continues:

Having got into his power all the blood royal of the land, yet he considered that his prospects were not sufficiently secure, without the removal or imprisonment of those who had been the closest friends of his brother, and were expected to be loyal to his brother's offspring. In this class he thought to include Hastings, the king's chamberlain; Thomas Rotheram, whom shortly before he had relieved of his office; and the Bishop of Ely.* Now Hastings had been from an early age a loyal companion of Edward, and an active soldier; while Thomas, though of humble origin, had become, thanks to his talent, a man of note with King Edward, and had worked for many years in the Chancery. As for the Bishop of Ely, he was of great resource and daring, for he had been trained in party intrigue since King Henry's time; and being taken into Edward's favour after the annihilation of King Henry's party, he enjoyed great influence. Therefore the protector rushed headlong into crime, for fear that the ability and authority of these men might be detrimental to him: for he had sounded their loyalty through the Duke of Buckingham, and learnt that sometimes they forgathered in each other's houses. One day these three and several others came to the Tower about ten o'clock to salute the protector, as was their custom. When they had been admitted to the innermost quarters, the protector, as prearranged, cried out that an ambush had been prepared for him, and they had come with hidden arms, that they might be first to open the attack. Thereupon the soldiers, who had been stationed there by their lord, rushed in with the Duke of Buckingham, and cut

*John Morton.

down Hastings on the false pretext of treason;* they arrested the others, whose life, it was presumed, was spared out of respect for religion and holy orders. Thus fell Hastings, killed not by those enemies he had always feared, but by a friend whom he had never doubted. But whom will insane lust for power spare, if it dares violate the ties of kin and friendship? After this execution had been done in the citadel, the townsmen, who had heard the uproar but were uncertain of the cause, became panic-stricken, and each one seized his weapons. But, to calm the multitude, the duke instantly sent a herald to proclaim that a plot had been detected in the citadel, and Hastings, the originator of the plot, had paid the penalty; wherefore he bade them all be reassured. At first the ignorant crowd believed, although the real truth was on the lips of many, namely that the plot had been feigned by the duke so as to escape the odium of such a crime . . .

He went on to discuss Richard's attitude:

. . . Thus far, though all the evidence looked as if he coveted the crown, yet there remained some hope, because he was not yet claiming the throne, inasmuch as he still professed to do all these things as an avenger of treason and old wrongs, and because all private deeds and official documents bore the titles and name of King Edward V. But after Hastings was removed, all the attendants who had waited upon the king were debarred access to him. He and his brother were withdrawn into the inner apartments of the Tower proper, and day by day began to be seen more rarely behind the bars and windows, till at length they ceased to appear altogether. Dr Argentine,[4] the last of his attendants whose services the king enjoyed, reported that the young king, like a victim prepared for sacrifice, sought remission of his sins by daily confession and penance, because he believed that death was facing him . . . I have seen many men burst forth into tears and lamentations when mention was made of him after his removal from men's sight; and already there was a suspicion that he had been done away with.

---

*Other contemporary authorities state that: (1) Hastings had gone to the Tower to attend a council meeting, was there accused of conspiracy and (2) he was taken out and beheaded.

Whether, however, he has been done away with, and by what manner of death, so far I have not at all discovered.(3)

When Polydore Vergil of Urbino first came to England in 1502 as deputy to the collector of papal revenues he was already an author of international reputation. History written in the new Italian humanist style was already regarded as good propaganda in courts north of the Alps: Paolo Aemiliani had been writing the history of the French monarchy since 1499. Henry VII had good reason to favour the production, in the new fashionable style, of a defence of his dynasty for its effect abroad. Polydore was seriously working on his *Anglia Historia* by 1506 and the first draft was finished by 1513. He had ample opportunity to discuss the events of Richard III's day with men who had taken a prominent part in them – though his general interpretation is, as one would expect, hostile:

> . . . revolving many matters in his mind, at last he bethought him of a device whereby the people, being seduced by a certain honest pretence, should the less grudge at his doings. And so the man, being blind with covetousness of reigning, whom no foul fact could now hold back, after that he had resolved not to spare the blood of his own house, supposing also all regard of honour was to be rejected, devised and bethought himself of such a sleight as followeth: He had secret conference with one Ralph Shaa,* a divine of great reputation as then among the people, to whom he uttered, that his father's inheritance ought to descend to him by right, as the eldest of all the sons which Richard his father the Duke of York had begotten of Cecily his wife; for as much as it was manifest enough, and that by apparent argument, thatf Edward, who had before reigned, was a bastard,† that is, not begotten of a right and lawful wife; praying the said Shaa to instruct the people thereof in a sermon at Paul's Cross, whereby they might once in the end acknowledge their true liege lord. And said that he greatly required the same, because he esteemed it more meet to neglect his mother's honour and honesty than to suffer so noble a realm to be polluted with such a race of kings . . .

*The brother of the Mayor of London.
†Accusations that Edward was illegitmate were an old scandal by this time (see *Mancini*, p. 133, n 12).

Shaa duly delivered his sermon at St Paul's in the presence of Richard, 'with a great guard of men armed', accusing the Duchess Cecily of adultery, stigmatizing Edward IV as a bastard and exhorting the nobility to make Gloucester king:

> . . . the true issue of the royal blood, and to forsake all others basely begot. When the people heard these words, they were wondrous vehemently troubled in mind therewith, as men who, abashed with the shamefulness of the matter, all to be cursed and detested as well the rashness, foolhardiness, and doltishness of the preacher as the madness of Richard the duke's wicked mind, who would not see how great shame it was to his own house and to the whole realm, how great dishonour and blot, to condemn, in open audience, his mother of adultery, a woman of most pure and honourable life; to imprint upon his excellent and good brother the note of perpetual reproach. Wherefore at the very instant you might have seen some, astonished with the novelty and strangeness of the thing, stand as mad men in a maze; others, all aghast with th'outrageous cruelty of th'horrible fact, to be in great fear of themselves because they were friends to the king's children; others, finally, to bewail the misfortune of the children, whom they ajudged now utterly undone. But there is a common report that King Edward's children were in that sermon called bastards, and not King Edward, which is void of all truth;* for Cecily, King Edward's mother, as is before said, being falsely accused of adultery, complained afterward in sundry places to right many noble men, whereof some yet live, of that great injury which her son Richard had done her . . .
>
> . . . Now by these means was it thought that Duke Richard had attained the sovereignty, and the same was everywhere so reported, though more for awe than goodwill; when, for fear of perils hanging every way over his head, he resolved that of necessity it was meet to stay a while, notwithstanding many of his friends urged him to utter himself plainly, and to dispatch at once that which remained, yet, lest his doings might easily be misliked, his desire was that the people might be

---

*Contemporaries differ as to the contents of Shaa's sermon. Cf. *The Great Chronicle of London*, pp. 231, 435.

earnestly dealt withal, and the whole matter referred to the determination of others as judges in that behalf. And so, about the 13th calends of June, he commanded the judges and magistrates of the city, Robert Bylles, lord mayor, Thomas Norland and William Maryn, sheriffs, with th'aldermen, to assemble in the Gild Hall, and to them he sent the Duke of Buckingham, with divers other noblemen that were of his counsel, to deal in his cause, and in his name to require that they, hearing the reasons concerning the dispatch of so weighty affair, would decree that which stood with the wealth of the whole realm and of th'inhabitants thereof. The Duke of Buckingham delivered, in long process, Duke Richard's mind, and in his behalf declared that there was not to enforce the cause any other thing but right, loyalty, constancy, honesty, and equity, seeing he demanded the kingdom from the which he had been defrauded before by his brother Edward, and therefore prayed that by their authority they would deal and determine of so weighty a matter, whereby he might, with good will of the commonalty, who would be ruled by their judgment, enjoy once at the last his royal right, which would be for the profit of the commonwealth; for as much as Duke Richard was of that wisdom and modesty that all men might well hope for, at his hand, both right and reason. This was the duke's demand and determination also, against which, because where force is right beareth no rule, no man durst gainsay. But Richard Duke of Gloucester, as though the terrified judges had decreed of his side, rode the next day after from the Tower through the midst of the city unto Westminster, in robes royal, and guarded with firm force of armed men, sitting in the royal seat. He then first of all took upon him as king; for some matters he determined, others he promised he would hear; to the magistrates he gave in commandment that from thenceforth they should do all things in his name ... (4)

According to the Croyland Continuator Gloucester advanced other claims:

From this day,* these dukes acted no longer in secret, but openly manifested their intentions. For, having summoned armed men, in

*i.e. the day of the removal of Richard, Duke of York, from the Westminster Sanctuary.

fearful and unheard-of numbers, from the north, Wales, and all other parts then subject to them,. the said Protector Richard assumed the government of the kingdom, with the title of king, on the twentieth day of the aforesaid month of June; and on the same day, at the Great Hall at Westminster, obtruded himself into the marble chair. The colour for this act of usurpation, and his thus taking possession of the throne, was the following: It was set forth, by way of prayer, in an address in a certain roll of parchment, that the sons of King Edward were bastards, on the ground that he had contracted a marriage with one Lady Eleanor Boteler, before his marriage to Queen Elizabeth; added to which, the blood of his other brother, George, Duke of Clarence, had been attainted; so that, at the present time, no certain and uncorrupted lineal blood could be found of Richard, Duke of York, except in the person of the said Richard, Duke of Gloucester. For which reason, he was entreated, at the end of the said roll, on part of the lords and commons of the realm, to assume his lawful rights. However, it was at the time rumoured that this address had been got up in the north, whence such vast numbers were flocking to London; although, at the same time, there was not a person but what very well knew who was the sole mover at London of such seditious and disgraceful proceedings.(5)

The great unsolved mystery of Richard's reign is the fate of his nephews – the Princes in the Tower. As early as January 1484 Gaillaume de Rochefort, the Chancellor of France, publicly accused Richard of murdering them. He probably based this accusation on talks with Dominic Mancini – and at the time it was probably no more than a plausible guess. Although various writers have tried to exonerate their uncle of guilt, circumstantial evidence, on balance, indicates that they died during his reign, most probably during the summer of 1483.[5] The best-known account is that of Sir Thomas More which now follows. Grave doubts, from time to time, have been cast upon its truth.[6] In spite of this it is still worth quotation, showing as it does the conflation of rumours circulating in the absence of certain knowledge. More himself frankly admitted that he was bewildered by conflicting stories. As he said, 'I shall rehearse you the dolorous end of those babes, not after every way that I have heard, but after that way that I have so heard by such men and such means as me thinketh it were hard but it should be true':

King Richard, after his coronation, taking his way to Gloucester to visit in hisnew honour the town of which he bare the name of his old, devised as he rode to fulfil that thing which he before had intended. And for as much as his mind gave him that, his nephews living, men would not reckon that he could have right to the realm, he thought therefore without delay to rid them, as though the killing of his kinsmen could amend his cause and make him a kindly king. Whereupon he sent one John Green, whom he specially trusted, unto Sir Robert Brackenbury, Constable of the Tower, with a letter and credence also that the same Sir Robert should in any wise put the two children to death. This John Green did his errand unto Brackenbury, kneeling before our Lady in the tower, who plainly answered that he would never put them to death, to die therefore; with which answer John Green, returning, recounted the same to King Richard at Warwick, yet in his way. Wherewith he took such displeasure and thought that the same night he said unto a secret page of his: 'Ah, whom shall a man trust? Those that I have brought up myself, those that I had weened would most surely serve me, even those fail me and at my commandment will do nothing for me.'

'Sir,' quoth his page, 'there lieth one on your pallet without, that I dare well; say, to do your grace pleasure, the thing were right hard that he would refuse', meaning by this Sir James Tyrell, which was a man of right goodly personage and for nature's gifts worthy to have served a much better prince, if he had well served God and by grace obtained as much truth and good will as he had strength and wit. The man had an high heart and sore longed upward, not rising yet so fast as he had hoped, being hindered and kept under by the means of Sir Richard Ratcliff and Sir William Catesby, which longing for no more partners of the prince's favour, and namely not for him whose pride they wist would bear no peer, kept him by secret drifts out of all secret trust, which thing this page well had marked and known.

Wherefore, this occasion offered, of very special friendship he took his time to put him forward and by such wise do him good that all the enemies he had, except the devil, could never have done him so much hurt. For upon this page's words King Richard arose (for this communication had he sitting at the draught,* a convenient carpet for

*i.e. privy.

such a counsel) and came out into the pallet chamber, on which he
found in bed Sir James and Sir Thomas Tyrell, of person like and
brethren of blood, but nothing of kin in conditions. Then said the king
merrily to them: 'What, Sirs, be ye in bed so soon!' and calling up Sir
James, broke to him secretly his mind in this mischievous matter; in
which he found him nothing strange. Wherefore, on the morrow, he
sent him to Brackenbury with a letter, by which he was commanded to
deliver Sir James all the keys of the Tower for one night, to the end he
might there accomplish the king's pleasure in such thing as he had
given him commandment. After which letter delivered and the keys
received, Sir James appointed the night next ensuing to destroy them,
devising before and preparing the means. The prince, as soon as the
protector left that name and took himself as king, had it showed unto
him that he should not reign, but his uncle should have the crown. At
which word the prince, sore abashed, began to sigh and said: 'Alas, I
would my uncle would let me have my life yet, though I lose my
kingdom.' Then he that told him the tale used him with good words
and put him in the best comfort he could. But forthwith was the
prince and his brother both shut up: and all others removed from them,
only one called Black Will or William Slaughter except, set to serve
them and see them sure. After which time the prince never tied his
points, nor aught wrought of himself, but with that young babe his
brother lingered in thought and heaviness till this traitorous death
delivered them of that wretchedness.* For Sir James Tyrell devised that
they should be murdered in their beds. To the execution whereof, he
appointed Miles Forest, one of the four that kept them, a fellow fleshed
in murder before-time. To him he joined one John Dighton, his own
horse-keeper, a big broad, square, strong knave. Then, all the others
being removed from them, this Miles Forest and John Dighton, about
midnight (the silly‡ children lying in their beds) came into the chamber

*An examination of the remains generally held to be those of the princes shows that
Edward V was suffering from a bone disease of the lower jaw and his state of
depression may well have been due to ill health rather than any premonition of his
fate. See L.E. Tanner and W. Wright, 'Recent Investigations Regarding the Fate of the
Princes in the Tower', *Archeologia*, lxxxiv, 1–26, 1934.
‡i.e. innocent.

and suddenly lapped them up among the clothes, so bewrapped them and entangled them, keeping down by force the feather bed and pillows hard unto their mouths, that within a while, smothered and stifled, their breath failing, they gave up to God their innocent souls into the joys of heaven, leaving to the tormentors their bodies dead in the bed. Which after that the wretches perceived, first by the struggling with the pains of death, and after long lying still, to be thoroughly dead: they laid their bodies naked out upon the bed, and fetched Sir James to see them. Which, upon the sight of them, caused those murderers to bury them at the stair foot, meetly deep in the ground, under a great heap of stones.(6)

After his coronation Richard made an extensive royal progress. At the beginning of August York, where his lavish lordship and patronage had made him popular with certain of the city cliques, received him with loud acclaim but in the home counties and in the south the murmurs of discontent grew louder. Richard's fellow conspirator, the Duke of Buckingham, to whom he owed so much and whom he had lavishly rewarded, went over to his enemies. Time and confusion have left his motives unfathomably obscure. By October a dangerous revolt was under way. The Croyland Continuator gives his opinion of its origins and describes its course:

In the meantime, and while these things were going on, the two sons of King Edward before-named remained in the Tower of London, in the custody of certain persons appointed for that purpose. In order to deliver them from this captivity, the people of the southern and western parts of the kingdom began to murmur greatly, and to form meetings and confederacies. It soon became known that many things were going on in secret, and some in the face of all the world, for the purpose of promoting this object, especially on the part of those who, through fear, had availed themselves of the privileges of sanctuary and franchise. There was also a report that it had been recommended by those men who had taken refuge in the sanctuaries, that some of the king's daughters should leave Westminster, and go in disguise to the parts beyond sea; in order that if any fatal mishap should befall the said male children of the late king in the Tower, the kingdom might still, in consequence of the safety of the daughters, some day fall again into the hands of the rightful heirs. On this being discovered, the noble church of the monks at Westminster, and all the neighbouring parts, assumed the appearance of a castle and fortress, while men of the greatest austerity were appointed by King Richard to act as the keepers thereof. The captain and head of these was one John Nesfeld, esquire, who set a watch upon all the inlets and outlets of the monastery, so that not one of the persons shut up could go forth, and no one could enter, without his permission.

At last, it was determined by the people in the vicinity of the City of London, throughout the counties of Kent, Essex, Sussex, Hampshire, Dorset, Devonshire, Somerset, Wiltshire, and Berkshire, as well as some others of the southern counties of the kingdom, to avenge their grievances before-stated; upon which, public proclamation was made, that Henry, Duke of Buckingham, who at this time was living at Brecknock in Wales,* had repented of his former conduct, and would be the chief mover in this attempt, while a rumour was spread that the sons of King Edward before-named had died a violent death, but it was uncertain how. Accordingly, all those who had set on foot this insurrection, seeing that if they could find no one to take the lead in their designs, the ruin of all would speedily ensue, turned their thoughts to Henry, Earl of Richmond, who had been for many years living in exile in Brittany. To him a message was, accordingly, sent, by the Duke of Buckingham, by advice of the Lord Bishop of Ely, who was then his prisoner at Brecknock, requesting him to hasten over to England as soon as he possibly could, for the purpose of marrying Elizabeth, the eldest daughter of the late king, and, at the same time, together with her, taking possession of the throne.

The whole design of this plot, however, by means of spies, became perfectly well known to King Richard, who, as he exerted himself in the promotion of all his views in no drowsy manner, but with the greatest activity and vigilance, contrived that, throughout Wales, as well as in all parts of the Marches thereof, armed men should be set in readiness around the said duke, as soon as ever he had set a foot from

---

*He had accompanied Richard in late July on a royal progress as far as Gloucester. There they had parted, Buckingham going to Brecknock, Richard to Worcester, Warwick and York.

his home, to pounce upon all his property; who, accordingly, encouraged by the prospect of the duke's wealth, which the king had, for that purpose, bestowed upon them, were in every way to obstruct his progress. The result was, that, on the side of the castle of Brecknock, which looks towards the interior of Wales, Thomas, the son of the late Sir Roger Vaughan, with the aid of his brethren and kinsmen, most carefully watched the whole of the surrounding country; while Humphrey Stafford partly destroyed the bridges and passes by which England was entered, and kept the other part closed by means of a strong force set there to guard the same.

In the meantime, the duke was staying at Webley, the house of Walter Devereux, Lord Ferrers, together with the said Bishop of Ely and his other advisers. Finding that he was placed in a position of extreme difficulty, and that he could in no direction find a safe mode of escape, he first changed his dress, and then secretly left his people; but was at last discovered in the cottage of a poor man, in consequence of a greater quantity of provisions than usual being carried thither.* Upon this, he was led to the city of Salisbury, to which place the king had come with a very large army, on the day of the commemoration of All Souls; and, notwithstanding the fact that it was the Lord's day, the duke suffered capital punishment in the public market-place of that city.

On the following day, the king proceeded with all his army towards the western parts of the kingdom, where all his enemies had made a stand, with the exception of those who had come from Kent, and were at Guildford, awaiting the issue of events. Proceeding onwards, he arrived at the city of Exeter; upon which, being struck with extreme terror at his approach, Peter Courtenay, Bishop of Exeter, as well as Thomas, Marquess of Dorset, and various other nobles of the adjacent country, who had taken part in the rebellion, repaired to the sea-side; and those among them who could find ships in readiness, embarked, and at length arrived at the wished-for shores of Brittany. Others, for a time trusting to the fidelity of friends, and concealing themselves in secret spots, afterwards betook themselves to the protection of holy places . . .

---

*Another authority states that he was betrayed by his own servant, Ralph Bannaster of Wem, with whom he had taken refuge.

Hearing the news Henry of Richmond, who with a small fleet from Brittany had arrived off the mouth of Plymouth harbour, immediately put to sea again.

Although Richard had put down Buckingham's rebellion, neither lavish bribery nor savage repression could destroy the hostility of many of his subjects. On the contrary, in certain parts of the country they increased it. The Croyland Continuator describes the results of the act of attainder passed against the defeated rebels in parliament:

> . . . what immense estates and patrimonies were collected into the king's treasury in consequence of this measure! All of which he distributed among his northern adherents, whom he planted in every spot throughout his dominions, to the disgrace and loudly expressed sorrow of all the people in the south who daily longed more and more for the return of their ancient rulers,* rather than the tyranny of these people.(7)

The essential truth of these accusations (especially in two groups of counties in the south-east and the south-west) has been demonstrated by recent research – and Richard's actions produced against him a tradition of hostility in southern England parallel to the favourable tradition of the north.

The *Great Chronicle of London* describes some of the events of the second half of 1484:

> In these days were chief rulers about the king, the Lord Lovell, and two gentlemen being named Mr Ratclyff and Mr Catesby of the which persons was made a seditious rhyme and fastened upon the Cross in Cheap and other places of the city whereof the sentence was as followeth, 'The cat, the rat, and Lovell our dog, rulen all England, under

---

*Sir Thomas More remarked that Richard with great gifts obtained unsteadfast friendships. British Library MS Harleian, 433, ff. 282ff, shows that he quickly granted away lands worth nearly £12,000 p.a. for reserved rents of only just over £750. In addition to the acto of attainder the King's Bench records show prosecutions of many of Richard's opponents. See also A.J. Pollard, 'The Tyranny of Richard III', in *Journal of Medieval History*, iii, 1977.

an hog.' This was to mean that the forenamed three persons as the Lord Lovell and the other two that is to mean Catesby and Ratclyff ruled this land under the king which bare a white boar for his cognisance. For the devisers of this rhyme much search was made and sundry accused to their charges, but finally two gentlemen named Turberville and Collingbourne were for that and other things laid to their charge, arrested and cast in prison, for whom shortly after as upon the (—)* was holden at the Guildhall an oyer and terminer‡ where the said two gentlemen were arraigned, and that one of them called Collingbourne convicted of that crime and other. For the which upon the (—)* following he was drawn unto the Tower Hill and there full cruelly put to death, at first hanged and straight cut down and ripped, and his bowels cast into a fire. The which torment was so speedily done that when the butcher pulled out his heart he spake and said JHESUS IHESUS. This man was greatly monyd of the people for his goodly personage and favour of visage. (8)

From then onwards, the Croyland Continuator once more narrates the events which led to the last great conspiracy against King Richard – the invasion of Henry of Richmond:

The feast of the Nativity was kept with due solemnity at the palace at Westminster, and the king appeared with his crown on the day of Epiphany. While he was keeping this festival with remarkable splendour in the great hall, just as at his first coronation, news was brought him on that very day, from his spies beyond sea, that, notwithstanding the potency and splendour of his royal state, his adversaries would, without question, invade the kingdom during the following summer, or make an attempt to invade it. Than this, there was nothing that could befall him more desirable, inasmuch as he imagined that it would put an end to all his doubts and troubles. Still, however, most shrewdly coming to the conclusion that money, which was now nearly failing him, forms the sinews of war, he had recourse to the modes of exaction which had been practised by King Edward, and which he himself had condemned

*Blank in MS.
‡i.e. a judicial commission of oyer and terminer (to hear and determine).

in full parliament; these were the so-called 'benevolences', a name detestable in every way. He accordingly sent chosen men, children of this world wiser in their generation than the children of light, who were by means of prayers and threats, by right or by wrong, to scrape up immense sums of money, after examining the archives of the realm, from persons of nearly all conditions.

Oh God! why should we any longer dwell on this subject, multiplying our recital of things so distasteful, so numerous that they can hardly be reckoned, and so pernicious in their example, that we ought not as much as suggest them to the minds of the perfidious. So too, with many other things which are not written in this book, and of which I grieve to speak; although the fact ought not to be concealed that, during this feast of the Nativity, far too much attention was given to dancing and gaiety, and vain changes of apparel presented to Queen Anne and the Lady Elizabeth, the eldest daughter of the late king, being of similar colour and shape; a thing that caused the people to murmur and the nobles and prelates greatly to wonder thereat; while it was said by many that the king was bent, either on the anticipated death of the queen taking place, or else, by means of a divorce, for which he supposed he had quite sufficient grounds, on contracting a marriage with the said Elizabeth. For it appeared that in no other way could his kingly power be established, or the hopes of his rival be put an end to.

In the course of a few days after this, the queen fell extremely sick, and her illness was supposed to have increased still more and more, because the king entirely shunned her bed, declaring that it was by the advice of his physicians that he did so. Why enlarge? About the middle of the following month, upon the day of the great eclipse of the sun, which then took place, Queen Anne, before-named, departed this life, and was buried at Westminster, with no less honours than befitted the interment of a queen.

The king's purpose and intention of contracting a marriage with his niece Elizabeth being mentioned to some who were opposed thereto, the king was obliged, having called a council together, to excuse himself with many words and to assert that such a thing had never once entered his mind. There were some persons, however, present at that same council, who very well knew the contrary. Those in especial who were unwilling that this marriage should take place, and to whose opinions the king hardly ever dared offer any opposition, were Sir Richard Ratclyff and William Catesby, esquire of his body. For by these persons the king was told to his face that if he did not abandon his intended purpose, and that, too, before the mayor or commons of the City of London, opposition would not be offered to him by merely the warnings of the voice; for all the people of the north, in whom he placed the greatest reliance, would rise in rebellion against him and impute to him the death of the queen, the daughter and one of the heirs of the Earl of Warwick, through whom he had first gained his present high position; in order that he might, to the extreme abhorrence of the Almighty, gratify an incestuous passion for his said niece. Besides this, they brought to him more than twelve Doctors of Divinity, who asserted that the Pope could grant no dispensation in the case of such a degree of consanguinity. It was supposed by many, that these men, together with others like them, threw so many impediments in the way, for fear lest, if the said Elizabeth should attain the rank of queen, it might at some time be in her power to avenge upon them the death of her uncle, Earl Anthony, and her brother Richard, they having been the king's especial advisers in those matters. The king, accordingly, followed their advice a little before Easter, in presence of the mayor and citizens of London, in the great Hall of the Hospital of Saint John, by making the said denial in a loud and distinct voice; more, however, as many supposed, to suit the wishes of those who advised him to that effect, than in conformity with his own.(9)

The records of the Mercers' Company describe the scene in London:

Where as long saying and much simple communication among the people by evil disposed persons contrived and sown to the very great displeasure of the king showing how that the queen as by consent and will of the king was poisoned for and th'intent that he might then marry and have to wife Lady Elizabeth, eldest daughter of his brother, late King of England deceased, whom God pardon, etc., for the which and other the king sent for and had tofor him at St John's as yesterday the Mayor and Aldermen where as he in the great Hall there in the presence of many of his lords and of much other people showed his grief and displeasure aforesaid and said it never came in his thought or mind to marry in such manner wise nor willing or glad of the death of his queen but as sorry and in heart as heavy as man might be, with much more in the premises spoken, for the which he then monished and charged every person to cease of such untrue talking on peril of his indignation. And what person that from henceforth telleth or reporteth any of the foresaid untrue surmised talking, that the said person therefore be had to prison unto the author be brought forth of whom the said person heard the said untrue surmised tale etc ... (10)

An enforced public denial of murder. Surely a uniquely shameful spectacle for an English kmg!

Rumours were spreading about an imminent invasion of Henry of Richmond at a place vaguely called Milford – but the name was so imprecise that it caused confusion. The Croyland Continuator again narrates:

For some say that there is a harbour in the neighbourhood of Southampton, called Milford, just as there is in Wales; and there being some persons endowed, as it were, with a spirit of prophecy, these predicted that those men would land at the harbour of Milford, and were in the habit of looking for the fulfilment of their prophecies to that effect, not at the most famous place, but most commonly at the other one which bore the same name. And then besides, the king, at this period, seemed especially to devote his attention to strengthening the southern parts of his kingdom. But it was all in vain: for, on the first day of August* the enemy landed with a fair wind, and without opposition, at that most celebrated harbour, Milford Haven, near Pembroke.

On hearing of their arrival, the king rejoiced, or at least seemed to rejoice, writing to his adherents in every quarter that now the long wished-for day had arrived, for him to triumph with ease over so contemptible a faction, and thenceforth benefit his subjects with the blessings of uninterrupted tranquillity. In the meantime, in manifold letters he dispatched orders of the greatest severity, commanding that no men, of the number of those at least who had been born to the inheritance of any property in the kingdom, should shun taking part in

*In fact on 7 August.

the approaching warfare; threatening that whoever should be found in any part of the kingdom after the victory should have been gained, to have omitted appearing in his presence on the field, was to expect no other fate than the loss of all his goods and possessions, as well as his life.

A little before the landing of these persons, Thomas Stanley, seneschal of the king's household, had received permission to go into Lancashire, his native county, to visit his home and family, from whom he had been long separated. Still, however, he was permitted to stay there on no other condition than that of sending his eldest son, George Lord Strange, to the king at Nottingham, in his stead; which he accordingly did.

The king's opponents, as already stated, having landed at Milford in Wales, made their way through rugged and indirect tracts in the northern parts of that province; where William Stanley, the brother of the said lord seneschal, as lord chamberlain of North Wales, was holding the sole command. Upon this the king sent word to the said Lord Stanley, requesting him without the least delay, to present himself before him at Nottingham. For the king was afraid lest that, as it really turned out, the mother of the said Earl of Richmond, whom the Lord [Thomas] Stanley had married, might induce her husband to go over to the party of her son.* On this, with wonderful (—)† he made an excuse that he was suffering from an attack of the sweating sickness, and could not possibly come. His son, however, who had secretly prepared to desert from the king, was detected by stratagem and taken prisoner; upon which, he discovered a conspiracy which had been entered into by himself and his uncle, Sir William Stanley before-mentioned, and Sir John Savage, to go over to the side of the Earl of Richmond; while at the same time, he implored the king's mercy, and promised that his father would with all speed arrive to the king's assistance. In addition to this, he sent word to his father by letter, of the danger to which he was exposed, and, at the same time, expressed his own wish that he would give the assistance before mentioned.

*Polydore Vergil gives another account of these conspiracies, attributing a more important role to Lady Margaret Beaufort.
†Blank in MS.

In the meantime the said two knights being publicly proclaimed at Coventry and elsewhere traitors against the king, and the enemy hastening on and directing his steps night and day to meet the king, it became necessary to move the army, though its numbers were not yet fully made up, from Nottingham, and to come to Leicester. Here was found a number of warriors ready to fight on the king's side, greater than had ever been seen before in England collected together in behalf of one person.* On the Lord's Day before the feast of Bartholomew the Apostle, the king proceeded on his way, amid the greatest pomp, and wearing the crown on his head; being attended by John Howard, Duke of Norfolk, and Henry Percy, Earl of Northumberland, and other mighty lords, knights and esquires, together with a countless multitude of the common people. On departing from the town of Leicester, he was informed by scouts where the enemy most probably intended to remain the following night; upon which, he encamped near the abbey of Mirival, at a distance of about eight miles from that town.(11)

Polydore Vergil, who undoubtedly drew his information from eyewitnesses, describes the battle of Bosworth and Richard's courageous last fight for his throne:

There happened in this voyage unto Earl Henry a chance worth memory; for though he were of noble courage, and that his forces augmented everywhere, yet was he in great fear, because he thought that he could not assure himself of Thomas Stanley, who, as I have shewed, for that he feared the danger that King Richard might do his son, did incline as yet to neither party; and as touching King Richard's causes, it was told him much otherwise than his friends had signified, which was, that nothing was more firm, nothing better furnished: wherefore, considering his fear was not for nothing, himself, accompanied with twenty armed men only, stayed by the way, uncertain what was best as to deliberate what he might do. Moreover

---

*This is exaggerated. Richard had possibly no more than 10,000 men, at most 16,000; Henry 5,000 plus 3,000 led by the Stanleys.

he heard that King Richard, with an host innumerable, was at hand. While he thus, somewhat sad, followed aloof, all th'army came to Tamworth, and when as by reason of the night which came upon him he could not discern the trace of them that were gone before, and so after long wandering could not find his company, he came unto a certain town more than three miles from his camp, full of fear; who, lest he might be betrayed, durst not ask questions of any man, but tarried there all that night, no more afraid for the present than for the peril to come; for he was afeared that the same might be a sign of some manner plague to ensue. Neither was the army less heavy for the sudden absence of their captain, when as Henry the next day after, in the grey of the morning, returned to the host, excusing himself that he was not deceived in the way, but had withdrawn from the camp of set purpose to receive some good news of certain his secret friends. After that he went privily to Atherstone, where Thomas Stanley and William lay encamped. Here Henry did meet with Thomas and William, where taking one another by th'hand, and yielding mutual salutation, each man was glad for the good state of th'others, and all their minds were moved to great joy. After that, they entered in counsel in what sort to darraigne* battle with King Richard, if the matter should come to strokes, whom they heard to be not far off. A little before th'evening of the same day, John Savage, Brian Sanford, Simon Digby, and many others, revolting from King Richard, came to Henry with a choice band of armed men, which matter both augmented the forces of Earl Henry, and greatly replenished him with good hope.

In the mean time King Richard, hearing that th'enemy drew near, came first to the place of fight, a little beyond Leicester (the name of that village is Bosworth), and there, pitching his tents, refreshed his soldiers that night from their travail, and with many words exhorted them to the fight to come. It is reported that King Richard had that night a terrible dream; for he thought in his sleep that he saw horrible images as it were of evil spirits haunting evidently about him, as it were before his eyes, and that they would not let him rest; which vision truly did not so much strike into his breast a sudden fear, as replenish the

---

*i.e. to set troops in battle array.

same with heavy cares: for forthwith after, being troubled in mind, his heart gave him thereupon that th'event of the battle following would be grievous, and he did not buckle himself to the conflict with such liveliness of courage and countenance as before, which heaviness that it should not be said he shewed as appalled with fear of his enemies, he reported his dream to many in the morning. But (I believe) it was no dream, but a conscience guilty of heinous offences, a conscience (I say) so much the more grievous as th'offences were more great, which, though at none other time, yet in the last day of our life is wont to represent to us the memory of our sins committed, and withal to show unto us the pains imminent for the same, that, being upon good cause penitent at that instant for our evil led life, we maybe compelled to go hence in heaviness of heart. Now I return to my purpose. The next day after King Richard, furnished thoroughly with all manner of things, drew his whole host out of their tents, and arrayeth his vanward, stretching it forth of a wonderful length, so full replenished both with footmen and horsemen that to the beholders afar off it gave a terror for the multitude, and in the front were placed his archers, like a most strong trench and bulwark; of these archers he made leader John Duke of Norfolk. After this long vanward followed the king himself, with a choice force of soldiers. In this mean time Henry, being departed back from the conference with his friends, began to take better heart, and without any tarry encamped himself nigh his enemies, where he rested all night, and well early in the morning commanded the soldiers to arm themselves, sending withal to Thomas Stanley, who was now approached the place of fight, as in the mid way betwixt the two battles, that he would come to with his forces, to set the solders in array. He answered that the earl should set his own folks in order, while that he should come to him with his army well appointed. With which answer, given contrary to that was looked for, and to that which th'opportunity of time and weight of cause required, though Henry were no little vexed, and began to be somewhat appalled, yet without lingering he of necessity ordered his men in this sort. He made a slender vanward for the small number of his people; before the same he placed archers, of whom he made captain John Earl of Oxford; in the right wing of the vanward he placed Gilbert Talbot to defend the same; in the left verily he sat John Savage; and himself, trusting to th'aid of

Thomas Stanley, with one troop of horsemen, and a few footmen did follow; for the number of all his soldiers, all manner of ways, was scarce 5,000 besides the Stanleyans, whereof about 3,000 were at the battle, under the conduct of William. The king's forces were twice so many and more. Thus both the vanwards being arrayed, as soon as the soldiers might one see another afar off, they put on their head pieces and prepared to the fight, expecting th'alarm with intentive ear. There was a marsh betwixt both hosts, which Henry of purpose left on the right hand, that it might serve his men instead of a fortress, by the doing thereof also he left the sun upon his back; but when the king saw th'enemies passed the marsh, he commanded his soldiers to give charge upon them. The making suddenly great shouts assaulted th'enemy first with arrows, who were nothing faint unto the fight but began also to shoot fiercely; but when they came to hand strokes the matter then was dealt with blades. In the mean time th'Earl of Oxford, fearing lest his men in fighting might be environed of the multitude, commanded in every rank that no soldiers should go above ten foot from the standards; which charge being known, when all men had throng thick togethers, and stayed a while from fighting, th'adversaries were therewith afeared, supposing some fraud, and so they all forbore the fight a certain space, and that verily did many with right goodwill, who rather coveted the king dead than alive, and therefore fought faintly. Then th'Earl of Oxford in one part, and others in another part, with the bands of men close one to another, gave fresh charge upon th'enemy, and in array triangle vehemently renewed the conflict. While that battle continued thus hot on both sides betwixt the vanguards, King Richard understood, first by espials where Earl Henry was afar off with small force of soldiers about him; then after drawing nearer he knew it perfitely by evident signs and tokens that it was Henry; wherefore, all inflamed with ire, he strick his horse with the spurs, and runneth out of th'one side without the vanwards against him. Henry perceived King Richard come upon him, and because all his hope was then in valiancy of arms, he received him with great courage. King Richard at the first brunt killed certain, overthrew Henry's standard, together with William Brandon the standard bearer, and matched also with John Cheney a man of much fortitude, far exceeding the common sort, who encountered with him as he came, but the king with great force drove him to the ground, making way with weapon on every side. But yet Henry abode the brunt longer than ever his own soldiers would have weened, who were now almost out of hope of victory, when as lo William Stanley with three thousand men came to the rescue: then truly in a very moment the residue all fled, and King Richard alone was killed fighting manfully in the thickest press of his enemies. In the mean time also the Earl of Oxford after a little bickering put to flight them that fought in the forward, whereof a great company were killed in the chase. But many mo forbare to fight, who came to the field with King Richard for awe, and for no goodwill, and departed without any danger, as men who desired not the safety but destruction of that prince whom they hated. There were killed about a thousand men, and amongst them of noblemen of war John Duke of Norfolk, Walter Lord Ferrers, Robert Brackenbury, Richard Ratclyff and many mo. Two days after at Leicester, William Catesby, lawyer, with a few that were his fellows, were executed. And of those that took them to their feet Francis Lord Lovell, Humphrey Stafford, with Thomas his brother and much more company, fled into the sanctuary of St John which is at Colchester, a town by the sea side in Essex. As for the number of captives it was very great, for when King Richard was killed, all men forthwith threw away weapon, and freely submitted themselves to Henry's obeisance, whereof the most part would have done the same at the beginning, if for King Richard's scurriers, scouring to and fro, they might so have done. Amongst them the chief were Henry Earl of Northumberland, and Thomas Earl of Surrey.* This man was committed to ward, where he remained long; he as friend in heart was received into favour. Henry lost in that battle scarce an hundred soldiers, amongst whom there was one principal man, William Brandon, who bare Earl Henry's standard. The field was foughten the 11th calends of September, in the year of man's salvation 1486,† and the fight lasted more than two hours . . .

. . . Henry, after the victory obtained, gave forthwith thanks unto Almighty God for the same; then after, replenished with joy incredible,

---

*Northumberland stood idle during the battle, but the story can hardly be true of Surrey. His father John, Duke of Norfolk, was slain fighting on Richard's side.
†In fact 22 August 1485.

he got himself unto the next hill, where, after he had commended his soldiers, and commanded to cure the wounded, and to bury them that were slain, he gave unto the nobility and gentlemen immortal thanks, promising that he would be mindful of their benefits, all which mean while the soldiers cried, God save King Henry, God save King Henry! and with heart and hand uttered all the shew of joy that might be; which when Thomas Stanley did see, he set anon King Richard's crown, which was found among the spoil in the field upon his head,* as though he had been already by commandment of the people proclaimed king after the manner of his ancestors, and that was the first sign of prosperity. After that, commanding to pack up all bag and baggage, Henry with his victorious army proceeded in the evening to Leicester, where, for refreshing of his soldiers from their travail and pains, and to prepare for going to London, he tarried two days. In the mean time the body of King Richard naked of all clothing, and laid upon an horse back with the arms and legs hanging down on both sides, was brought to th'abbey of monks Franciscans at Leicester, a miserable spectacle in good sooth, but not unworthy for the man's life, and there was buried two days after without any pomp or solemn funeral. He reigned two years and so many months, and one day over. He was little of stature, deformed of body, th'one shoulder being higher than th'other, a short and sour countenance, which seemed to savour of mischief, and utter evidently craft and deceit. The while he was thinking of any matter, he did continually bite his nether lip, as though that cruel nature of his did so raise against it self in that little carcase. Also he was wont to be ever with his right hand pulling out of the sheath to the middest, and putting in again, the dagger which he did always wear. Truly he had a sharp wit, provident and subtle, apt both to counterfeit and dissemble; his courage also haut and fierce, which failed him not in the very death, which, when his men forsook him, he rather yielded to take with the sword, than by foul flight to prolong his life, uncertain what death perchance soon after by sickness or other violence to suffer.(12)

---

*Documents in the Papal Archives, recently printed, however, throw some doubt on this incident and on the story of the conference at Atherstone. It is there stated that Derby himself dated his meeting with Henry as 24 August. See K.B. McFarlane, *E.H.R.*, lxxviii (1963), 771–2.

NOTES

1. For a full account of his life and works see C.A.J. Armstrong, *The Usurpation of Richard III* (1936).
2. See A.F. Pollard, 'The Making of Sir Thomas More's Richard III', in *Historical Essays in Honour of James Tait* (Manchester, 1933), pp. 223–38.
3. E.F. Jacob, *The Fifteenth Century, 1399–1485* (1961), p. 614 casts doubt on this story about the great seal, but the evidence which he cites does not disprove it.
4. See Mr Armstrong's amendment to his translation, 'An Italian Astrologer at the Court of Henry VII', in *Italian Renaissance Studies*, (ed.) E.F. Jacob (1960), p.449; John Argentine, from 1501 Provost of King's College, Cambridge, was a theologian and physician.
5. There are detailed discussions by P.M. Kendall, *Richard the Third* (1955), Appendix 1, criticized as unconvincing by E.F. Jacob, *The Fifteenth Century, 1399–1485* (1961), pp. 623–5; and *The Complete Peerage*, xii, pt. ii (1959). See also S.B. Chrimes, 'The Fifteenth Century', in *History*, xlviii (1963), 22–23.
6. See Kendall, *Richard the Third* (1955), pp. 398–406.

SIX

Henry VII and the Last of the Wars

In a postscript to *The Croyland Chronicle* a third anonymous author gives his somewhat sour appraisal of Henry VII's first parliament and his tide to the throne:

After the coronation of King Henry had been solemnly performed on the day above-mentioned, a parliament was held at Westminster, on which so many matters were treated of (I wish I could say 'all *ably* treated of'), that the compenious nature of this narrative cannot aspire to comprise an account of the whole of them. Among other things, proscriptions, or, as they are more commonly called, 'attainders', were voted against thirty persons;* a step which, though bespeaking far greater moderation than was ever witnessed under similar circumstances in the time of King Richard or King Edward, was not taken without considerable discussion, or, indeed, to speak more truly, considerable censure, of the measures so adopted. Oh God! what assurance, from this time forth, are our kings to have, that, in the day of battle, they will not be deprived of the assistance of even their own subjects, when summoned at the dread mandate of their sovereign? For, a thing that has been too often witnessed, it is far from improbable, that deserted by their adherents, they may find themselves bereft of inheritance, possessions, and even life itself.

In this parliament, the sovereignty was confirmed to our lord the king, as being his due, not by one, but by many titles: so that we are to believe that he rules most rightfully over the English people, and that, not so much by right of blood as of conquest and victory in warfare. There were some persons, however, who were of opinion that words to that effect might have been more wisely passed over in silence than

*There were twenty-eight attainders in this parliament.

inserted in our statutes; the more especially, because, in the very same parliament, a discussion took place, and that, too, with the king's consent, relative to his marriage with the Lady Elizabeth, the eldest daughter of King Edward; in whose person it appeared to all that every requisite might be supplied, which was wanting to make good the title of the king himself.(1)

It was not long before revolts broke out against Henry's rule both in Yorkshire and the West Country. After their suppression Polydore Vergil commented that from the time when Edward IV had overthrown Henry VI 'men were so nourished on sectionalism that they could not later desist from it.' It had become almost a habit. Yet another rebellion soon occurred:

Latest among such adventurers was a lowborn priest called Richard, whose surname was Simons, a man as cunning as he was corrupt. He evolved a villainous deed of this sort, by which he might trouble the country's tranquillity. At Oxford, where he devoted himself to scholarship, he brought up a certain youth who was called Lambert Simnel.* He first taught the boy courtly manners, so that if ever he should pretend the lad to be of royal descent (as he had planned to do) people would the more readily believe it and have absolute trust in the bold deceit. Some time having elapsed since Henry VII had (as soon as he had gained power) flung Edward, the only son of the Duke of Clarence, into the Tower of London, and since it was popularly rumoured that Edward had been murdered in that place, the priest Richard decided that the time had arrived when he might profitably execute the villainy he had projected. He changed the boy's name and called him Edward, by which name the Duke of Clarence's son was known, and forthwith departed with him to Ireland. There he secretly summoned a meeting of a considerable number of Irish nobles whom he understood by popular report to be ill-disposed to Henry. Having secured their trust, he described to them how he had saved from death the Duke of Clarence's son, and how he had brought him to that land, where (so he had heard) the name and family of King Edward were

*He was probably the son of an organ builder, though his father has been variously described as a carpenter, a baker and a tailor.

always cherished. The story was readily believed by the nobles and was soon communicated to others. It was accepted without dispute to such an extent that Thomas Fitzgerald, the Irish-born chancellor of King Henry in the island, was among the first to entertain the boy as if he were of royal descent and to begin to give him all his support. Fitzgerald first called together all his own followers, informed them of the boy's arrival and how the Kingdom of England was his by right as the only male of royal descent, and exhorted them on that account to support him in an attempt to restore the boy to the throne. He then communicated the project to other nobles who, having heard his plan, promised all the help in their power. Thus it quickly came about that the news spread to all Irish cities, which spontaneously transferred their allegiance to the youth and called him king. Then the leaders of the conspiracy sent secret messengers to those in England whom they knew had been of King Richard's party, to implore them to remain loyal and decide upon supporting the boy. Other messengers were dispatched to Edward's sister Margaret in Flanders, the widow of Charles Duke of Burgundy, to demand her assistance also. . . . The woman Margaret was not indeed unaware that the House of York had been almost utterly destroyed by her brother Richard, but she was not satisfied with the hatred which had almost obliterated the family of Henry VI, nor mindful of the marriage which, as we have shown, finally united the two Houses of York and Lancaster. She pursued Henry with insatiable hatred and with fiery wrath never desisted from employing every scheme which might harm him as a representative of the hostile faction. Consequently, when she learnt of the new party which had recently arisen against Henry, although she considered the basis of it to be false (as indeed it was), she not only promised assistance to the envoys, but took it upon herself to ally certain other English nobles to those already active in the new conspiracy. Furthermore, Francis Lord Lovell, who had crossed to Flanders at this time, encouraged the woman to undertake more ambitious plans . . .

To resist the threat Henry VII, with the advice of a council of nobles, issued a general pardon of treason and other offences to win over waverers and issued many orders dealing with improvements in public administration. To counteract the deceit he also ordered the real Edward, the Duke of

Clarence's son, to be led from the Tower through London to St Paul's
Cathedral:

> . . . But this medicine was of no avail for diseased minds. For John Earl of
> Lincoln, the son of John Duke of Suffolk and King Edward's sister
> Elizabeth, together with Thomas Broughton and many more who
> longed for revolution, joined the conspiracy against Henry, and decided
> to cross over to Margaret so that they could unite with the other
> originators of the rebellion. Therefore as soon as the council had been
> dismissed by the king, the earl fled secretly to Flanders and there busied
> himself with Margaret and Francis Lord Lovell in preparations for war . . .

The king raised troops, marched to Norwich, prayed devoutly at the
shrine of our Lady of Walsingham* and proceeded to Cambridge:

> Meanwhile John Earl of Lincoln and Francis Lovell, having received
> from Margaret an army of about two thousand Germans, whose
> commander was that most martial man Martin Schwartz, crossed over
> to Ireland and in the city of Dublin crowned as king the lad Lambert,
> of ignoble origin and, having changed his name, called Edward, whom
> falsely (as they very well knew) they called the Duke of Clarence's son.
> After this, having assembled a great number of the destitute and almost
> unarmed Irish under the leadership of Thomas Geraldine,† they sailed
> to England with their new king. They landed according to plan on the
> west coast not far from Lancaster, putting their trust in the wealth and
> assistance of Thomas Broughton, who was of great authority in that
> part and who (as was explained above) was one of the conspirators.
>   King Henry indeed had anticipated what actually happened, and had
> a little prior to the arrival of the enemy dispatched Christopher
> Urswick to find out whether the ports on the Lancashire coast were
> capable of handling large ships; so that if they proved likely to be useful
> to his enemies he could at once so place his soldiers as to deny them

---

*Walsingham was probably the most popular pilgrimage centre in England in the
fifteenth century.
†i.e. Sir Thomas Fitzgerald, the Irish Chancellor.

the coast. Christopher carried out these orders and, after he had learnt from the depth of the bed of the sea that the ports were deep, returned to the king. But on his way he was informed of the sudden landing of the enemy, sent ahead a messenger to tell the king of the approach of his enemies and, following on the heels of the messenger, himself gave a fuller account of the whole matter. The king was at Coventry when he received the messenger, and, abandoning all other business, he judged he must set out forthwith against the foe wherever he might betake himself, lest time should be given him for assembling greater forces. He marched to Nottingham and encamped not far from the town in a wood which is called Banrys in the vernacular. Accompanied by a great number of armed men, George Talbot Earl of Shrewsbury, George Lord Strange, and John Cheyney, all outstanding captains, with many others well versed in military affairs, came to him there . . .

Meanwhile the Earl of Lincoln had entered Yorkshire. Although his following was small he determined to gamble on the fortunes of war and in the event of victory to ditch Lambert Simnel and then seize the throne for himself. After marching south the rebels were defeated at Stoke near Newark:

. . . it was only then, when the battle was over, that it was fully apparent how rash had been the spirit inspiring the enemy soldiers: for of their leaders John Earl of Lincoln, Francis Lord Lovell, Thomas Broughton, and the most bold Martin Schwartz and the Irish captain Thomas Geraldine were slain in that place, which they took alive in fighting [sic]. Lambert the false boy king was indeed captured, with his mentor Richard: but each was granted his life – the innocent lad because he was too young to have himself committed any offence, the tutor because he was a priest. Lambert is still alive to this very day, having been promoted trainer of the king's hawks; before that for some time he was a turnspit and did other menial jobs in the royal kitchen.(2)

The Great Chronicle of London gives interesting details of the battle of Stoke.

. . . the victory whereof fell unto the king, loved be God, how be it that by subtle ways men were set atween the place of the field and many of the king's subjects which were coming toward his Grace, showing unto them that the king had lost the field and was fled. By such subtle mean and report many a true man to the king turned back again, and some men of name for fear rode unto sanctuary, and tarried there till to them was brought better tidings. This field was the sorer foughten by reason that forenamed Martin Schwartz was deceived, for when he took this voyage upon him he was comforted and promised by th'Earl of Lincoln, that great strength of this land after their landing would have resorted unto the said earl. But when he was far entered and saw no such resort, then he knew well he was deceived, wherefore he said unto th'earl, Sir, now see I well that ye have deceived yourself and also me, but that notwithstanding, all such promise as I made unto my lady the duchess, I shall perform, exhorting th'earl to do the same. And upon this sped them toward the field with as good a courage as he had had twenty thousand men more than he had, and there held promise in such wise that he and th'earl both were slain upon the field, with much of their people.(3)

Despite the victory at Stoke unrest continued. Discontent easily coincided with pro-Yorkist sentiment. Early in 1489 parliament voted £100,000 for war against France. A rising, or at least very serious riots, followed attempts to collect the tax from the people of Yorkshire and Durham who considered themselves already burdened enough with defence against the Scots. Yorkist hopes still centered round the Duke of Clarence's son, the young prisoner, the Earl of Warwick. In December 1489 the Abbot of Abingdon was implicated in a plot to set him free and was executed for his share in it. Even then conspiracy still went on. In September 1490* John Taylor, an Exeter merchant and former Yorkist customs official, then in exile in France, wrote the following letter to John Hayes, once one of the Duke of Clarence's estate administrators and now in Henry VII's service:

Right Reverend and Worshipful Sir. I heartily recommend me unto you, praying you to take to your remembrance, the words we spake

---

*This is the year usually given, but the correct date may be 1491. The letter was written at Rouen on 15 September and received at Winchester on 26 November.

together in St Peter's Church of Exeter, and at the Black Friars, when ye were at your breakfast, and I made mine errand unto you, for seeing of evidence; Sir, ye shall understand, that the king's grace of France, by th'advice and assent of his council, will aid and support your master's son* to his right, and all his lovers and servants, and take them as his friends, both by land and by water, and all they may well be assured safely to come unto France, both bodies and goods, and such as have no goods they may come hither and be relieved, if they be known for true men to the quarrel; and over that, he will give help of his own subjects, with ships, gold and silver, to come into England, and with such number as shall be thought by you, and by other your master's son's frients, necessary and behoveful for his help and succour, and they to be ready and land at such time and place, as ye with other shall appoint; and therefore I pray you show this matter unto such as ye know well will give their good counsel and assistance to the same; and if ye may, bring the answer of the mind therein yourself, or else send it by Thomas Gale of Dartmouth; and ye may speak with him by the same token, that he and I communed together of matters touching your master's son in Stockingham Park, when Sir John Halwell hunted therein; and be you not afeared to shew all your mind unto to him, for he is trusty in this matter. . . . Sir, ye remember, that the token between you and me is, that such as I shall send unto you, shall take you by the thumb, as I did you, when ye and I went up out of the Cloister into St Peter's Church, and by that token ye should be assured of all things, and fear nothing, and so ensure ye all your friends and mine. Sir, ye shall hear by other friends, Sir, the convenable time of help is come, and therefore now endeavour yourself, and put to your hand, and spare for no cost, for there shall be help in three parties out of realm, but here is the place most meetly for you, and where ye shall lack nothing; the bearer hereof shall show you more, to whom I pray you give credence. Written at Rouen in Normandy, the 15th day of September, by your old acquaintance, John Taylor, th'elder.(4)

In 1491 the Yorkist plot discussed in England and France, by chance entered its active stage in Ireland. In the autumn John Taylor and two citizens

---

* i.e. the Earl of Warwick.

of Cork, Hubert Burgh and John Walter, induced a handsome, seventeen-year-old Fleming, then in the town, to impersonate Richard, Duke of York, the younger of Edward IV's two murdered sons. The Fleming was Perkin Warbeck, who, for the next six years, became a notorious international figure and a dangerous embarrassment to Henry VII. Polydore Vergil tells of the next stages in Perkin's career:

> While this was in hand, a rumour of it came to France; Charles summoned Peter to him in order to arm him against Henry, who was then attacking him.* Peter was most agreeably surprised by this message, for now he had begun to number kings among his friends, and he at once betook himself to Charles, by whom he was kindly received honoured with a retinue and all the other dignities which were fitting for a man of royal descent. Soon after this, however, peace having been made with the English . . .,† Charles dismissed the man, who returned his hopes dashed, to Margaret in Flanders. Margaret received Peter on his return‡ as though he had been raised from the dead and as if (so she dissembled) she had never cast eyes on him before; so great was her pleasure that her happiness seemed to have disturbed the balance of her mind. So that her rejoicing should be noted by all, she publicly congratulated her nephew on his preservation and took pleasure in hearing him repeat the tale of how, having been saved by a ruse from death, he had wandered among many peoples, in order by this means that she might convince all that he was indeed Richard the son of her brother Edward. Thereafter she started to treat the youth with great respect and for her sake the Flemings likewise all exalted him. The more the deceit was given an appearance of truth, the more people professed that they believed the youth had escaped the hand of King Richard by divine intervention and had been led safely to his aunt.
>
> The rumour of so miraculous an occurrence rapidly spread to neighbouring countries and even more quickly crossed into England,

*He was at Charles VIII's court when Henry invaded France in October 1492.
†The treaty of Étaples, 3 November 1492. Charles VIII undertook not to assist English rebels.
‡Polydore Vergil asserted that the conspiracy had begun in Burgundy and that Warbeck's appearance in Cork was not a matter of chance.

where the story was not believed merely by the common people, but where there were many important men who considered the matter as genuine. As a result, when it began to be rumoured that Richard, King Edward's son, was alive and that among the Flemings he was held in great esteem, conspiracies immediately began to multiply, just as in spring the trees always clothe themselves in a multitude of flowers. On the one hand there were the desperadoes who, on account of the various crimes they had committed, were taking refuge in sanctuaries; these were induced by poverty or bribes to break forth and flock to Peter in Flanders. On the other hand, many among the nobility turned to conspiracy; some were actuated by mere foolhardiness; others, believing Peter to be Edward's son Richard, supported the claim of the Yorkist party; others again, considering themselves ill-rewarded by King Henry for the services they had zealously rendered on his behalf, were moved partly by resentment and partly by greed; lastly, there were others whose desire for a revolution flung them headlong into this conspiracy. But all this happened somewhat later . . .

. . . Meanwhile the rumour of Richard, the resuscitated Duke of York, had divided nearly all England into factions, filling the minds of men with hope or fear. For there was no one who was not deeply concerned over such an affair. Each, according to his disposition, anticipated either peril or profit. The king indeed and his friends marvelled that anyone could have fabricated such a fiction as to make a transparent untruth gain such currency as truth, and to make many of his magnates (for already he perceived plainly that this had happened) consider it as established fact. Hence Henry feared that, unless the deception was quickly recognised as such by all, some great upheaval would occur. There were some who were pleased by the new situation and considered the facts to be true and not false, hoping thereby to benefit themselves; the conspirators in particular were confident that it would come about. And since this type of crime is always more dangerous actually to attempt than merely to plot, it was accordingly decided by the conspirators to send some of their number to Margaret in Flanders, who should learn when Richard Duke of York would be ready to make his way to England; and who should promptly inform them so that, when he did arrive, they could come forward with timely support. With general consent Sir Robert Clifford was sent to Flanders, with William Barley, and he revealed to Margaret all the plans of the conspirators. Margaret was exceedingly pleased by Robert's arrival and easily persuaded him that all which had been rumoured concerning Duke Richard was true. Later she showed him her Peter, who had assumed the part of Richard with great skill. Having seen the youth, Robert forthwith believed him to be of royal descent and reported in this sense to the conspirators. Having received Robert's message, the conspirators, in order to rouse up a popular upheaval, everywhere asserted that to be true which had previously been spoken of publicly concerning the Duke of York. But they did this with such artfulness, that none who heard could be certain as to who was responsible for the rumour.

When the king saw the pernicious tale gather authority among the people, he suspected what was in fact the case, that some members of the nobility were conspiring against him (indeed evidence of this was the sudden departure of Robert Clifford); and he at once sent some knights with carefully picked troops to guard the coast and ports. They were to prevent anyone being able to sail, so that no one should be able to cross to the continent or land in the island; and to guard diligently all roads and footpaths lest anyone should approach the shore, and lest anywhere there should be gatherings of many men . . .*

During this time the king sent spies into Flanders, some indeed who, pretending they fled to the rediscovered Duke of York, were to find out the conspirators' plans and their names; and yet others who, with an offer of forgiveness, were to persuade Robert Clifford and William Barley to return. These emissaries performed both their duties well, they learnt the names of some of the conspirators and persuaded Robert Clifford to return. William Barley, indeed, would hear nothing of returning then, but two years later, having been forgiven by Henry, he came to his senses and returned home. In this fashion the spies secretly left the false duke one at a time and coming back to Henry carefully reported all that they had found out. Several of them remained in order to accompany Robert when he returned. All the conspirators

---

*I have omitted an account of an embassy which Henry sent to the Archduke Philip's counsellors in Flanders to give the lie to Warbeck's story and to protest against Margaret of York's activities.

identified by the spies were ordered by the king to be arrested and brought to him at London. Among the nobles arrested were John Ratcliffe Lord Fitzwalter, Sir Simon Mountford, Sir Thomas Thwaites, William Daubeney, Robert Ratcliffe, Richard Lacy and many more. There were also several priests, who were more sound in body than in mind, to wit brother William Richford, provincial of the English Dominicans, and William Sunon, both learned men and distinguished preachers, William Worsley Dean of St Paul's, Robert Layborne and Thomas Powys, Prior of Langley and a Dominican. The other conspirators, when they heard that the conspiracy had been found out, fled to various sanctuaries. They were all taken and condemned for treason; from their number Simon Mountford, Robert Ratcliffe and William Daubeney were executed as the leaders and instigators of the plot. The remainder, including the priests (out of reverence for their cloth), were spared. The penalty was remitted for John Lord Fitzwalter, but he was sent to Calais; because, while imprisoned there, he had bribed the guards and tried to escape, he also was soon beheaded . . .

Robert Clifford now abandoned any hope of success and, also induced by promises from Henry, secretly fled out of Flanders into England. Under interrogation he revealed that Henry's own chamberlain, Sir William Stanley, was implicated. Although he was the brother of Henry's own step-father, Thomas, Earl of Derby,* the king, fearing that lenience might encourage others in treason, caused Sir William to be condemned and beheaded. To suppress the revolt in Ireland Henry sent Sir Edward Poynings there with four battalions of soldiers. Polydore Vergil divided the Irish into two categories – the wealthier and more civilized who had become anglicized and the native Irish 'wild men of the woods'. Perkin Warbeck had launched his appeal mainly to this second group:

In order, therefore, to harry those who had supported Peter, Edward Poynings turned his forces against the wild Irish, especially since all the other Irish enemies of the king had fled to them so that, having joined forces, they might together defend themselves. Edward, however, when

*The fourth husband of Henry's mother, Lady Margaret Beaufort.

the Irish nobles did not send the aid they had promised, made little progress against the barbarous natives whom he was unable to bring to battle in any one place because they confined themselves to wandering among the forests and marshes on account of their lack of soldiers. Then Edward, suspecting that all this had happened through the guile and deceit of Gerald Earl of Kildare who was governor of the island, suddenly arrested Gerald and led him as a prisoner to the king in England. Although he was charged with many offences he so successfully excused himself that not long afterwards the king sent him back with honour to his governorship in Ireland.* This action had been prompted in the king by a variety of considerations – the man's authority among the barbarous Irish, the critical situation (in which Henry considered a war might well occur), and the trust which had hitherto been placed in the earl. Matters having been settled in this fashion, to obtain some relaxation the king went about midsummer tothe district (that is the 'county') of Lancashire, in order to see his mother Margaret who was then living there with her husband, Thomas, Earl of Derby.(5)

Early in 1495 the wildest rumours were going round England and in the midst of all the turmoil Warbeck and his followers struck in Kent. *The Great Chronicle of London* relates their attack:

Also upon the third day of July arrived at a place or haven in Kent named the Deal, a certain persons to the number of five hundred or moo, the which were of the adherents of that ungracious mawmet in Flanders, that had deceived so many men by th'aid and comfort of a few lewd persons as after will appear. This now being accompanied with fourteen small sails, and thinking that by the commons of Kent that he should have been aided, caused the said number to land, and himself with other rascal hoved still upon the water fast by. And when those other had been a certain season upon land, and saw no comfort of people drawing to them ward, but rather tokens of discomfort, they

*Kildare was Lord Deputy 1486–92, arrested 27 February 1495, re-appointed Lord Deputy 6 August 1496. According to the *Book of Howth* 'as all Ireland could not rule Kildare Henry thought him meet to rule all Ireland.'

withdrew little and little toward their ships. Whereof the Mayor of Sandwich being ware, with such a company as tofore he had provided, came so fast upon them that some were compelled to fight, while the other fled to their ships. In the which fight a few were slain, and upon an hundred and sixty taken on live, among the which were four named captains called Mountford, Corbet, White and Belt, which Mountford was the son of Sir Simon Mountford before beheaded.* And when the chief rebel with the residue of his lewd company saw his men thus slain and taken, seeing well that there was no tarrying to his profit, in all haste hysid up his sails and after drew westward, and the other thus taken, were led unto Sandwich, and so forth toward London, that upon the 12th day of July foresaid, Sir John Pecche then Sheriff of Kent brought them railed in cart ropes as horses been traced to draw in a cart and some in carts unto London bridge foot where the Sheriffs of London being ready received of the said rebels by tale an hundred and fifty-nine, of the which, forty-two were sent unto Newgate, and the remnant were had to the Tower. These were most Flemings and other outlandish men as gunners and other such as lived by theft and ravine.(6)

After this miserable fiasco Warbeck sailed for Ireland. An attack on Waterford failed, and after visiting Cork he fled to Scotland. In July 1496 Giovanni de Bebulcho wrote home from Bruges to Milan giving the latest information about Perkin and the state of affairs in England:

When I asked what news there was of the Duke of York, he† replied that the duke was in Scotland, making a marriage with a cousin of the king there.‡ I asked him if he had heard anything about the Scots invading England. He said he had not, and that the King of Scotland was very poor as regards money, but he had an abundance of men, and that the Scots were the enemies of the English and the friends of the French. I asked him about English affairs. He said that the king is rather

---

*In 1495.
†A Florentine, Aldobrandini, who had been in London at Easter and was then in Bruges.
‡He married Lady Catherine Gordon.

feared than loved, and this was due to his avarice. I asked who ruled
him and had control over him. He said there was only one who can do
anything, and he is named Master Bray,* who controls the king's
treasure. The king is very powerful in money, but if fortune allowed
some lord of the blood royal to rise and he had to take the field, he
would fare badly owing to his avarice; his people would abandon him.
They would treat him as they did King Richard, whom they
abandoned, taking the other side because he put to death his nephews,
to whom the kingdom belonged.(7)

In September 1496 James IV of Scotland and Perkin Warbeck invaded
England. Their expedition was a failure. Although the Scots advanced little
more than four miles across the border and retired panic-stricken within a
few days, their invasion provoked the most dangerous reaction in England.

Taxation and levies of ships and men in the south-west, particularly in
Cornwall, for a punitive expedition, were far in excess of the burdens placed
on the rest of the country, and drove the inhabitants to rebellion. This south-
western rising roused Perkin's hopes once more. James IV proposed to
cooperate with the rebels by a new invasion of the north while Perkin was
to lead an expedition by sea to Cornwall. James persisted although the
Cornish rebellion had been suppressed before his own preparations were
complete. He was soundly defeated early in September by the Earl of Surrey.
After the victory the Milanese ambassador, Raimondo de' Raimondi, visited
Henry VII at Woodstock. Extracts from three letters which he wrote to
Milan between the 8 and 16 September follow:

... On the 2nd we were taken to Oxford, a place for general study, and
the Venetian ambassador was lodged in one of the colleges for the
students and I in another. On the morrow we were fetched to go to
the royal quarters, seven miles from Oxford. When we were a mile off
the Bishop of London and the Duke of Suffolk came to meet us and
received us with a little Latin speech on the part of the bishop. We went
to the royal quarters, where they took us into a room to rest awhile, and
then the same lords and others took us into the royal presence. The

*Sir Reynold Bray, one of Henry's most prominent servants. He was denounced by
the Cornish rebels in 1497.

king was standing and remained so until our departure. The royal seat was adorned with cloth of gold, and besides the multitude of nobles and gentlemen, six bishops, the Cardinal of Canterbury and the Spanish ambassador were also present. There also was the king's eldest son Arthur, Prince of Wales, about eleven years of age, but taller than his years would warrant, of remarkable beauty and grace and very ready in speaking Latin. His Majesty, in addition to his wonderful presence, was adorned with a most rich collar, full of great pearls and many other jewels, in four rows, and in his bonnet he had a pear-shaped pearl, which seems to me something most rich . . .

. . . Your lordship has heard from many of this king's wisdom and ways. I can testify to this, and need add no more. He speaks French, but in such a way that everyone can understand, and above all he evidently has a most quiet spirit . . .

. . . the letter of congratulation, dated 17th July, on the victory gained by the king, came opportunely, though rather late. The victories were two; the first against the Cornishmen, who, some ten thousand in number, took up arms under a blacksmith, declaring that they would not pay the subsidy; the other against the King of Scotland, who raised his camp, not very gloriously, to express myself no less modestly than this most sage king himself did. Another matter also which his Majesty did not tell me, is that the youth, the reputed son of King Edward, has fled incognito, and his wife is said to be a prisoner, so that I consider that this youth called Perkin, has vanished into smoke . . .

. . . this kingdom is perfectly stable, by reason first of the king's wisdom, whereof everyone stands in awe, and secondly on account of the king's wealth, for I am informed that he has upwards of six millions of gold,* and it is said that he puts by annually more than five hundred thousand ducats. This he can accomplish easily, for his revenue is great and real, not merely on paper, nor does he spend anything.

He garrisons two or three fortresses, contrary to the custom of his predecessors, who garrisoned no place. Besides this, he has neither ordnance nor munitions of war, and his bodyguard I suppose does not

*But see *E.H.R.*, lxxix (1964) 254. The amount is grossly exaggerated. Henry left, at most, about £300,000, mainly in jewels and plate; no more than three years' income.

amount to one hundred men,* although he is now living in a forest district which is unfortified . . .

. . . The pope is entitled to much praise, for he loves the king cordially, and strengthens his power by ecclesiastical censures, so that at all times rebels are excommunicated. The efficacy of these censures is now felt by the Cornishmen, who are in this trouble that all who eat grain garnered since the rebellion, or drink beer brewed with this year's crops, die as if they had taken poison, and hence it is publicly reported that the king is under the direct protection of almighty God . . .

. . . Everything favours the king, especially an immense treasure, and because all the nobles of the realm know the royal wisdom and either fear him or bear him an extraordinary affection and not a man of any consideration joins the Duke of York, and the state of the realm is in the hands of the nobles not of the people . . .(8)

Perkin Warbeck, unfortunately for Henry's peace of mind, had not 'vanished into smoke'. Taking a last desperate gamble he landed in Cornwall† with three small ships and about 120 men 'or fewer'. With the addition of local malcontents his forces reached perhaps an untrained rabble of 3,000 men. Two assaults on Exeter were beaten off, an appeal to Taunton failed. Then, after fleeing into the sanctuary at Beaulieu near Southampton, he surrendered.

On 5 October at Taunton Perkin made the following confession, revealing the course of his early life and the origins of his fantastic royal career:

First it is to be known that I was born in the town of Tournai, and my father's name is called John Osbek; which said John Osbeck was controller of the town of Tournai. And my mother's name is Kateryn de Faro. And one of my grandsires upon my father's side was called Deryk Osbeck, which died; after whose death my grandmother was married

---

*The Venetian envoy thought Henry's armaments more considerable, though he admitted that they were less than he expected them to be.
†He wrecked his last chance of success by sailing first to Ireland. His more powerful friends there held aloof, and thus, without additional reinforcements he came to Cornwall too late.

unto the w'in [sic] named Peter Flamme; and that other of my grandsires was called Peter Flam, which was receiver of the foresaid town of Tournai and dean of the boatmen that be upon the water or river of Leystave.* And my grandsire upon my mother's side was called Peter Faro, the which had in his keeping the keys of the gate of St. John's, within the above-named town of Tournai. Also I had an uncle named Master John Stalyn dwelling in the parish of St Pyas within the same town, which had married my father's sister, whose name was Johane or Jane, with whom I dwelled a certain season; and afterward I was led by my mother to Antwerp for to learn Flemish in an house of a cousin of mine, officer of the said town, called John Stienbek, with whom I was the space of half a year. And after that I returned again unto Tournai by reason of the wars that were in Flanders. And within a year following I was sent with a merchant of the said: town of Tournai named Berlo, and his master's name Alex, to the mart of Antwerp, where as I fell sick, which sickness continued upon me five months; and the said Berlo set me to board in a skinner's house, that dwelt beside the house of the English nation. And by him I was brought from thence to the Barowe Mart, and lodged at the Sign of th'Old Man, where I abode the space of two months. And after this the said Berlo set me with a merchant in Middleburgh to service for to learn the language, whose name was John Strewe, with whom I dwelled from Christmas unto Easter; and then I went into Portugal in the company of Sir Edward Brampton's wife in a ship which was called the Queen's ship. And when I was comen thither I was put in service to a knight that dwelled in Lisbon, which was called Peter Vacz de Cogna, with whom I dwelled an whole year, which said knight had but one eye; and then because I desired to see other countries I took licence of him. And then I put myself in service with a Breton, called Pregent Meno, the which brought me with him into Ireland. And when we were there arrived in the town of Cork, they of the town, because I was arrayed with some clothes of silk of my said master's, came unto me and threped† upon me that I should be the Duke of Clarence son, that was before time at Dublin. And for as much as I denied it there was brought

*The River Escaut.
†i.e. asserted, imputed.

unto me the Holy Evangelist and the Cross by the mayor of the town, which was called John Lewelyn; and there in the presence of him and other I took mine oath as truth was that I was not the foresaid duke's son, nother of none of his blood. After this came unto me an English man, whose name was Steffe Poytron, with one John Water, and said to me in swearing great oaths, that they knew well I was King Richard's bastard son; to whom I answered with high oaths that I were not. And then they advised me not to be a-feared but that I should take it upon me boldly, and if I would so do they would aid and assist me with all their power again the King of England; and not only they, but they were well assured that th'Earls of Desmond and Kildare should do the same, for they forsid* not what party so that they might be revenged upon the King of England; and so against my will made me to learn English, and taught me what I should do and say. And after this they called me Duke of York, the second son of King Edward the fourth, because King Richard's bastard son was in the hands of the king of England. And upon this the said John Water, Steffe Poytron, John Tiler, Hubert Bourgh, with many other, as the foresaid earls, entered into this false quarrel. And within short time after this the French king sent unto me an embassy into Ireland, whose names was Loyte Lucas and Master Steffes Frion, to advertise me to come into France; and thence I went into France, and from thence into Flanders, and from Flanders into Ireland, and from Ireland into Scotland, and so into England.(9)

In November Perkin was taken to London and conveyed, a public spectacle, through Cheapside and Cornhill to the Tower. A few days later two of his followers were hanged at Tyburn. The Venetian envoy wrote home that he had seen Perkin, 'Who was in a chamber of the king's palace and habitation. He is a well favoured young man, twenty-three years old, and his wife a very handsome woman; the king treats them well, but did not allow them to sleep together.'[1] His turbulent career was over.‡

Yet at home plots continued. In 1499 the *Great Chronicle of London* tells how:

*i e. cared, regarded.
‡He escaped in June 1498 but was soon recaptured and was executed in November 1499. See below p. 235.

In this passing of time in the borders of Norfolk and Suffolk was a new mawmet areared which named himself to be the forenamed Earl of Warwick, the which by sly and covert means essayed to win to him some adherents. But all in vain. In conclusion he was brought before th'Earl of Oxford, to whom at length he confessed that he was born in London, and that he was son unto a cordyner* dwelling at the Black Bull in Bishopsgate Street, after which confession he was sent up to the king and from him to prison, and upon that arraigned and convict of treason, and finally upon Shrove Tuesday hanged at St Thomas Watering in his shirt, where he so hung still till the Saturday following, and then for noyance of the way passers he was taken down and buried, being of the age of nineteen years or twenty. And as it was of him after reported, he confessed that being at Cambridge at school he was sundry times stirred in his sleep that he should name himself to be the Duke of Clarence's son and he should in process obtain such power that he should be king.(10)

The Ralph Wulford affair (such was the foolish young man's name) seems to have determined Henry that the pretext for such treason must be removed. In November Perkin Warbeck and the innocent Earl of Warwick – he had been a prisoner since boyhood – were both executed. One last pretender now remained – Edmund de la Pole, Earl of Suffolk, the oldest surviving son† of Edward IV's sister Elizabeth. He fled abroad from Henry's court in 1499, returned forgiven, only to flee again in 1501. Until the Archduke Philip of Hapsburg surrendered him to Henry in March 1506, Edmund de la Pole wandered from one European court to another with the incurable, feckless optimism of the émigré, leaving a trail of unpaid bills behind him, depending on charity even for the clothes on his back, an undignified pawn pushed or manipulated into various shady schemes – always a diplomatic embarrassment but, in Henry's eyes, at times a genuine threat to the Crown. The following letter written, probably about 1505, by Thomas Killingworth to the earl shows the desperate straits into which the would-be king had fallen:

*i.e. cordwainer.
†His elder brother John, Earl of Lincoln, had been killed fighting against Henry VII at the battle of Stoke (1487).

Sir, and if your friend* here had not been, I had sent to you ere this
time. He tarried so long ere he sent to you to th'intent he would have
certified you of some news out of England; but as yet he hath heard
none. And he bade me write to you, that touching you he heareth no
thing but good; and also he bade me write to you of th'arresting of the
ships in the king's§ lands; which men say secretly should be for you.
And, Sir, upon the case he saw you in himself, he sendeth you four ells
of the best satin he can buy here, and lining thereunto, and cloth for
two pair hosen and lining. And with this gear he sendeth a servant of
his own for fear it might be taken from Sir Walter¶ [and also, as me
seemeth, to th'intent his servant may see how ye stand; for I perceived
by the sculken‡ he mistrusteth your case.]†

For your gown he asked me how many ells velvet would serve you. I
told him fourteen English yards; and then he said, 'What lining
thereunto?' I answered 'Sarcenet, because of the least cost to help it
forward'. And he said to me, 'Well, I shall see what I can do therein'. So,
Sir, if it please you to write to him in Dutch, and thank him, and give
but one word therein touching your gown, I doubt not ye shall havet
it. And as to the help of my Lord Neville** and your servants, and for
the host in Zwolle,†† I moved him therein after your mind, and thus
much I perceive that [seeing the poverty ye be in] my Lord Neville, I
think he will help of a gown and a bonnet, but further he speaketh not,
neither for the payment of the host nor yet for the help of your
servants. And also he sayeth ye spake not to him of no such things. And,
Sir, and ye had therein spoken plainly to him, it had been otherwise.
For he is a kind and a friendly man, and one word of your own mouth
had been worth an hundred of another man's ...

    ... Now, Sir, this day on Lady D[ay] Mr Paul shewed me certain

*Probably Paul Zachtlevent of Amsterdam.
§Probably Philip of Castile.
¶De la Pole's chaplain.
‡i.e. scout, spy (?)
†Passages in square brackets have been struck out in the original.
**Most probably Sir George Neville, 3rd Baron Abergavenny.
††De la Pole had evidently left Zwolle without paying his bill at the inn.

specialities and writings under the sign and seal of the Duke of York*
concerning money as was due to him by my Lord of York; and, Sir,
under this manner he brake to me. He would fain help you and be also
able to do you good service at the point, and this is his meaning. How
be it, therein no thing will he do, but after your own mind and
pleasure. If it pleased you to be content, he would send by a body of
this town to King Harry the copies of such writings and duties as the
Duke of York oweth him under notaries' signs, desiring him where as
he hath lent his goods unto the duke of York [which was the right
King of England and that] seeing that he is dead without paying, that it
would please King H to pay to him the same money: and if King H
will not do so, as he is sure he will not, then he would show King H
plainly that he will lean to you and aid you with his body and goods to
his power. This is one way whereby he would perceive King H answer.
Item, Sir, another way is this. Paulus was born in the Estland in the
Duke of Pombernes lands joining upon the King of Denmark lands,
whither daily resort merchants of England, where the princes of the
lands are his friends; and therefore, if it pleased your grace, this is his
desire for that purpose. Ye know well th'abusion King H hath made
against the Duke of York that he was a counterfeit. He desireth
therefore to have your certificate that it is untrue, and your authority,
and if it please you to set your sign manual to this parchment that this
bringer shall, [sic] and upon that the same writing shall be made here, if
it be your pleasure. And thereupon he trusteth by the help of the King
of Denmark and the Duke of Pombernes to have recovery shortly of
this good upon some English merchants, and that in short time [if your
cause go not well] and help you therewith; and to th'intent your grace
shall perceive it is his own desire he hath subscribed it with his own
hand, and also he sendeth your grace therewith the secret token betwix
your grace and him; which secret token he beseecheth your grace to
send him again by this bringer . . .(11)

Edmund de la Pole was the last serious pretender, but evidence of
discontent and latent disloyalty came to light again and again. Nearly twenty
years after the battle of Bosworth Henry VII's only surviving son was still a

---

*i.e. Perkin Warbeck.

child and in private conversations prominent men could still ignore his claims to the succession. About the year 1504 John Flamank reported to the king a long discussion between some of the officers of the Calais garrison. One of them, Sir Hugh Conway, the treasurer, had told the following tale:

> . . . the same Sir Hugh said, that 'we be here now together the king's true servants to live and die, and also to spend all that we have in the world to do his grace service. Therefore what so ever we speak or commune for his surety, and for the surety of this his town, can be no treason; so good it is that we look and speak of things to come as well as those present. I do speak this for a cause that is good that we look sadly to, for the king's grace is but a weak man and syklow,* not likely to be no long lives man. It is not long sithens his highness was sick and lay then in his manor of Wanstead.† It happened the same time me to be amongst many great personages, the which fell in communication of the king's grace and of the world that should be after him if his grace happened to depart.' Then he said that some of them spake of my Lord of Buckingham, saying that he was a noble man and would be a royal ruler. Other there were that spake, he said, in likewise of your traitor Edmund de la Pole, but none of them, he said, that spake of my lord prince.(12)

At the last, though even in his final years he still dreaded conspiracy, Henry came though all his perils and his son, Henry VIII, peacefully succeeded him in 1509. Polydore Vergil thus ends his acount of the reign:

> Henry reigned twenty-three years and seven months. He lived for fifty-two years. By his wife Elizabeth he was the father of eight children, four boys and as many girls. He left three surviving children, an only son Henry Prince of Wales, and two daughters; Margaret married to James King of Scotland, and Mary betrothed to Charles Prince of Castile. His body was slender but well built and strong; his height above the average. His appearance was remarkably attractive and his face was cheerful, especially when speaking; his eyes were small and blue, his teeth few, poor and blackish; his hair was thin and white; his complexion

*i.e. sickly.
†Henry bought the manor of Wanstead in 1499.

sallow. His spirit was distinguished, wise and prudent; his mind was brave and resolute and never, even at moments of the greatest danger, deserted him. He had a most pertinacious memory. Withall he was not devoid of scholarship. In government he was shrewd and prudent, so that no one dared to get the better of him through deceit or guile. He was gracious and kind and was as attentive to his visitors as he was easy of access. His hospitality was splendidly generous; he was fond of having foreigners at his court and he freely conferred favours on them. But those of his subjects who were indebted to him or who did not pay him due honour or who were generous only with promises, he treated with harsh severity. He well knew how to maintain his royal majesty and all which appertains to kingship at every time and in every place. He was most fortunate in war, although he was constitutionally more inclined to peace than to war. He cherished justice above all things; as a result he vigorously punished violence, manslaughter and every other kind of wickedness whatsoever. Consequently he was greatly regretted on that account by all his subjects, who had been able to conduct their lives peaceably, far removed from the assaults and evil doing of scoundrels. He was the most ardent supporter of our faith, and daily participated with great piety in religious services. To those whom he considered to be worthy priests, he often secretly gave alms so that they should pray for his salvation. He was particularly fond of those Franciscan friars whom they call Observants, for whom he founded many convents,* so that with his help their rule should continually flourish in his kingdom. But all these virtues were obscured latterly only by avarice.[2] . . . This avarice is surely a bad enough vice in a private individual, whom it forever torments; in a monarch indeed it may be considered the worst vice, since it is harmful to everyone, and distorts those qualities of truthfulness, justice and integrity by which the state must be governed.

> Blessed be our Lord God Jesus Christ
> Mary mother of God
> Pray for us all
> Amen.(13)

---

*At Henry's death there were, in fact, only six convents of Friars Observant in England, of which the king had founded five, three of which were transferred from the order of Friars Conventual.

NOTES

1. *Cal. State Papers Venetian* i, 335, *Pollard*, i, 1897. Abstract of dispatches.
2. This has been disputed. See the controversy between G.R. Elton and J.P. Cooper in *The Historical Journal*, i (1958), ii (1959) and iv (1961).

SEVEN

The Fortunate Island

Although we tend to think of fifteenth-century England as torn apart by civil strife, contemporaries, both English and foreign, held very different opinions. William Worcester recommending that the sons of nobles and gentlemen be trained to arms lamented:

> But now of late days, the greater pity is, many one that been descended of noble blood and born to arms, as knights' sons, esquires, and of other gentle blood, set themself to singular practik, strange faculties from that fet,* as to learn the practique of law or custom of land, or of civil matter, and so wasten greatly their time in such needless business, as to occupy courts' holding, to keep and bear out a proud countenance at sessions and shires' holding, also there to embrace† and rule among your poor and simple commons of bestial countenance that lust to live in rest. And who can be a ruler and put him forth in such matters, he is, as the world goeth now, among all estates more set of than he that hath dispended thirty or forty years of his days in great jeopardies in your antecessours' conquests and wars. So would Jesus they so will well learned them to be as good men of arms, chieftains, or captains in the field that befalleth for them where worship and manhood should be showed, much better rather than as they have learned and can be a captain or a ruler at a sessions or a shire day, to indict or amerce your poor bestial people, to their impoverishing, and to enrich themself or to be magnified the more, but only they should maintain‡ your justices and your officers using the good custom of your laws. And then ye should have right little heed to have thought, anguish or business for to conquer and win again your rightful inheritance, or to defend you

---

*Set, i.e. tendency, inclination.
†i e. to attempt to corrupt.
‡i.e. support, give countenance to.

realm from your enemies. And that such singular practik should not be accustomed and occupied unduly with such men that be come of noble birth, but he be the younger brother, having not whereof to live honestly.(1)

Nor were the nobility less powerful or esteemed at the end of the century than they were at its beginning.* John Russell, Bishop of Lincoln, described by Sir Thomas More as 'as wise man and a good, and of much experience, and one of the best learned men, undoubtedly, that England had in his time,' set down his opinion of the nobility in a sermon intended for the opening of parliament in 1483:

If there be any surety or firmness here in this world, such as may be found out of heaven, it is rather in the isles and lands environed with water than in the sea or in any great Ryvers,** *Nam qui mare navigant pericula narrant.* And therefore the noble persons of the world, which some for the merits of their ancestors, some for their own virtues, been endowed with great havours,† possessions and riches, may more conveniently be resembled unto the firm ground that men see in the islands than the lower people, which for lack of such endowment, not possible to be departed amongst so many, and therefore living by their casual labours, be not without cause likened unto the unstable and wavering running water ... Noblesse is virtue and ancient riches.

. . . The cause why nobles and noble men ought more to be persuaded to accord, and each amiably to hearken upon other, than the whole generality of the people, is plain and evident inowe, considering how the politic rule of every region well ordained standeth in the nobles ...

. . . To you then my lords pertaineth principally the office of hearing of the state of every case falling among yourself, yourself to be reduced by loving treaty, the people by true justice. Ye to be like to Moses and

---

*Contrary to the opinions of several contemporaries and many modern historians the Wars of the Roses made little or no difference to the numbers of the nobility. See Introduction, p. 13ff.

**A punning reference to the Wydeville family.

†i. e. property, wealth.

Aaron, which ascend unto the mount where the law is given. The
people must stand afar, and not pass the limits; ye speak with the prince,
which is *quasi deus noster in terris,* as they did with God mouth to
mouth; but it sufficeth the people to receive with due obeisance the
prince's commandments by the direction of his wise ministers and
officers.(2)

Yet, as the observant Venetian envoy wrote home in 1497, the powers of
the English nobility were restricted within very narrow limits. In his opinion
by continental standards they possessed no wide powers of jurisdiction,
'English noblemen are nothing more than rich gentlemen in possession of a
great quantity of land.'* According to the same writer England was a
disorderly place, not from war, but from the defects of its police and judicial
system due to the earlier over-centralization of the royal courts:

It is the easiest thing in the world to get a person thrown into prison in
this country; for every officer of justice, both civil and criminal, has the
power of arresting anyone, at the request of a private individual, and the
accused person cannot be liberated without giving security, unless he
be acquitted by the judgment of the twelve men above named;§ nor is
there any punishment awarded for making a slanderous accusation.
Such severe measures against criminals ought to keep the English in
check, but, for all this, there is no country in the world where there are
so many thieves and robbers as in England; insomuch, that few venture
to go alone in the country, excepting in the middle of the day,† and
fewer still in the towns at night, and least of all in London.(3)

Sir John Fortescue, while in exile with Queen Margaret in the 1460s,
wrote his book De Laudibus Legum Anglie for the instruction of the young
Prince Edward. In this book he describes the condition of England and
France:

*i.e. a reference to feudal tenures.
§i.e. a jury.
†This statement receives no support from contemporary English writers.

England is indeed so fertile that, compared area to area, it surpasses almost all other lands in the abundance of its produce; it is productive of it own accord, scarcely aided by man's labour. For its fields, plains, glades, and groves abound in vegetation with such richness that they often yield more fruits to their owners uncultivated than ploughed lands, though those are very fertile in crops and corn. Moreover, in that land, pastures are enclosed with ditches and hedges planted over with trees, by which the flocks and herds are protected from the wind and the sun's heat; most of them are irrigated, so that the animals, shut in their pens, do not need watching by day or by night. For in that land there are neither wolves, bears, nor lions, so the sheep lie by night in the fields without guard in their cotes and folds, whereby their lands are fertilised. Hence, the men of that land are not very much burdened with the sweat of labour, so that they live with more spirit, as the ancient fathers did, who preferred to tend flocks rather than to distract their peace of mind with the cares of agriculture. For this reason the men of that land are made more apt and disposed to investigate causes which require searching examination than men who, immersed in agricultural work, have contracted a rusticity of mind from familiarity with the soil. Again, that land is so well stocked and replete with possessors of land and fields that in it no hamlet, however small, can be found in which there is no knight, esquire, or householder of the sort commonly called a franklin, well-off in possessions; nor numerous other free tenants, and many yeomen . . .

. . . You remember, most admirable prince, you have seen how rich in fruits are the villages and towns of the Kingdom of France, whilst you were travelling there, but so burdened by the men-at-arms, and their horses, of the king of that land, that you could be entertained in scarcely any of them except the great towns. There you learned from the inhabitants that those men, though they might be quartered in one village for a month or two, paid or wished to pay absolutely nothing for the expenses of themselves and their horses, and, what is worse, they compelled the inhabitants of the villages and towns on which they descended to supply them at their own charges with wines, meats, and other things that they required, and from neighbouring villages with more choice provender than they found there. And if any declined to do so, they were quickly compelled by cudgelling to do it at once; and then these men, having consumed the victuals, fuel and fodder for their horses in one village, hastened to another, to devastate it in the same manner, paying not a penny for any of their own necessaries nor those of their concubines, whom they always carried with them in great numbers, nor for shoes, hose, or other items of the same sort, even to the smallest strap; on the contrary, they made the inhabitants of the villages where they stayed pay all their expenses of every kind. This is done in every village and town that is unwalled in the whole of that country, so that there is not one small town which is free from this calamity, and which is not plundered by this abominable extortion once or twice a year. Moreover, the king does not suffer anyone of his realm to eat salt, unless he buys it from the king himself at a price fixed by his pleasure alone. And if any poor man prefers to eat without salt rather than buy it at excessive price, he is soon compelled to buy as much salt at the king's price as is proportionate to the number of persons he supports in his home. Furthermore, all the inhabitants of that realm give to their king every year a fourth part of all the wines that accrue to them, and every innkeeper a fourth penny of the price of the wines that he sells; and yet again all villages and towns pay to the king annually hugh sums assessed on them for the wages of men-at-arms, so that the king's troops, which are always very numerous, are kept in wages every year by the poor of the villages, towns, and cities of the realm. In addition, each village always maintains at least two archers, and some more, sufficiently accoutred and equipped to serve the king in his wars as often as it pleases him to summon them, which he frequently does. Notwithstanding all these, other very heavy tallages are levied to the use of the king every year, on every village of the realm, from which they are relieved in not a single year.

Exasperated by these and other calamities, the people live in no little misery. They drink water daily, and they taste no other liquor unless at solemn feasts. They wear frocks or tabards of canvas like sackcloth. They do not use woollens, except of the cheapest sort, and that only in their shirts under their frocks, and wear no hose, unless to the knees, exposing the rest of their shins Their women are barefooted except on feast days; the men and women eat no flesh, except bacon lard, with which they fatten their pottage in the smallest quantity. They do not taste other meats, roast or boiled, except occasionally the offal and heads of animals killed for the nobles and merchants. On the contrary, the men-at-arms eat their poultry, so that they are left with scarcely their eggs for themselves to eat as a rare delicacy. And if anyone grows in wealth at any time, and is reputed rich among the others, he is at once assessed for the king's subsidy more than his neighbours, so that forthwith he is levelled to their poverty. This, unless I am mistaken, is the condition of the plebeian people's estate in that realm; yet the nobles are not thus oppressed with exactions ...

... In the realm of England, no one billets himself in another's house against its master's will, unless in public hostelries, where even so he will pay in full for all that he has expended there, before his departure thence; nor does anyone take with impunity the goods of another without the permissionof the proprietor of them; nor, in that realm, is anyone hindered from providing himself with salt or any goods whatever, at his own pleasure and of any vendor. The king, indeed, may, by his officers, take necessaries for his household, at a reasonable price to be assessed at the discretion of the constables of the villages, without the owners' permission. But none the less he is obliged by his own laws to pay this price out of hand or at a day fixed by the greater officers of his household, because by those laws he cannot despoil any of his subjects of their goods without due satisfaction for them. Nor does the king there, by himself or by his ministers, impose tallages, subsidies, or any other burdens whatever on his subjects, nor change their laws, nor make new ones, without the concession or assent of his whole realm expressed in his parliament.

Hence every inhabitant of that realm uses at his own pleasure the fruits which his land yields, the increase of his flock, and all the emoluments which he gains, whether by his own industry or that of others, from land and sea, hindered by the injuries and rapine of none without obtaining at least due amends. Hence the inhabitants of that land are rich, abounding in gold and silver and all the necessities of life. They do not drink water, except those who sometimes abstain from other drinks by way of devotional or penitential zeal. They eat every kind of flesh and fish in abundance, with which their land is not meanly stocked. They are clothed with good woollens throughout their garments; they have abundant bedding, woollen like the rest of their furnishings, in all their houses, and are rich in all household goods and agricultural equipment, and in all that is requisite for a quiet and happy life, according to their estate.(4)

Fortescue's depressing account of the poverty and degradation of the French peasantry was not the prejudiced vision of a homesick *émigré*. It is amply confirmed by the Cahier of the Third Estate presented two decades later at the meeting of the Estates General at Tours in 1484, part of which follows:

As to the common people (menu peuple), who cannot imagine the persecutions, poverty and wretchedness, which they have suffered and suffer in many ways.

First, since the said time,* there has been no district where they have not always been men-at-arms coming and going, living on the poor people, now men-at-arms of the ordnance, now the nobles of the ban,† now the franc-archers, formerly the halbardiers and at other times the Swiss and the spearsmen who have done them infinite wrongs.

And there should be noted and piteously considered the injustice and iniquity with which the poor people have been treated, for the men of war are paid for the resistance of oppression, and these are they who oppress most. The poor peasant must pay and support those who beat him, who turn him out of his house, who make him sleep on the ground, and who rob him of his substance; and wages are paid to the men-at-arms to preserve and defend them, and guard their possessions!

All this evil is obvious enough; for when the poor peasant has worked all the day, with great effort and sweat of his body, and has gathered in the fruit of his said work, on which he expects to live, someone comes to carry off the fruit of his said work, to hand it over to such people as will perhaps beat the poor peasant before the end of the month, and will come and carry off the horses which work the land which yields the crops with which the man of war is paid. And when the poor peasant works to pay with great difficulty his share of the taille for the pay of the men-at-arms and what he believes left to him for his support, hoping that he will be able to live and get through

* Since *c.* 1415.
† i.e. those called out for feudal military service.

the year, or for sowing, there come some or other men-at-arms who will eat and consume the little which the poor man has kept in order to live . . .

The account continues to elaborate the misdeeds and oppressions of the soldiery and to complain of the ruinously increased burden of French royal taxation:*

. . . because of which have followed many great and piteous inconveniences: for some [of the people] have fled and retired into England, Brittany and elsewhere; and others dead of hunger in great and uncountable numbers: and others out of despair have killed wives, children and themselves seeing that they had nothing on which to live. And many men, women and children, for lack of beasts, are forced to labour, yoked to the plough; and others work at night, for fear that they will be taken and arrested for the said tailles by day. By reason of which, part of the land is left untilled, and all because they are subject to the will of those who desire to enrich themselves from the goods of the people, and without the consent and deliberation of the three estates. And in like manner the district of Languedoc has been marvellously vexed and tormented with tailles and imposts; so that during the lifetime of the said King Charles VII they paid only about fifty thousand pounds *tournois*, and at the time of the death of the last deceased king, they amounted to more than six hundred thousand pounds. Matters have gone the same way in France, Guienne, Bourbonnais, Rouergue, Quercy, Languedoc [sic], Auvergne, Forez, Beaujolais, Champagne, Vermandois, Nivernais, Rethelois, Lyonnais, and Gatinois, Poitou, Limousin, Artois, Picardy, Berri and the other districts of the kingdom, each in its place, the which districts by reason of the said charges have mostly fallen in piteous and dolorous case, which would be too long to tell . . .(5)

So far as we know these heart-rending accusations were never denied. From England, by contrast, we have no descriptions of the hideous, brutalizing effects of war. Englishmen would certainly have chronicled such

*The amount of the taille rose from 1,200,000 livres in 1462 to 4,600,000 in 1481.

horrors had they existed, for they denounced the evils inflicted upon the people by the greed of the landowning classes. The year before the meeting of the Estates General at Tours Bishop Russell wrote:

[Let] there by alway ordained officers to oversee, and not to permit any owner to abuse the possession of his own thing, *Ne civitas defloreteur ruinis*, lest that by the several sloth and negligence of the land lords, cities and towns should fall to extreme decay and ruin. If this be not so well accepted in this land as liberty, it is light to see what is grown thereof, by the decay of well nigh all the cities and boroughs of the same.(6)

The Warwickshire antiquarian, John Rous, who died in 1491, denounced enclosures long before the Tudor pamphleteers:

What shall be said of the modern destruction of villages which brings Dearth to the commonwealth? The root of this evil is greed. The plague of avarice infects these times and it blinds men. They are not sons of God, but of Mammon ... As Christ wept over Jerusalem so do we over the destruction of our own times. There are men who rejoice: and Christ's sorrow is their pleasure. The Church suffers also and our land looks as if an enemy had passed over it. How many outrageous things do men perform!

They enclose the area of a village with mounds and surround it with ditches. In such places the king's highway is blocked and poor people cannot pass through. Where villages decay, there also do tithes. The word of God to Noah is mocked: Grow multiply and fill the earth.

If such destruction as that in Warwickshire* took place in other parts of the country it would be a national danger. Yet not all my list is of Warwickshire villages: some albeit a few, are in Gloucestershire and Worcestershire.(7)

Although most travellers remarked upon the vast tracts of uncultivated land in England they were also at pains to emphasize the country's obvious

---

*He gives a list of fifty-eight places depopulated in Warwickshire, all but two of which have been identified.

prosperity. The intelligent, well-informed, if occasionally somewhat over-caustic Venetian envoy of 1497 wrote home his final considered opinions to his Doge and Senate. We may also adopt them as a fitting epilogue to the civil wars:

> ... The riches of England are greater than those of any other country in Europe, as I have been told by the oldest and most experienced merchants, and also as I myself can vouch, from what I have seen. This is owing, in the first place, to the great fertility of the soil, which is such, that, with the exception of wine, they import nothing from abroad for their subsistence. Next, the sale of their valuable tin brings in a large sum of money to the kingdom; but still more do they derive from their extraordinary abundance of wool,* which bears such a high price and reputation throughout Europe. And in order to keep the gold and silver in the country, when once it has entered, they have made a law, which has been in operation for a long time now, that no money, nor gold nor silver plate should be carried out of England under a very heavy penalty. And every one who makes a tour in the island will soon become aware of this great wealth, as will have been the case with your Magnificence, for there is no small innkeeper, however poor and humble he may be, who does not serve his table with silver dishes and drinking cups; and no one, who has not in his house silver plate to the amount of at least £100 sterling, which is equivalent to 500 golden crowns with us, is considered by the English to be a person of any consequence. but above all are their riches displayed in the church treasures; for there is not a parish church in the kingdom so mean as not to possess crucifixes, candlesticks, censers, patens and cups of silver; nor is there a convent of mendicant friars so poor, as not to have all these same articles in silver,† besides many other ornaments worthy of a cathedral church in the same metal. Your Magnificence may therefore imagine what the decorations of those enormously rich Benedictine,

---

*In fact by this time the exports of wool had steeply declined, mainly owing to the demands of the domestic cloth industry.
†This is exaggerated. In his will Henry VII directed that a silver pyx engraved with the royal arms should be given to every parish and friary church which possessed only a wooden one.

Carthusian, and Cistercian monasteries must be. These are, indeed, more like baronial palaces than religious houses . . .

. . . The population of this island does not appear to me to bear any proportion to her fertility and riches . . .

. . . all the beauty of this island is confined to London; which, although sixty miles distant from the sea, possesses all the advantages to be desired in a maritime town; being situated on the River Thames, which is very much affected by the tide, for many miles (I do not know the exact number) above it: and London is so much benefited by this ebb and flow of the river, that vessels of 100 tons burden can come up to the city, and ships of any size to within five miles of it; yet the water in this river is fresh for twenty miles below London. Although this city has no buildings in the Italian style, but of timber or brick like the French, the Londoners live comfortably, and, it appears to me, that there are not fewer inhabitants than at Florence or Rome. It abounds with every article of luxury, as well as with the necessaries of life: but the most remarkable thing in London, is the wonderful quantity of wrought silver. I do not allude to that in private houses, though the landlord of the house in which the Milanese ambassador lived, had plate to the amount of 100 crowns, but to the shops of London. In one single street, named the Strand,* leading to St Paul's, there are fifty-two goldsmith's shops, so rich and full of silver vessels, great and small, that in all the shops in Milan, Rome, Venice, and Florence put together, I do not think there would be found so many of the magnificence that are to be seen in London. And these vessels are all either salt cellars, or drinking cups, or basins to hold water for the hands; for they eat off that fine tin,† which is little inferior to silver. These great riches of London are not occasioned by its inhabitants being noblemen or gentlemen; being all, on the contrary, persons of low degree, and artificers who have congregated there from all parts of the island, and from Flanders, and from every other place . . . Still, the citizens of London are thought quite as highly of there, as the Venetian gentlemen are at Venice . . .

*Not the Strand but Cheapside.
†i.e. pewter.

The English are, for the most part, both men and women of all ages, handsome and well-proportioned; though not quite so much so, in my opinion, as it had been asserted to me, before your Magnificence went to that kingdom; and I have understood from persons acquainted with the countries, that the Scotch are much handsomer; and that the English are great lovers of themselves, and of everything belonging to them; they think that there are no other men than themselves, and no other world but England; and whenever they see a handsome foreigner, they say that 'he looks like an Englishman', and that 'it is a pity that he should not be an Englishman'; and when they partake of any delicacy with a foreigner, they ask him, 'whether such a thing is made in *their* country?' They take great pleasure in having a quantity of excellent victuals, and also in remaining a long time at table, being very sparing of wine when they drink it at their own expense. And this, it is said, they do in order to induce their other English guests to drink wine in moderation also; not considering it any inconvenience for three or four persons to drink out of the same cup. Few people keep wine in their own houses, but buy it, for the most part, at a tavern; and when they mean to drink a great deal, they go to the tavern, and this is done not only by the men, but by ladies of distinction. The deficiency of wine, however, is amply supplied by the abundance of ale and beer, to the use of which these people are become so habituated, that, at an entertainment where there is plenty of wine, they will drink them in preference to it, and in great quantities. Like discreet people, however, they do not offer them to Italians, unless they should ask for them; and they think that no greater honour can be conferred or received, than to invite others to eat with them, or to be invited themselves; and they would sooner give five or six ducats to provide an entertainment for a person, than a groat to assist him in any distress.

They all from time immemorial wear very fine clothes, and are extremely polite in their language; which, although it is, as well as the Flemish, derived from the German, has lost its natural harshness, and is pleasing enough as they pronounce it. In addition to their civil speeches, they have the incredible courtesy of remaining with their heads uncovered, with an admirable grace, whilst they talk to each other. They are gifted with good understandings, and are very quick at every thing they apply their minds to; few, however, excepting the clergy, are addicted to the study of letters ...

They have a very high reputation in arms; and from the great fear the French entertain of them, one must believe it to be justly acquired. But I have it on the best information, that when the war is waging most furiously, they will seek for good eating, and all their other comforts, without thinking of what harm might befal them.

They have an antipathy to foreigners, and imagine that they never come into their island, but to make themselves masters of it, and to usurp their goods; neither have they any sincere and solid friendships amongst themselves, insomuch that they do not trust each other to discuss either public or private affairs together, in the confidential manner we do in Italy. And although their dispositions are somewhat licentious, I never have noticed any one, either at court or amongst the lower orders, to be in love; whence one must necessarily conclude, either that the English are the most discreet lovers in the world, or that they are incapable of love. I say this of the men, for I understand that it is quite the contrary with the women, who are very violent in their passions. Howbeit the English keep a very jealous guard over their wives, though any thing may be compensated, in the end, by the power of money.(8)

LIST OF ABBREVIATIONS

B.I.H.R.	*Bulletin of the Institute of Historical Research.*
Commynes	P. de Commynes, *Mémoires*, ed. J. Calmette et G. Dunille, 3 vols., Paris, 1924–5; translated by A.R. Scoble, Bohn's Antiquarian Library, 2 vols., London, 1855–6.
Croyland	'Historiae Croylandensis Continuatio' in *Jerum Anglicarum Scriptorum Veterum*, tom. 1. ed. W. Fulman, Oxford, 1684; translated by H.T. Riley, *Ingulphus Chronicle of the Abbey of Croyland*, Bohn's Antiquarian Library, London, 1854.
C.S.	Camden Series.
C.S.P.M.	*Calendar of State Papers and Manuscripts existing in the Archives and Collections of Milan*, i, ed. and translated by A.B. Hinds, 1912.
Davies	*An English Chronicle of the Reigns of Richard II, Henry IV, Henry V, and Henry VI*, ed. J.S. Davies, C.S., 1856.
E.E.T.S.	Early English Text Society.
E.H.L.	C.L. Kingsford, *English Historical Literature in the Fifteenth Century*, Oxford, 1913.
E.H.R.	*English Historical Review.*
Flenley	*Six Town Chronicles of England*, ed. R. Flenley, Oxford, 1911.
G.C.L.	*The Great Chronicle of London*, ed. A.H. Thomas and I.D. Thornley, London, 1938.
Gregory	'Gregory's Chronicle', in *The Historical Collections of a Citizen of London*, ed. J. Gairdner, C.S., 1876.
Mancini	*The Usurpation of Richard III (Dominicus Mancinus ad Angelum Catonem de Occupatione Regni Anglie Per Riccardum Tercium Libellus)*, ed. and translated by C.A.J. Armstrong, Oxford, 1936.

More	'The History of King Richard III', in *The English Works of Sir Thomas More*, ed. W.E. Campbell, i, 1931.
P.L.	*The Paston Letters*, ed. J. Gairdner, 4 vols., Edinburgh, 1910.
Pollard	A.F. Pollard, *The Reign of Henry VII from Contemporary Sources*, 3 vols., London, 1913–14.
P.R.O.	Public Record Office.
P.V.(E)	*Three Books of Polydore Vergil's English History*, ed. Sir H. Ellis, C.S., 1844, from a sixteenth-century translation.
P.V.(H.)	*The Anglica Historia of Polydore Vergil, A.D. 1485–1537*, ed. and translated by D. Hay, C.S., 1950.
R.P.	*Rotuli Parliamentorum*, 6 vols., London, 1767.
R.S.	Rolls Series.
Stevenson	*Letters and Papers Illustrative of the Wars of the English in France During the Reign of Henry VI*, ed. J. Stevenson, 2 vols., R. S., 1861–4.
Warkworth	J. Warkworth, *A Chronicle of the First Thirteen Years of the Reign of King Edward the Fourth*, ed J.O. Halliwell, C.S, 1839.

SOURCES

One: The House of Lancaster

1. *R.P.*, iii, 422–3.
2. *Chronicon Adae de Usk*, A.D. 1377–1421 ed. and trans. E. Maunde Thompson. pp. 133, 319–20, 1904.
3. Extracts from Sir John Fastolf's Report upon the Management of the War in France upon the Conclusion of the Treaty of Arras', Stevenson, ii Pt. ii, 575–85, sections on pp. 579–82.
4. 'Collectarium Mansuetudinum et Bonorum Morum Regis Henrici VI, ex Collectione Magistri Joannis Blakman bacchalaurei theologiae, et post Cartusiae monachi Londoni,' ed. and trans. M.R. James as *Henry the Sixth*, pp. 4–5, 7–8, 13–14, 26–27, 29–30, 35–36, 1919.
5. P.R.O., Warrants for Issues, E. 404/57/166.
6. P.R.O., Warrants for Issues E. 404/62/188.
7. T. Basin, *Histoire de Charles VII*, ed. C. Samaran, i, 84–89, 1933–44.
8. Davies, Appendix, pp. 116–17.
9. 'A Chronicle for 1445 to 1455', in *E.H.L.*, p. 344.
10. *Davies*, p. 64.
11. *R.P.*, v, 176.
12. *R.P.*, v, 177–81.
13. *P.L.* i, 124–5.
14. *Gregory*, pp. 190–4.
15. *R.P.*, v, 346.
16. P.R.O., Ancient Indictments, Suffolk K.B. 9/118/30.
17. *P.L.* i, 150–3.
18. Stevenson, ii, Pt. ii, 770.
19. 'London Chronicle for 1446–1452', in *E.H.L.*, pp. 297–8.
20. *P.L.*, i, 263–4, 265–7. 'News Letter' of John Stodeley.
21. *R.P.*, v, 241.
22. *R.P.*, v, 242.
23. *P.L.*, i, 315.
24. *R.P.*, v, 280–1.

25. 'The Dijon Relation'; Dijon, Archives de la Côte d'Or, B. 11942, no. 258, printed by C.A.J. Armstrong in 'Politics and the Battle of St Albans, 1455', in *B.I.H.R.*, xxxiii (1960), 63–65.

26. *P.L.*, i, 345–6.

27. *R.P.*, v. 284–5.

28. G.H. Radford, 'Nicholas Radford, 1385(?)–1455', in *Trans. of the Devonshire Association*, xxxv (1903), 265–8, printed from a petition (then in the Duke of Northumberland's collections) exhibited to the king in parliament by John Radford, cousin and executor of Nicholas Radford.

29. *R.P.*, v, 285.

30. *Historical Poems of the 14th and 15th Centuries*, (ed.) R.H. Robbins (1959), pp. 189–90.

31. *Davies*, pp. 75, 79–83.

32. *R.P.*, v, 348–9.

33. J. de Waurin, *Recueil des Croniques etAnchiennes Istories de la Grant Bretaigne, a present Nomme Engleterre*, ed.W. Hardy (R.S., 1864–91), v, 275–6.

34. *Davies*, p. 89.

35. *P.L.*, i, 535, Letter of 23 October 1460.

36. J.P. Gilson, 'A Defence of the Proscription of the Yorkists in 1459', in *E.H.R.* xxvi (1911), 512–25, especially pp. 516–18.

Two: The Fight for the Throne

1. *P.L.*, i, 506.

2. *Davies*, 90.

3. Ibid., p. 91.

4. *C.S.P.M.*, i, 24.

5. *Davies*, pp. 94–98.

6. *Registrum Abbatiae Johannis Whethamstede, Abbatis Monasterii Sancti Albani*, ed. H.T. Riley (R.S. 1872–3), i, 376–8.

7. *Waurin*, op. cit., v, 313–15.

8. *R.P.*, v, 375–9.

9. *Gregory*, pp. 208–10.

10. *Davies*, pp. 106–7.

11. *Croyland*, p. 531, Bohn's trans. pp. 421–3.

12. *Gregory*, p. 211.

13. *Gregory*, pp. 211–14.

14. *C.S.P.M.*, i, 49–50.

15. *G.C.L.*, pp. 194–6.

16. *Stevenson*, ii, Pt. ii, 777.

17. *C.S.P.M.*, i, 58.
18. *C.S.P.M.*, i, 58–59.
19. *C.S.P.M.*, i, 61–62.
20. *C.S.P.M.*, i, 69.
21. *C.S.P.M.*, i, 74–77.

Three: Edward of York and Warwick the Kingmaker

1. *R.P.*, v, 463–7.
2. *C.S.P.M.*, i, 106–7.
3. *P.L.*, ii, 91.
4. 'B.M. Vitellius A XIV', printed in C.L. Kingsford, *Chronicles of London* (1905), pp. 177–8.
5. *Gregory*, pp. 219–26.
6. R. Fabyan, *The New Chronicles of England and France*, ed. H. Ellis (1811), p. 654.
7. *Stevenson*, ii, Pt. ii, 783–6.
8. *Œuvres de Georges Chastellain*, (ed.) M. le Baron Kervyn de Lettenhove (1863–5), iv, 278–80, 284–6.
9. *C.S.P.M.*, i, 116, Letter of 6 February 1465.
10. *Warkworth*, p. 5.
11. *C.S.P.M.*, i, 117–18. Letter of 14 February 1467 written from Bourges-en-Berri.
12. *C.S.P.M.*, i, 120. Letter of 19 May 1467.
13. J. de Waurin, *Recueil des Croniques et Anchiennes Istories de la Grant Bretaigne, a present Nomme Engleterre*, ed. Mlle Dupont (1858–63), iii, 186–95; trans. L.D. Thornley, *England Under the Yorkists* (1921), pp. 33–36.
14. *C.S.P.M.*, i 124–5.
15. *Stevenson*, ii, Pt. ii, 788–9.
16. *G.C.L.*, pp. 205–8.
17. *Croyland*, pp. 551–2; Bohn's trans., pp. 457–9.
18. 'Chronicle of the Rebellion in Lincolnshire, 1470', ed. J.G. Nichols in *Camden Miscellany*, i (1847), 5–12.
19. *Commynes*, i, 193–6; Bohn's trans., i, 184–6.
20. 'B.M. Harleian 543, f. 169 b,' printed in H. Ellis, *Original Letters Illustrative of English History*, 2 Ser., i (1827), 132–5.
21. *Warkworth*, pp. 10–13.
22. *Historie of the Arrivall of Edward IV in England and the Finall Recouverye of his Kingdomes from Henry VI. A.D. M. CCCC LXXI*, ed. J. Bruce (C.S., 1838), pp. 2–4, 5–11, 12–14, 15, for the last four extracts.

23. *G.C.L.*, p. 215.
24. *Commynes*, i, 213; Bohn's trans., i, 200.
25. *Arrivall*, op. cit., pp. 18–30.
26. *Warkworth*, pp. 19–22.

Four: Peace and Success, 1471–1483

1. *Croyland*, p. 557; Bohn's trans., pp. 469–70.
2. *Warkworth* pp. 26–27.
3. *C.S.P.M.*, i, 164–8.
4. *R.P.*, vi, 121.
5. *G.C.L.*, p. 223.
6. *C.S.P.M.*, i, 189. Letter *c.* 1475.
7. *Commynes*, ii, 54–60, 62–67, 69–70; Bohn's trans., i, 268–73, 274–7, 279.
8. *Croyland*, p. 559; Bohn's trans., P. 473.
9. *R.P.*, v, 572.
10. *The Plumpton Correspondence*, ed. T. Stapleton (C.S., 1839), p. 33.
11. *P.L.*, iii, 235.
12. *The Boke of Noblesse*, op. cit., pp. 80–81.
13. *Croyland*, pp. 561–2; Bohn's trans., pp. 477–80.
14. *More*, pp. 56–57, 431–2.   i
15. *Croyland*, pp. 562, 563–4; Bohn's trans., pp. 480, 481–2, 483–4.
16. *Mancini*, pp. 78–85.

Five: Richard III

1. *Mancini*, pp. 85–91.
2. *More*, pp. 42–43, 407–11.
3. *Mancini*, pp. 107–115.
4. *P.V. (E)*, pp. 183–6.
5. *Croyland*, pp. 566–7; Bohn's trans., p. 489.
6. *More*, pp. 67–68, 449–51.
7. *Croyland*, pp. 567–8, 570; Bohn's trans., pp. 490–3, 495, for the last three extracts.
8. *G.C.L.*, p. 236.
9. *Croyland*, pp. 571–3; Bohn's trans., pp. 498–500.
10. *Acts of Court of the Mercers' Company, 1453–1537*, ed. L. Lyell and F.D. Wamey (1936), pp. 173–4.
11. *Croyland*, pp. 573–4; Bohn's trans., pp. 500–502.
12. *P.V. (E)*, pp. 220–7.

Six: Henry VII and the Last of the Wars

1. *Croyland*, p. 581; Bohn's trans., pp. 511–12.
2. *P.V. (H.)*, pp. 10–27, for the last five extracts.
3. *G.C.L.*, p. 241.
4. *R.P.*, vi, 454–5; Pollard, i, 82–84.
5. *P.V. (H.)*, pp. 64–81.
6. *G.C.L.*, pp. 258–9.
7. *C.S.P.M.*, i, 299–300, Pollard, i, 135–6.
8. *C.S.P.M.*, i, 321–6; part printed in Pollard, i, 159–60, 164.
9. 'B.M. Vitellius A XVI,' printed in C.L. Kingsford, *Chronicles of London* (1905), pp. 219–221; Pollard, i, 183–5.
10. *G.C.L.*, p. 289.
11. J. Gairdner, *Letters and Papers Illustrative of the Reigns of Richard III and Henry VII* (R.S., 1861–3), i, 263–5.
12. J. Gairdner, *Letters and Papers etc.*, op. cit., i, 231–40; *Pollard*, i, 240–50. Dated by Gairdner *c.* 1503, but Pollard suggests *c.* 1504 at the earliest.
13. *P.V. (H.)*, pp. 142–7.

Seven: The Fortunate Island

1. *The Boke of Noblesse*, op. cit., pp. 77–78.
2. 'Brit. Mus., MS. Cott. Vitellius E.x. Art 23, f. 177' printed in *Grants of King Edward the Fifth*, ed. J.G. Nichols (C.S., 1854), pp. 1–li; see also p. lix.
3. *A Relation, or Rather a True Account, of the Island of England* ed. and trans. C.A. Sneyd (C.S., 1847), pp. 33, 34, 36.
4. *Sir J. Fortescue, De Laudibus Legum Anglie*, ed. and trans. S.B. Chrimes (1949), pp. 67–71, 81–85, 87–89.
5. *Journal des États Généveux de France Tonus à Tours en 1484*, ed. J. Messelin et A. Bernior (Collections de Documents Inédits sur l'Histoire de France, Paris, 1835), pp. 672–5.
6. *Grants of King Edward V*, op. cit., pp. 1–li.
7. J. Rous, *Historie Regum Anglie*, ed. T. Hearne (1745), pp. 113–18. I have used the very free translation and condensation of Rous' excessively long and garrulous denunciation made by M. Beresford in *The Lost Villages of England* (1954), p. 81.
8. *Italian Relation*, op. cit. pp. 28–9, 31, 41–3, 20–4.

Chronological Table

1399	30 September	Usurpation of Henry IV.
1411	21 September	Birth of Richard of York.
1421	6 December	Birth of Henry VI.
1422	31 August– 1 September	Death of Henry V.
1434	April–May	York takes part in a Great Council at Westminster.
1435	1 July– 6 September	Congress of Arras.
	September	Fastolf's Report upon the Management of the War in France.
	14–15 September	Death of John, Duke of Bedford.
	21 September	Reconciliation of Burgundy and France.
1436–7		Richard of York Lieutenant-General of France and Normandy.
1436	12 December	Henry VI signs his first royal warrant.
1439	September	Failure of Anglo-French peace negotiations at Oye.
1440–5		York Lieutenant-General of France and Normandy.
1443	30 March	John Beaufort, Duke of Somerset, appointed Captain-General of France and Guienne.
1444	24 May	Betrothal of Henry VI and Margaret of Anjou.
	28 May	Truce with France.
1445	9 April	Margaret of Anjou lands at Portsmouth.
	September– December	York returns to England.
1447	February	Parliament of Bury St Edmunds. Death of Humphrey, Duke of Gloucester.
	11 April	Death of Cardinal Beaufort.
	9 December	York appointed Lieutenant of Ireland.
1449	24–25 March	Sack of Fougeres.
1449	(March)– 1450 (April)	Loss of Normandy.
1450	22 January	Suffolk's Apologia in parliament.
	17 March	Suffolk banished for five years.

	2 May	Suffolk murdered.
	21 May–12 July	Cade's rebellion.
	August	York returns from Ireland.
	September (?)	Somerset returns from Calais.
1451	June	Thomas Yonge's petition that York be recognized as heir to the throne.
1452	February–March	York's insurrection at Dartmouth.
1453	By 10 August	Henry VI insane.
	13 October	Birth of Henry VI's heir, Edward, Prince of Wales.
1454	(3 April)–	York's First Protectorate.
	1455 (February)	
1455		Henry VI recovers sanity.
1455	22 May	Battle of St Albans I. Death of Edmund, Duke of Somerset.
1455–	19 November–	York's Second Protectorate
1456	25 February	
1455–6		York and the Nevilles obtain control of Calais.
1459	23 September	Battle of Blore Heath.
	12–13 October	Flight of York, March, Salisbury and Warwick from Ludford.
	November	Parliament of Devils at Coventry. Attainder of the Yorkists.
1460	26 June	March, Salisbury and Warwick cross from Calais and land in Kent.
	10 July	Battle of Northampton
	September	York returns from Ireland.
	October	York's claim put to parliament. Act of Accord. York recognized as heir to the throne.
	30 December	Battle of Wakefield. Death of York.
1461	2 February	Battle of Mortimer's Cross.
	17 February	Battle of St Albans II.
	4 March	Edward IV accepted as king.
	29 March	Battle of Towton.
1462	February	Arrest and execution of the Earl of Oxford.
1462	16 April	Margaret of Anjou in Brittany.
	September	Margaret of Anjou and Pierre de Brezé land in Northumberland. Their fleet wrecked. Escape to Berwick.
1462	(December)–	Lancastrians surrender the Northumbrian castles.
	1463 (January)	

1463	Spring (?)	Lancastrians recover Northumbrian castles.
	August	Margaret of Anjou and Prince Edward sail to Flanders.
1464		Defection of Henry, Duke of Somerset. Lancastrian risings in the north.
	25 April	Skirmish at Hedgeley Moor.
	1 May	Edward IV secretly marries Elizabeth Wydeville.
	14 May	Battle of Hexham.
	June	Lancastrians finally ejected from Northumbrian castles.
1465	July	Capture of Henry VI.
1468	June–November	Treason scares, arrests and executions.
	3 July	Marriage of Charles the Bold of Burgundy and Margaret of York.
1469	June	Robin of Redesdale's rebellion.
	11 July	Marriage of George, Duke of Clarence and Isabel Neville at Calais.
	26 July	Battle of Edgecote.
	August	Edward IV Warwick's prisoner at Middleham.
1470	February–March	The Lincolushire rising.
	12 March–	Battle of Empingham (Losecote Field). Flight of Clarence and Warwick.
	April	Refused entrance to Calais.
	5 May	Clarence and Warwick land at Honfleur.
	mid-July–	Reconciliation of Margaret of Anjou and Warwick at
	August	Angers.
	13 September	Warwick's invasion force lands at Dartmouth and Plymouth.
	29 September	Edward IV flees from Lynn to Holland. Restoration of Henry VI. (The Readeption, 6 October 1470–11 April, 1471).
1471	14 March	Edward IV lands at Ravenser.
	14 April	Battle of Barnet. Death of Warwick. Margaret of Anjou and Edward, Prince of Wales land at Weymouth.
1473	30 September	John, Earl of Oxford, takes St Michael's Mount.
1474	15 February	John, Earl of Oxford, surrenders St Michael's Mount.
1475	4 July	Edward IV crosses to Calais for the French campaign.
	29 August	Meeting at Pécquigny.
1478	18 February	Death of George, Duke of Clarence.
1483	9 April	Death of Edward IV.
	11 April	Edward V proclaimed king.
	14 April	News of Edward IV's death reaches Ludlow.

	24 April	Edward V leaves Ludlow for London.
	29 April	Meeting between Gloucester, Buckingham and the Wydevilles at Northampton.
	30 April–1 May	Queen Elizabeth takes sanctuary at Westminster.
	4 May	Edward V enters London.
	13 June	Execution of Lord Hastings.
	16 June	Richard, Duke of York, taken from the Westminster Sanctuary.
	—	Richard of Gloucester acclaimed as King Richard III.
	June (?)	Murder of Edward V and Richard, Duke of York.
	October	Buckingham's rebellion.
	2 November	Execution of Humphrey, Duke of Buckingham.
1485	7 August	Henry of Richmond lands in Milford Haven.
	22 August	Battle of Bosworth.
1486	18 January–April	Henry VII marries Elizabeth of York. Rising of Lord Lovell and Humphrey and Thomas Stafford.
1487	January (?)	Lambert Simnel in Ireland.
	16 June	Battle of Stoke.
1489	December	Abbot of Abingdon's conspiracy.
1491	Autumn	Perkin Warbeck appears in Ireland.
1492	Spring–Summer	Charles VIII invites Perkin Warbeck to France.
	3 November	Treaty of Étaples.
	—	Perkin Warbeck goes to Burgundy.
1493	November	Perkin Warbeck in Austria.
1495	16 February	Execution of Sir William Stanley.
	July	Perkin Warbeck's failure in Kent.
	July–August	Perkin Warbeck's failure at Waterford.
	November	Perkin Warbeck in Scotland.
1496	September	James IV of Scotland and Perkin Warbeck invade northern England.
1497	June	Rebellion in Cornwall.
	July	Thomas, Earl of Surrey's expedition against Scotland.
	September–October	Surrender of Perkin Warbeck.
1499	23 November	Execution of Perkin Warbeck.
	28 November	Execution of Edward, Earl of Wanwick.
1509	21 April	Death of Henry VII.

Index